Fela Anikulapo-Kuti

Fela Anikulapo-Kuti

Afrobeat, Rebellion, and Philosophy

Adeshina Afolayan and Toyin Falola

BLOOMSBURY ACADEMIC
NEW YORK • LONDON • OXFORD • NEW DELHI • SYDNEY

BLOOMSBURY ACADEMIC
Bloomsbury Publishing Inc
1385 Broadway, New York, NY 10018, USA
50 Bedford Square, London, WC1B 3DP, UK
29 Earlsfort Terrace, Dublin 2, Ireland

BLOOMSBURY, BLOOMSBURY ACADEMIC and the Diana logo are trademarks of Bloomsbury Publishing Plc

First published in the United States of America 2022
Paperback edition first published 2023

Cover design by Louise Dugdale
Cover image: "Fela," Toyin Falola Private Collections.

Library of Congress Cataloguing-in-Publication Data
Names: Afolayan, Adeshina, author. | Falola, Toyin, author.
Title: Fela Anikulapo-Kuti : Afrobeat, rebellion, and philosophy / Adeshina Afolayan and Toyin Falola.
Description: New York : Bloomsbury Academic, 2022. | Includes bibliographical references and index. |
Summary: "Reappraises the life, musical dynamics, and philosophy of Afrobeat legend Fela Anikulapo Kuti, and positions his music within the context of Africa's search for freedom"– Provided by publisher.
Identifiers: LCCN 2021040021 (print) | LCCN 2021040022 (ebook) | ISBN 9781501374715 (hardback) | ISBN 9781501374753 (paperback) | ISBN 9781501374722 (epub) | ISBN 9781501374739 (pdf) | ISBN 9781501374746 (ebook other)
Subjects: LCSH: Fela, 1938-1997–Criticism and interpretation. | Fela, 1938-1997–Philosophy. | Fela, 1938-1997–Political and social views. | Afrobeat–Social aspects–Nigeria. | Afrobeat–Political aspects–Nigeria. | Nigeria–Politics and government–20th century.
Classification: LCC ML410.F2955 (print) | LCC ML410.F2955 (ebook) | DDC 781.63092–dc23
LC record available at https://lccn.loc.gov/2021040021
LC ebook record available at https://lccn.loc.gov/2021040022

ISBN: HB: 978-1-5013-7471-5
PB: 978-1-5013-7475-3
ePDF: 978-1-5013-7473-9
eBook: 978-1-5013-7472-2

Typeset by Integra Software Services Pvt. Ltd.

To find out more about our authors and books visit www.bloomsbury.com and sign up for our newsletters.

Contents

Preface

Of all the great musicians that have come out of Nigeria, none have Fela Anikulapo-Kuti's undisputable reputation for achievements, notoriety, and global recognition. Fela, as he came to be known at the height of his fame, combined socially engaged music with an entertaining dexterity unrivaled by any other. He was a sociopolitical activist, a pan-Africanist, a nationalist, a polygamist, the creator of Afrobeat, and a multitalented instrumentalist, all rolled into a skinny but outspoken and fiery one-man scourge of Africa's ideological poverty and Nigeria's bad leadership.

Fela's many roles have made him both one of the most studied and one of the most misunderstood figures in Africa's cultural history. In fact, this reputation has become the focus of essays, monographs, books, documentaries, conferences, and panel discussions all addressing and offering sociological, cultural, and political analyses of his personality, his politics, his music, and his ideology. The almost saturated industry of Fela studies therefore poses a serious challenge to new attempts at examining Fela's multifaceted personality.

This new volume provides a fascinating biographical and philosophical interrogation of Fela Anikulapo-Kuti: the narrative of a man who brought the sting of Afrobeat music to the Afrocentric liberation philosophies already enlivened by Franz Fanon, Kwame Nkrumah, Patrice Lumumba, and Steve Biko. It applies a historical and critical approach to answer the questions: How does Fela's life and struggles against military dictatorship in Nigeria and maldevelopment in Africa enable us to understand the contextual ramifications of the philosophy of freedom? In what unique ways have Fela and his music redefined liberation philosophies on the African continent? How did he transform Nigeria's political landscape? How did he influence the content and context of a socially engaged and politically committed form of music that entertains the masses even as it irritates the elites?

Fela's life and times were both revolutionary and anomic. Just as he gathered a widespread following with his rebel art, he was also widely targeted for his many anti-social tendencies and eccentricities. This volume ties together the multiple narratives and impulses of Fela's life, including his mother's influence, his many wives, his unique Afrobeat music, his battles with the Nigerian society and the governments he battled, his philosophy and ideology. And above all, his Africanism. As a musician and philosopher, Fela is a historic continental figure, not only in the context of Nigeria's democratic evolution and Africa's liberation struggle but also within the global anti-imperialist movements for freedom and justice.

Introduction

Nigeria gained political independence from Britain on October 1, 1960. The end to decades of political, cultural, and economic denigration brought on a huge euphoria and a rising hope within the population founded on the capacity of the Nigerian nationalists to take charge and redirect the ship of state that had been steered by the colonial administrative calculation in service of the Western metropoles. From the tragic trans-Atlantic slave trade to the 1885 Scramble for Africa, and all the way to the 1960 year of independence, Africa was the site of numerous horrors and devastating policies that had the objective of subjugating and exploiting Africans while also denigrating their cultural heritage and achievements. There is no single story of colonialism in Africa; each African country went through its own unique scripting of the colonial tragedy. Nigeria was no exception.

When independence came for many African states, especially in 1960, it was the climax to many years of suffering and hardship. Nigerian literature, for example, offers a glimpse into the complexities of colonization and their effects on the social configuration and psyche of Nigerians. In *Things Fall Apart* (1958), Chinua Achebe's magnum opus, we are treated to a fictional representation of how colonialism disrupted an entire cultural framework and defiled its moral order. When Okonkwo, the eponymous hero of the novel, dies, it signals the capitulation of an entire way of life to the colonialists' onslaught. It was in this context that Kwame Nkrumah uttered his strident call for taking by force the political kingdom as the initial condition for Africa's liberation and freedom: "Seek ye first the political kingdom, and all other things shall be added."

The year 1960, named the African Year of Independence, saw twenty-seven African states, including Nigeria, become ex-colonies laden with shining dreams and aspirations of postcolonial liberation and social reconstruction. For the Nigerian and other African nationalists, it was sufficient for the colonialists to leave for the national predicament to be transformed for good, but it did not take many years after independence for this bubble of euphoria to burst. It took Nigeria just six years, from October 1960 to January 1966, for the first military putsch to happen following a massive reversal of hope and an even more massive corruption of the commonweal by those who fought for independence, leading to one of the most tragic civil wars in African history. The Nigerian Civil War became a brutal metaphor for a postcolonial predicament that circumscribes the promises that were to follow entry into the political kingdom.

From this point on, postcolonial Nigeria became compromised in terms of its political development, governance, and every other attribute that should have made the exit of the colonialists a good development for Nigerians. At the global level, Nigeria's economic fate had been sealed by its unwitting insertion into the global neoliberal capitalist hegemony, accomplished through the crippling conditionalities of the infamous Washington Consensus, the set of economic frameworks, dynamics, and policies that the World Bank and International Monetary Fund (IMF) set up for transforming the economies of developing countries, especially in Africa. The shape of postcolonial conditions in Nigeria, as well as most African states, was defined by a stalled decolonization process that resulted from an inadequate deconstruction of the colonial legacies. In Nigeria, it quickly dawned on the nationalists that the structural and institutional inheritances they had received were not going to be adequate for the task of social reconstruction and national development. The consequences were complex political dynamics that inevitably led to economic underdevelopment and sociocultural disarticulation.

It was within the juncture of the colonial and postcolonial sociopolitical complexity in Nigeria that Fela Anikulapo-Kuti and his family were born. Fela's life, music, as well as philosophy, were a fitting reaction to a postcoloniality gone bad. His entire life bore the brunt of the Nigerian state's attempts to police its citizens and maintain the colonial borders. Thus, Fela represents an anticolonial consciousness pushing at the stalled decolonization project toward liberation and genuine independence. His entire musical oeuvre, at least from the commencement of Afrobeat, speaks to an African philosophical consciousness drawing from the older pan-Africanist and Afrocentric discourses of Kwame Nkrumah and Marcus Garvey, as well as the black consciousness rhetoric of Malcolm X and Martin Luther King, Jr. In Fela's hand, that anticolonial sensibility became a double-edged sword that cut both continentally and nationally. Fela's voice constituted a stentorian rebuke against all forms of political and cultural anomaly afflicting both leadership and followership. And in Nigeria, he was the scourge of military dictators, from Buhari to Obasanjo. By the time of his death in 1997, Olufela Anikulapo-Kuti (the One-that-Holds-Death-in-the-Quiver) was only fifty-nine years old, but he left—on the one hand—an ambivalent social legacy that drew the youth to simultaneously conflicting messages and—on the other—a solid philosophy of rebellion and social change that still offers a valuable perspective to reflect on the Nigerian and African predicament.

Fela's entire life trajectory can be described as a search for freedom—the personal freedom to be his own person, as a mischievous boy growing up under the stern supervision of his parents; the developmental freedom to chart his own path, when he traveled out of Nigeria to study music; the artistic freedom to create a distinct style for his music; and the ideological freedom to rebel against perceived injustice at the national and continental levels. This iteration of the search for freedom becomes deepened once one understands the extent to which freedom and unfreedom are intertwined in any attempt to define the realms and extent of freedom on the continent. The sources of unfreedom are both internal and external to Africa—slave trade, colonialism, imperialist subjugation, globalizing neoliberal capitalism, and post-independence authoritarian regimes. In outlining the dialectic between freedom and unfreedom, Crawford Young argues for three historical moments in Africa, each of which "constituted a field of metaconflict over the idea of freedom"—the trans-Saharan and trans-Atlantic slave trade, from the seventeenth to the nineteenth century; colonization, from late nineteenth century through the 1950s and 1960s; and then the aggressive authoritarian regimes of the postcolonial period. Each of these moments created a framework of unfreedom that generated an antithesis in a longing for freedom. During the moment of slavery, freedom, "as a powerful and eventually triumphant idea, meant the abolition of unfreedom, or chattel slavery."[1] With colonialism and colonization, freedom became iterated through the anticolonial and independence movements across Africa. And finally, when the newly independent African states delineated the space of independence as that of unfreedom, "[t]he idea of freedom now spread into multiple sites: democratization, economic liberalization, human rights, gender equality."[2]

The crises of Africa's postcolonial states in itself thus engendered multiple sites of freedom, within which citizens seek to find relief. These crises created an architecture of trauma and suffering; it drove people in multiple directions, either into legal engagement with the state and its apparatuses or out of politics into informality, resignation, or criminality. It is in this sense that William Foltz identifies four forms of freedom: their dynamics configure the existence of the state, its citizens, and the relationship between them. The first is juridical freedom for the African state, deriving from independence and the newly found capacity to maneuver within the global community of sovereign states. The year 1960 has been dubbed the African year of independence. This is because it was the year that exactly seventeen African countries became independent. Other states followed in quick succession. With independence therefore, the African states were now opened up to the benefits and opportunities that accrue to other states in the international scheme of things. This is what Foltz calls the *freedom for the African state*. This freedom that the African state got at independence was, however, circumscribed by so many things that were the results of the colonial exploitation. The first was the political map of the continent which was redrawn in line with the colonial power tussle. The second was the economic integration of the continent and its states into the global capitalist framework within which the African states were ill-prepared to operate. These two fundamental postcolonial factors have serious implication for how these states could manage their newfound freedom. For Foltz,

> Weak at home, the new African states were objectively weaker abroad. Unable to project power effectively within their own boundaries, they had even less ability to project power or influence beyond them. In that sense all African states really were born equal: whatever the differences in size or natural endowments, during the first years of independence none of them had the ability to coerce another. The new African states did have one trump card they could play in the international arena, however; that was the juridical sovereignty that came with officially recognized membership in the international community of sovereign states.[3]

The result was that even though these states have gained juridical freedom, it was a freedom that lacked effectiveness in transforming the lives of their citizens. The adoption of African socialism and the one-state governance dynamics as a response to the neocolonial impulse of the international community further led to the impoverishment of the ideology of liberation.

The second form of freedom, deriving from the first, is *freedom from the African state*—the freedom that African states achieved at independence led to the accumulation of benefits for their leadership, to the detriment of their citizens. Once the leadership of these states realized the essence of the various structural traps that the colonialists have put them, they came to the realization of their predicaments. The essence of that predicament is that there was no way they could use the structures of exploitation as the fulcrum for jumpstarting social reconstruction in postcolonial Africa. The unfortunate result was that most of the leadership entered into a framework of internal colonialism which required using the same structure the colonialists used to subject their own citizens. This led to the immediate loss of legitimacy by the state in the eyes of the citizens. It also led to an increasingly weaker status on the international scene. But the more the state lost legitimate status, the more it increased its extractive and repressive dynamics. On the one hand, the African state's juridical capacity went into extracting Africa's rich resources; on the other hand, the state commenced preying on the citizens.

> Part of this predation might be centrally controlled and co-ordinated, with profits collected by the state apparatus on behalf of the ruler and his immediate political family. Some of it was decentralized and poorly-ordered freebooting, as state agents were given license to supplement (or replace) their salaries by squeezing the local citizenry. As the Camerounian phrase has it, "The goats graze wherever they are tethered." Paradoxically, rents from export of highly-valued natural resources often worsened rather than improved the lot of the ordinary citizen. Most immediately, it was often the case that inhabitants of producing areas suffered environmental damage. This was the plight of Nigeria's Ogoni people; their fishing resources and farmland were polluted by international oil companies, but virtually none of the royalty payments to the government ever returned to ameliorate the Ogoni's lot. More generally in Africa the export of highly valued resources, petroleum in particular, appears to have a *depressing* effect on economic growth, probably by increasing governmental corruption. As a result, frustrated, ordinary citizens have sought freedom *from* the African state.[4]

In other words, there was an increase in the level of deprivation such that citizens looked for ways to escape from repression. Thus, while the African state got its freedom at independence, it denied the same freedom to its citizens in the post-independence period. In fact, the African state rather became predatory in ways that endangered the lives of the citizens. The African state therefore sets in motion the dynamics that led to its citizens trying to seek for their freedom elsewhere. Freedom from the African state took two dimensions. The first type of response to the predatory state in Africa is exit from the state. The refugee situation in most of Africa is a gruesome attestation to this option of exit. The second option can be referred to as an exit-in-place where the citizens simply just drop out of the gaze of the state, mostly into the informal sector.

Not many citizens took this path. There were those who instead sought *freedom within the African state*, a new form of freedom, to challenge the authoritarian structures and apparatuses of the African state in pursuit of human rights, human dignity, and democracy. From the beginning of the 1990s, after the end fall of the USSR and the official end to the Cold War, there was an increasing pressure on authoritarian regimes across the world to transform and bow to the emerging call for democracy and democratization. Freedom during this dispensation was characterized in terms of the readiness to democratize and allow popular participation. Foltz argues:

> Taken together, these external factors [multi-party democracy, declining per capita GDP, the rejection of authoritarianism on the continent by the foreign powers, and increasing call for democratization], interacting with domestic pressures [the independence of South Africa and the emergence of good governance], opened a political space in which Africans seeking political freedoms could maneuver. Where not savagely repressed, myriad organizations belonging to the broad category of "civil society" stepped to the fore, much as civil organizations ranging from syncretist churches to trade unions to ethnic-based "friendly associations" had helped provide the social infrastructure for nationalist independence movements some 40 years earlier. Some of these were mere fronts for autocratic rulers, rural bigmen, or unsuccessful politicians left over from another era. Others demonstrated unexpected vitality and organizational capacity and called forth financial support (and some political protection) from Western non-governmental organizations (NGOs) and aid agencies.[5]

It is within these series of internal and external pressures against authoritarian regimes that the political space became opened up to allow for political freedoms for the citizens. Thus, together with those who refused to flee with their feet or drop out of place, the civil society organizations mostly geared up to battle the African state and wrest from its some degrees of political freedoms. There were increasing agitations in most African states for the enthronement of democratic governments. The last form of freedom, *freedom through the African state*, derived from the wave after wave of democratic agitations that engulfed despotic African governments. These agitations enabled a state, amenable to transformation itself, to intervene on behalf of the citizens of a neighboring state when they were oppressed under the jackboot of a despotic government.[6] For instance, there was an increasing lack of tolerance for military intervention in politics as well as for any kind of government that refuses popular sovereignty.

Fela's adult life and mature philosophy are firmly situated within Foltz's third form of freedom: the freedom *within* the African state. This volume critically explores how his life, music, philosophy, and activism manifest within the context of the unfreedom that the Nigerian state created after independence. Chapter 1 provides a trajectory of critical studies that explore different and varying dimensions of Fela's music, performance aesthetics, and lifestyle. This is with the objective of grounding the significance of this volume. Chapter 2 stretches these intellectual perspectives into more general outlining of Fela's life and achievements. It is a flowing narrative of the historical trajectory within which Fela could be situated, and which gives birth to his persona and philosophy. This chapter snapshots the important themes that the volume enlarges subsequently. Apart from these two introductory chapters, the volume is structured into five parts. The first part is made up of three chapters. Chapter 3 explores Fela's beginning and his family's deep influence on his socio-political maturation. Fela was born into a "stubborn" family; both of his parents were activists who contributed to the shaping of postcolonial Nigeria. The contrasts defining his family composition and upbringing—between discipline and unruliness, talent and deviance, middle-class wealth and Spartan existence, Christianity and cultural traditions, patriotism and rebellion—played a huge, definitive role forming Fela's worldview later in life. Born in the waning years of colonialism, and maturing during the early-but-turbulent period of Nigeria's postcolonial consolidation, Fela felt the full weight of Africa's struggle to liberate itself from the external and internal forces that stifled its potentialities. Arguably, Fela's mother played one of the most formidable roles in his upbringing.

Chapter 4 outlines the professional trajectory of Fela's life, from highlife to Afrobeat. His music constitutes a fundamental part of his political philosophy and social activism. His musical metamorphosis within the cosmopolitan cultural ambience of London, from highlife to highlife jazz to Afrobeat, was matched by his growing political awareness. It began with his immersion into London's racial dynamics, and his ideological formation matured in the United States. Afrobeat, once it had fully evolved, became the embodiment of all that Fela had learned, believed, and preached. Chapter 5 interrogates the symbiotic relationships between Fela, his wives, and the other women who were significant in the definition of his persona. Apart from his mother, part of Fela's complexity is defined by his relationship with women in general, and with his wives in particular. Orthodox interpretation describes a "patriarchal" Fela, but the truth is that these women—Remilekun in London, Sandra in Los Angeles, the twenty-seven wives in Lagos, and his entire concubinage—exerted significant influence on Fela's political maturation. His twenty-seven "Queens" in particular had a life of their own that reflected Fela's influences but also transcended them.

The four chapters that make up the second part of this volume tie together specific aspects of Fela's life and music. Chapter 6 investigates Fela's connection to the postcolonial condition of Nigeria's political economy. Chapter 7 explores the political undertone of Fela's Afrobeat's radical tone. In Chapter 8, we excavated the language dynamics that undergirds Fela's radicalism. Chapter 9 interrogates the relationship between postcoloniality and Fela's art. In the third part of the volume, consisting of six chapters, we critically unraveled what has come to be known as "Felasophy"—the entire ensemble of sociopolitical and ideological fragments and thoughts that define Fela's philosophical thought. By the time he returned to Nigeria in 1970, with a full philosophical and Africanist sensibility, he had been completely transformed in thought, and Afrobeat had been born as a musical conveyor of political, philosophical, and ideological concepts addressing blackness, African personality, and the black race and black pride. Contemporaneously, Africa was slowly but steadily getting mired in the dynamics of underdevelopment. In Nigeria, the Civil War had just ended; Nigerians had to face the severe challenge of reconstituting the façade of unity it had shredded. Fela's strident engagement with successive Nigerian military governments primed his ideological confrontation with neocolonialism and imperialism throughout the African continent. Chapters 10 to 14 are unique in their attempt to bring together his distinct set of ideas and beliefs—which may not have translated into a coherent worldview—about what ails Nigeria and the black race, and how a rehabilitation of black consciousness can be achieved, the first condition for achieving black human well-being. His ideas and ideologies connect with current arguments about pan-Africanism, negritude, and the black power movement. The chapters altogether interrogate the elements of Fela's blackism and the inspiration, from Yoruba culture and pan-African philosophical dynamics that gave flesh to it.

Chapter 14 specifically discusses Fela's social deviance and eccentricities. He was no saint. He could be considered a deviant who alienated many with his eccentric lifestyle. He smoked marijuana, had extramarital affairs, was rabidly abusive, and consistently offended social sensibility with his lewdness and obscenity. His night club, "The Afrika Shrine," and his "Kalakuta Republic" home became hotspots for all manner of undesirable social elements. His paradoxical deviancy alienated him from the elite, but it also endeared him to the poor.

Chapters 15 and 16, which make up the last part of the volume, situate Fela within contemporary milieu that enables the memorialization of his ideological and musical efforts in post-Fela frameworks ranging from musical celebrations to intellectual discourses. More than twenty-five years after Fela's death in 1997, how do we measure the philosophical influence of Afrobeat in the contemporary understanding of nation-building and continental unity? Is Fela as relevant as others, like Fanon, in terms of a collective attempt to come to terms with black consciousness? Where is Afrobeat situated today in an entertainment scene dominated by hip-hop? Can we still hear Fela's strident voice in Nigeria? Chapter 16 specifically interrogates the ideological and global influences of Fela. By the time of his death, Fela's influence had grown beyond the shores of Nigeria and Africa. His voice reverberates in pan-African circles as an ideological force comparable to a potent figure like Bob Marley. This chapter narrates Fela's complicated legacies in music, politics, activism, and culture.

In life and even after death, Fela Anikulapo-Kuti remains an enigma that was too hard for Nigeria's authoritarian regimes to unravel. His life's trajectory, from childhood through his musical maturation and ideological consciousness, constitutes a unique and aesthetically interesting existence—especially within the strictly intellectual pan-African context. The Nigerian military government had its revenge on Fela, through the violence of naked power, but he had the last laugh: the military regime ended under the deluge of democratic aspirations, while Fela's music and ideas live on. This book provides an opportunity to looks at Africa's anticolonial and anti-imperial liberation struggles through the historical, unfolding life of an iconoclast who was similar to other African revolutionaries, but also critically unlike them in the sheer forcefulness of his lyrical voice that spat fire and entertainment in equal measure.

1

Fela Anikulapo-Kuti and Fela Studies

Introduction

This chapter contains a critical review of scholarly engagements in different disciplines and from academic backgrounds with the music and ideas of Fela Anikulapo-Kuti, a global figure whose musical productions and lyrics generated tremendous attention and reflections during and after his lifetime. Fela was a force whose commitment to the course of freedom and political emancipation cost him personal freedom and shredded him beyond imagination as he became a constant target of political victimization, a victim of authoritarian politics, a prisoner of societal acrimony, and in consolation, a dignified activist who was celebrated in his time and also posthumously. There is no doubt that the annexation of music for the sole purpose of antagonizing an oppressive government with its regimental system was a revolutionary action by Fela. In some aspects of African life and politics, there was no recorded precedence of such musical genre in relation to social relevance and political utility. Fela was not a public official or politician, yet he was engaged critically in political thinking. The public accepted him as its voice.

The most appropriate way to describe this historical figure is to establish the connections between his ideology and his irreversible commitment to it for social advancement, as this would enable us to generate a coherent cognitive picture. Apparently, Fela's ideology, readily espoused in his music, is an assortment of protest and resistance to predatory political and social behavior and actions that seek to deny the people their fundamental rights and freedom to the advantage of some elite and power structures that are chiefly interested in exploiting their innocence and helplessness. An entrenched political elite would consider any act of resistance or any engagement, that seeks to undermine the enthroned lopsided structure that profits only the few, as potential impediment and would therefore throw their weight against it since they would naturally challenge anything that threatens the status quo and their class identity and interest. In this sense, any radical or revolutionary act that challenges the status quo is considered anti-society by the powerful individuals. Fela, however, was unapologetic in claiming the identity of a political rebel.

Attacks on him, therefore, led to the unending abuse of his human rights and the denigration of his identity. Successively, he was harassed and embarrassed for choosing to identify with the masses against the brutal actions of the (military) governments, who appeared to be uninterested in how their actions affect the common people. Without doubt, Fela's rise to stardom was filled with challenges, trials, and bitter experiences that naturally almost imploded into identity struggles as those who share the messages of the enigma became impatient at a time, and would not remain silent when brutal actions are meted out against their idol for no obvious violation of the law. The aspirations of the common people are amplified in Fela's ideologies and continuously represented even in his daily life. He attracted countless vilifications and endured innumerable traumas, but the fact that his opponent was the government gave him the necessary encouragement to continue to press his anti-establishment critique, knowing that his success or otherwise would not be put under the carpet, for the society remembers its heroes, even if they cannot identify with them during their trying times.

The entirety of Fela's life, as contained in his upbringing, family history, musical trajectory, lyrical dynamics, life's experience, ideological contestations, philosophical explorations, and social eccentricities, has become the source of critical and celebratory intellectual and scholarly engagements and explorations. Different books and essays have been written on different and interrelated dimensions of his life—his mother, his wives, Afrobeat, his sojourns abroad, his "Felasophy," contributions to postcolonial critique and decolonization, his relationship with pan-Africanism and Afrocentric scholars, his love for Africa and her traditions, his countercultural effluence, and many more. This objective of this volume is to tie all these dimensions of Fela's life together into a philosophical dynamic defined around a pursuit of freedom. It is this thread that determines this volume's relationship with other critical material already in existence about Fela and his significance. In other words, while other significant studies of Fela's life, music, and philosophical sensibility have been done in piecemeal fashion—as this review of the significant literature will demonstrate—this volume brings all the issues of Fela's philosophical maturation and ideological dynamics together in stark relief.

Fela: This Bitch of a Life by Carlos Moore

Carlos Moore examines the life of the Afrobeat star using scholarly frameworks that assist in the interpretation of Fela's works and the evaluation of the sociopolitical atmosphere that propelled them. As a political scientist, Moore was able to interrogate the political rascality generated by the African postcolonial environment in the music of Fela, and therefore understood the imperative of his protest. As an ethnologist, however, he considered the African cultural scaffoldings that strongly influenced the perception of Fela Anikulapo-Kuti. Moore's intellectual compilation was foreworded by Gilberto Gil, a composer, and a bandleader, who was able to easily relate to the artistic brilliance of the music genius. *This Bitch of a Life* is also introduced by a sound critic, Margaret Busby. Collectively, they all celebrate the fecundity of Fela's messages and art, not leaving behind the revolutionary spirit of a man who refuses to be silenced. The fact that Carlos Moore spent a considerable amount of time with Fela to retrieve personal classified information for his biographical account adds to the credibility that the book has in public intellectualism.

Apart from the book taking us through a terrific journey into the heart of Fela, his life, and works, it competently reveals how the man became an assortment of techniques and ideas with which to combat the overindulging elite, who, according to him, refused to see beyond their noses in relation to a future that would throw Africa behind others (if they fail to rescue the situation by taking bold steps that would instigate African development). The book, no doubt, accentuates the contributions of Fela, with the burden of protest animating his entire being. Fela roared against injustices so much that his voice travels the world around. His commitment to African struggles and true freedom is succinctly summarized by Margaret Busby: "Fela Anikulapo-Kuti was a fearless maverick for whom music was a righteous and invincible weapon. His self-given second name, Anikulapo—which translates as 'the one who carries death in his pouch'—spoke of indestructibility and resilience."[1] It is fair to conclude that in no place did Fela's music fail to win the heart of anyone with the taste for good music, style, and artistic content during his lifetime. And this is still a posthumous fact.

One does not need to travel far into the work of Moore, *Fela: This Bitch of a Life*, before one gets to be educated about the prescience, directness, and ideologically controversial nature of the man in question. Just a few words from him and one gets to know about the African cultural nuances especially as related to the belief in the supernatural. He gladly talks about himself as an *abiku*—a socio-ethnological phenomenon among the Yoruba people that explains children with unknown power for reincarnation. This signals why he was eventually referred to as *Abami Eda* (an enigma). Within the same breath, Fela already reveals his aversion to Eurocentric imposition and identity politics which seek to erase the African identity in place of their own. Fela categorically recollects that "So to make some white man happy, my father asked this German missionary to … name me. Can you imagine that, man? A white man naming an African child! In Africa, man, where names are taken so seriously."[2]

Fela: The Life and Times of an African Musical Icon by Michael E. Veal

This book, apart from Carlos Moore's *Fela: This Bitch of a Life*, is about the most popular of all Fela's intellectual biographies. Published in 2000, three years after Fela's death, Veal's volume contained a detailed trajectory of the emergence of Fela as a musical force. In eight chapters, Veal painstakingly outlined Fela's historical trajectory from Abeokuta, where he grew up between 1938 and 1957 to the height of his musical maturation before his death in 1997. The book also contained a critical appendix of the personnel of Fela's bands, from the Koola Lobitos to the Egypt 80, as well as a detailed discography.

As an accomplished ethnomusicologist, Veal came to the writing of the Fela book with a certain depth of understanding of Fela's musical competence. And this was further accentuated by his historical methodology, fieldwork, and participant observation assisted by Fela's willing collaboration. Veal's interest in Fela's Afrobeat came from his realization that Fela's music "seemed to recontextualize and extend musical ideas" with which he was familiar.[3] Afrobeat contains

> unmistakable echoes of diasporic African musical innovators and styles: James Brown, John Coltrane, modal jazz, big-band jazz, funk, rhythm-and-blues, and salsa. At the same time, I recognized an overall spirit and use of many musical devices I associated with West African music: tightly woven rhythm patterns, vocal chants, call-and-response choruses, and an overall percussive approach to articulation, among others. Compositionally, I admire Fela's ability to compose a seemingly endless series of complex, catchy groove patterns, chorus lines, and horn riffs. Compositions rarely clocked in at less than fifteen minutes, with

> sections allotted for scored ensemble passages, jazz-styled solo improvisations, choral singing, and the vocal song proper, which itself comprised a number of movements.[4]

Veal calls Afrobeat "a long-form highlife-funk-jazz fusion" that undermined and even refashioned all the known conventions underlying the musical styles, especially of the Afro-American music context.

Veal insists that his work is situated between being "a musical study and an ethnography."[5] As what he calls a "semi-biographical narrative," Veal concentrated on Fela as a musician, as a social figure, and then Fela's work and influence across Africa and the diaspora. According to him,

> First, I analyze Fela the musician, in his various roles as composer/arranger, bandleader, vocalist and instrumentalist. In so doing, I survey his various musical influences, provide a continuous stylistic analysis that charts the development of his art throughout his career, and discuss concurrent trends in related musical genres. Second, I analyze Fela the social figure and the way his role as political musician, derisive social/political critic, heir to a family protest tradition, social maverick, and creator of a distinct artistic subculture shaped his analysis and articulation of the major social, political, and cultural themes of his time in Nigeria. third, I analyze Fela's works within two wider spheres: post=colonial Africa, and a dynamic of cross-cultural influences operating between Africa and cultures of the African diaspora.[6]

Arrest the Music! Fela and His Rebel Art and Politics by Tejumola Olaniyan

If one intends to understand the resistance undercurrents of Fela's music, one needs to acquaint oneself with the copiously informative book of Tejumola Olaniyan, *Arrest the Music! Fela and His Rebel Art and Politics*, as it is filled with sufficient textual content capable of enriching one's knowledge. One would not only get to know about the African political travails and socioeconomic challenges ahead of them, one would perhaps understand the ineluctable necessity warranting the revolutionary protest of courageous individuals like Fela. In ten rigorously argued chapters, Olaniyan attempted to situate Fela within the context of the African postcolonial state, and what he called the "postcolonial incredible": "that which cannot be believed; that which is too improbable, astonishing, and extraordinary to be believed. The incredible is not simply a breach but an outlandish infraction of 'normality' and its limits" (2004: 2).[7] Olaniyan's objective was to map Fela's complex and paradoxical reactions to the postcolonial incredible. Olaniyan sees it as a relationship of transcendence and sustenance: "The one is transcendentalist in aspiration—a powerful exploration of the wherewithal to surmount the incredible and its rule—while the other wallows in a sustaining relationship with it."[8] And Olaniyan pursues the arduous task of situating Fela within his space and time in the Nigerian postcolony.

One thing that makes the intellectual evaluation of Olaniyan on Fela's music very captivating is his ability to produce cultural valuations and validations which are readily suggestive of Fela's wider sense of African sociocultural values. This is perhaps possible partly because they share similar cultural and political realities that encourage a deep-seated interest in whoever pictures a better environment. Obviously, the book is calculated to expose how Fela's music uncovered the indiscriminate political scheming of the elite and inadvertently committed cultural and economic genocide in the process. Once the political class is adequately catered for, the survival of African economy, culture, and leadership takes a rear concern in their minds. Whereas everything in the human society is connected which means that when one aspect of human life malfunctions, the effects spread to other aspects of the people's lives. Once the Nigerian political class is indifferent to the overall safety of the people, they have therefore declared their disinterest on things that appear more important to the people. Therefore, Olaniyan interrogates the songs of Fela and his personal life and comes to the conclusion that he was an iconic activist with rebellious mindset against any trace of oppression.

Arrest the Music! is a piece that elaborates eloquently the rascality of the Nigerian leadership which was determined to censure Fela and his arts because of the obvious eruption of discontent that his songs provoked in their minds. Olaniyan captures this in his introduction: "Fela had innately more and real violent visitations from the security agents of successive Nigerian governments over the course of the three decades of his musical career."[9] He supplements this with the occasion of the brutal destruction of Fela's instruments and arts to the dismay of the miffed audience who watched the totalitarian actions with utmost disdain and disbelief. The book therefore marvels at the contributions of the artist to the sociological activities and political trajectories of the country and the continent at large.

Afrobeat: Fela and the Imagined Continent by Sola Olorunyomi

It is critically impossible that Fela with his diverse and dynamic arts did not generate multiple and multidisciplinary scholarly engagements. The fact that Sola Olorunyomi complements what different authors have recorded about Fela attests to this claim. Even though there are numerous contributions in literary scholarship, historical exploration, and sociological interpretations of Fela's works, Olorunyomi yet again offers an impressive voice to the evaluation of Fela's arts and sees his musical productions from a riveting perspective. In *Afrobeat*, Olorunyomi examined Fela's songs vis-à-vis their anticolonial activism and his commitment to the emancipation agenda of a continent. It is a critical fact that studies into Afrobeat were lacking in sufficient literature during the beginning of Olorunyomi's scholarly intervention on the works of Fela Anikulapo-Kuti, an experience that was suggestive of the rigorously critical condition of any worthwhile past academic research into his music.

Olorunyomi's title has a contextual implication for the elaboration of African repression and then the corresponding resistance Africans offered to these predatory forces. When examined carefully, the selection of topics reflected in the different chapters of the book demonstrates the critical role of independence and emancipatory struggles that African intellectual considered imperatively expedient. From Kwame Nkrumah of Ghana, Obafemi Awolowo of Nigeria at the political spectrum, to Kenneth Onwuka Dike, Mahmoud Mamdani, Valentin Mudimbe, Ngugi wa Thiong'o, among many others in the intellectual community, the independence of Africa not in the ceremonial sense but basically in all endeavors reverberates all through their yearnings and activism. Surprisingly, Fela would lend his voice to the movements albeit in more appealing ways and his contributions recorded a considerable amount of success as the political class becomes embattled and their energy for mis-governance was effectively enervated. Against this background, his music, just as the intellectual productions of political or intellectual Africans were analyzed and evaluated for important information, became the field of research where different scholars of various disciplines come to perform their academic ritual.

Outside of the purely biographical and ethnological materials that preceded his work, Olorunyomi critically focused on answering the question, "What is Afrobeat?" This is strategic. It was Olorunyomi's means of teasing out the aesthetic and performance subtext in Fela's music as an instrument for social change. And so, for him,

> From the outset, the multidisciplinary imperative of such a venture had dawned on me, and I felt somewhat compelled to heed the warning of Houston A. Baker concerning the need for a theoretical approach that would be cognizant of an "Improvisational flexibility and a historicizing of form that are not always characteristic of academic responses to popular cultural forms." My inclination in this bid is two-fold. One is to explore the theoretical overlaps that are implicit in such a discourse; and, also, to bring into focus the theorizing of the "self" by the aesthetic subculture, in order not to foist arbitrary theory on a form that can express a subtle but most profound mode of signification.[10]

In understanding Fela, and his aesthetic and political performances, one needs to come at them from a plural perspective that deploys textual reading, conceptual analysis, and practical experience. Afrobeat is essentially a lyrical and critical response to its post-independence context, as well as to the crisis of modernity.

To demonstrate that Africans are capable of resistance to the cultural praxis bequeathed by the colonialists and their European imperialists, Fela needed to show an act of rebellion. This stands to obviate the misconception of the West that Africans are incapable of independent thinking or creativity. The invalidation of this unfounded claims is demonstrated through substituting the inherited structures with indigenous one as a means of protest. Even when the music content of Fela was castigating and casting aspersions on the African leaders who were serial neocolonial oppressors, Fela's styles were a clear rejection of the Western system as that would uncharacteristically overshadow the African identity and then rubbish it beyond imagination. When it is understood that Fela went to Trinity College to study music and came to create a style that was entirely different from what he got from the school, one would understand that Fela was a revolutionary who wanted a different Africa from the one the colonizers bequeathed or envisaged. Olorunyomi uses the track "Gentleman" to buttress his points. Here, Fela contrasts the African worldview, and those molded by it, to the European worldview.

Fela: Kalakuta Notes by John Collins

Collins' *Kalakuta Notes* is appropriately titled because it brings a refreshing dimension to Fela studies. This is because it is a record of Collins' observation which he noted in the diary kept after starring in Fela's autobiographical film *The Black President* in 1977. He supplemented this reflections and observations in his diary with copious interviews with Fela and everyone else in close contact with him, from friends to members of the band. Collins' emphasis was on Fela and his Ghanaian connections and relationships. The original title of the book was "Fela through Ghanaian Eyes." According to him,

> I began writing this book in 1998 after receiving a very positive response to the diary I had kept when I worked with Fela in 1977, and published just after Fela's death in the Nigerian *Glendora* magazine. It was then that I decided to go ahead and write a full book that would be based on my personal knowledge of Fela—as well as that of other Ghanaian musician [*sic*] and promoters who played and worked with Fela over the years.[11]

There is no Fela biography that would not be drawn into his iconoclastic lifestyle and the radical blaring of Afrobeat. Collins regarded Fela as a "musical warrior who drew heavily on age-old connections between music, militancy, and violence."[12] This separates him from James Brown, Bob Dylan, or Bob Marley. Fela initiated a connection between African music and direct action: "Indeed, if there was not sufficient confrontation to inspire a song, he would create that confrontation first—a unique creative device that often resulted in direct battles with the Nigerian authorities."[13]

Fela was radical and there can never be any attempt to erase that for that remains the legacy of the icon which continues to provide him the unending opportunity to increase his fame even long after his demise. Fela's radicality, however, does not come at the detriment of the unassuming innocent masses. Instead, Fela took a bigger and a more challenging opponent in the African, especially Nigerian, leadership in its taciturnity with regard to the well-being of the defenseless Nigerians. Fela was himself aware of the danger involved in taking on the political authority, and especially the brutal Nigerian military, who have at their disposal the battalion of security operatives and agents to whom they can dedicate the duty of frustrating imagined or confirmed detractors. Nigerian government was adamant, Fela Anikulapo-Kuti was equally uncompromising. Only one of them would bear the brunt of the brutal experiences. It was Fela.

In "Black President," a chapter in the book, Collins recalls one of the many experiences Fela had with the Nigerian military over an issue that was blown out of proportion deliberately, and which allow the authority to seize a well-sought opportunity to inflict maximum pain on the revolutionary for taking an opposing position against the government. As Collins narrated, one of Fela's drivers had accidentally knocked down an officer in the Nigeria army and, to escape the search for him, had dashed into Fela's abode, Kalakuta Republic, for safety. Military officials insisted that Fela must release the culprit so he could face punitive measures for his careless driving and traffic violation. Fela, in his usual habit of defending the defenseless, refused and noted that the nature of the situation does not fall within the domain of the military but the police.

The military officials, however, were hell-bent on showing that they were in control being in control and would therefore spare no opportunity to nail Fela, who had been a serial impediment combating them courageously at every given opportunity, to the coffin. Coincidentally, Fela just recently released one of his beautiful tracks that he titled "Zombie". The military officers who were confronting him therefore could be said to be showing an annoyance over a man who has rubbished what they consider as their career path. Collins reports that Fela responded to "them by playing his recently released 1976 "Zombie" on his saxophone. The officers left in a furious mood after questioning Fela's right to call his house a 'republic' and surround it with an electric fence. They said that as far as they were concerned there was only one republic, and that was the Nigerian one."[14] Because Fela has committed an offense against the men in khaki prior to the incidence—an offense of relegating their career to laughable stock and dispiriting them in the process—the soldiers created an excuse to visit their anger on the popular revolutionary. The government, against who the activist has always directed his campaigns, remained mute after all, in an action that shows complicity than diplomatic indifference. This book therefore exposes the dedicated life of Fela to freedom and independence of Africans and it explores the various themes connected to his artistic productions.

Fela: From West Africa to Broadway by Trevor Schoonmaker

There is a deluge of scholars who x-ray the evolutionary growth of Fela's music, detailing the attributes and the characteristics it shares with some other genres of music. Among a number of intellectual works produced in this respect, however, Trevor Schoonmaker's *Fela: From West Africa to Broadway* remains classic. Schoonmaker's volume is unique because it is an edited volume that brought together established Fela scholars, philosophers, and cultural enthusiasts to reflect on Fela and his music. This was a culmination of the Fela Project which the editor began in 2003. This project started with an art exhibition and catalogue called *Black President: The Art and Legacy of Fela Anikulapo-Kuti*. The collection of brilliant scholars brought together for the *Fela* volume is meant to further contribute to the unravel the complexity of Fela's life and time.

Fela: From West Africa to Broadway presents an insightful description of Fela's work and yet does not fail in its attempts to record the revolutionary spirit infused into the Afrobeat structure of the music legend. The fact that a number of Africans today joyously identify with the Afrobeat brand and also extend the dominance of the style to the world around confirms the conclusion that the tentacle of the music genre is strong and indestructible. This book comprises fourteen different chapters all of which interrogate different dimensions of the Fela legacy, from his pan-Africanism and its spiritual dimension, his *Black President* film and his album jackets, to Fela's women, Fela's relationship with Lagos, his education, the aesthetics of Afrobeat, and the revolutionary power of his music. Altogether, the chapters further reinforce the argument that Fela was an Africanist force that confronted colonialist ideology and bad governments in Nigeria. According to Schoonmaker:

> Through the many voices in this collection you will experience Fela's legacy and meet the man—a man of the people, a political gadfly, a musical revolutionary, a spiritual leader, a distant father, a loyal son, a husband to 28 and a lover to more. You will meet how he challenged dictators, composed more than 77 hit albums and was king of a commune. You will hear how he was a leader to millions and yet was led astray. You will hear about Nigeria, the tales of Fela's life and the diasporic reverberations of his action and music.[15]

The book shows that Fela Anikulapo-Kuti was a nonconformist, and his deviant disposition was not provoked by a determination to become an outcast. Rather, he chose the style because the targets of his flagellating protest were not ordinary. For anyone who is familiar with postcolonial African environment, it is very easy to spot their excessive use of force and power for the benefit of their cartel. The fact that Nigeria was assuredly heading to a brick wall given the concentration on the personal aggrandizement of her political elites at the expense of the ordinary Nigerians, there was no doubt that a revolutionary action was expedient. However, in a society made tensed by the despotic regime of the military, alternating with the civilian government (of similar authoritarian posture), calling out the government is a nearly suicidal act. Despite the risks involved, Fela thrived in a surrounding full of thorns. Fela's music is synonymous with protest, and his personal is representational of struggles.

Fela Anikulapo-Kuti: Bruised. Battered. Beloved by Tade Makinde

Fela Anikulapo-Kuti: Bruised. Battered. Beloved is an interesting deviation from the other books that have been produced about Fela Anikulapo-Kuti. While other books centered their arguments on the musical productions of the icon, Makinde undertakes the assignment of knowing the man by looking at his personal life. And this the author does through a unique interview method. This is a build-up on the significance of the interview and personal method which had been a feature of some of the previous books. The author mined the relationship that Fela had with so many others who shared some of Fela's legacy and experiences.[16]

The book presents the philosophical side of Fela and how the society was complicit in the shaping of his views about life in the direction he saw it. Contrary to the available misconceptions that were informed by the courageous involvement of Fela which makes him appear like an outcast, Fela was a great figure with a humble spirit. Fela was a loving father of adorable children with capacity for love and confounding affection. When the female members of his band were facing an onslaught of criticism from the public mischievously taunting them for working with Fela, he married them to ease the public opprobrium. Besides, Fela showed incredible interest in the yearnings and travails of the common people who he believed were victims of bad leadership. It was this mindset that made him undertake courageous tasks that would lead to social change.

The title of Makinde's book indicates something ominous about the off-camera experience of Fela with the government of the country. The government, which felt excessively threatened by the continuous existence of the revolutionary, took different measures to ensure that he was frustrated. The book, for example, recounts the 1977 experience where the military regime masterminded series of raids and attacks on the armless man, exploiting all opportunities to censure his voice. While the terror of the government against the man was unceasing, Fela's personal life therefore did not collapse as imagined by his detractors. To win the war against Fela, the government imagined, it was necessary to defeat him physically and then emotionally. This is readily deductible from the invasion of his Kalakuta Republic during the period where the men in khaki visited maximum damage on his household. His wives were raped, and his mother, molested. Fela was expected to become voiceless after the incidence or become too weak to engage the government. Unfortunately for the government, the ferocious force with which Fela always resurge after each attack revealed his unreadiness to bow out.

Fela's songs, for instance, question the loyalty of the military officials who execute instructions from their superiors without checking the sense in such orders. The military took this as the excuse to invade his Kalakuta Republic. And Fela was beaten, bruised, and then battered to the satisfaction of those who meant to silence him.

Fela Anikulapo-Kuti: The Primary Man of an African Personality by Jawi Oladipo-Ola

Jawi Oladipo-Ola, in addition to the bulky intellectual materials produced about the African star, chronicles the ideology of Fela in this engaging book. The impression is already registered that Fela was an open book with an expensive capacity to generate thoughts and produce ideas. Hardly would anyone decide to take an intellectual assignment over the music and the lifestyle of the man without eventually being overwhelmed by available materials. Apart from the reality that one would encounter different types of conclusions about him, it is not equally impossible that the man's lifestyle and arts can be given multiple interpretations, without losing focus. Oladipo-Ola examines the life and songs of Fela and realizes that the man was not an average individual whose emergence to stardom was exclusively reinforced by his courageous engagement of the government for fame.[17] He was not an attention-seeking individual whose works showed a dearth of intellectual input. Contrary to this mindset, Fela's songs are revelation of a man of informed reasoning, logically arranged protest and intellectually resplendent individual with taste for class.

The fact that his music became a rallying point for people across the class divide tells about the fact that Fela was classy and brainy. Unlike many musicians whose engagement of music was only dictated by their interests and not competence, Fela was particularly adept to attract growing attention he had during and after his existence. Fela provoked an intellectual redefinition where it is established behind his name that he encouraged a reawakening of revolutionary mindset that seeks to dislodge man inhumanity to man. To the extent that the posthumous relevance of Fela can be spotted in the confidence that the public has toward anything carrying his trademark and how they are socially celebrated and promoted. The book establishes that the contemporary ascription of Fela's ideology to any musician with taste for human liberation speaks extensively about the regards and acceptance that people still have to the legacy bequeathed by the man. In actuality, during the time when the government was excessively reactionary to the songs, arts, and speeches of the man, the most creative works of the man were produced.

This book therefore presents the philosophical positions of Fela, his belief in equality, democracy and his dedication to humanitarian services without occupying elected positions. He continued to give much attention to this even at the detriment of his health. Whenever a defenseless individual is harmed or suffered from the leadership gap of the society, Fela gave his voice, his arts, and his freedom to identify with these people and project their anguish for the consumption of the government. He did this to provoke change. Among people who lived during his time, Fela's ideologies stood him apart from the rest. Oladipo-Ola likens the intellectual capacity of Fela to a man with hunger for adding values to himself. Fela consumed books written by great people of the continent and above. This explains why he was at the forefront of decolonization revolution. He identified virtually all the traces of identity politics and divisional agenda of the European imperialists and would therefore produce counter-narratives to challenge such instances in his music. This is predictably one of the reasons he attracted minimal human rights intervention in international community because Fela was never pretentious of his own aversion to avarice, subjugated leadership system, and the expansionist ideology of the West to the African people.

"Identity and Ideological Representation in Selected Fela Anikulapo-Kuti's Songs" by Temitope Ajayi

As the title suggests, Ajayi's essay examines the ideological representation of the artistic productions of Fela Anikulapo, in relation to the identity they espouse.

One of the most intellectually reinforcing arguments made by Ajayi is contained in his citation of Bloor and Bloor (2007), where he concludes that "ideologies are established belief systems, values, attitude, and assumptions shared by members of a particular social group, as opposed to members of another group. In other words, what distinguishes a people of a given social group from another is what they do differently from the members of the other group."[18] This argument establishes the basis for ideological constructions and their cultural components that necessitate dissimilarities when placed side by side with others. In essence, it is apparent that the emergence of ideologies is precipitated by the human history and experience, and their evaluation. When one examines one's past and therefore conducts an objective analysis of the situation at hand, it provides one the opportunity to project or predict the future with some exactitude.

Ajayi's analysis of Fela's songs focuses on the unraveling of the ideologies rooted in his artistic productions. By extending the definition of ideology to mean the set of ideas employed by people for the justification of their actions in their process of rebuilding their social and economic systems, Ajayi therefore implies that the personage of Fela Anikulapo builds sturdy ideological database used to rationalize his commitment against repressive government at every given opportunity. His ideologies therefore are carved from the familiar experience of unproductive leadership that was consuming the Nigerian space at the time of his musical activism. Knowing that the Nigerian government in the postcolonial environment was irreversibly anti-masses, he uses his Afrobeat as a means to amplify the yearnings of the citizens and highlight the negative impact of unproductive leadership to the society generally. The Nigerian people are bounded by common history of colonialism and slavery, and therefore had a unifying experience of anguish filtered into them through the colonialists and eventually the neocolonialist Africans. Necessarily, when people are confronted with a dedicated authoritarian, there are always reactionary forces in the place who take the position of calling out the government no matter the consequences. Interestingly, Fela is that figure in the music industry.

Ajayi's objective is to outline the values and aspirations decidedly represented by Fela. Without doubt, the activism of the man in question began with the discovery that virile development is usually reliant on the amount of objective criticism which can be organized against the government. Governance upholds the statutory duties to advance the society from its current position to the next when continuously engaged. However, this assignment is susceptible to abandonment especially when the euphoria of power and its corresponding gains are too overwhelming. Successive Nigerian governments therefore intended to add values to their people and initiate projects that would bring about desirable development to them. However, majority of these political elites become distracted with the intoxicating power of politics and therefore subsequently abandon their principles when they get power. As such, this creates the need for voices which would continuously challenge them to come alive to their statutory duties and fixate their attention of full development and not frivolities. Ajayi x-rays Fela's music and reveals why and how Fela's ideologies are attempts to create groups' identity in order to champion an emancipatory role.

To the extent that Ajayi defines "Otherness" as a social phenomenon that distinguishes groups from one another, the artistic productions of Fela place the government in a diametrically opposing position to the people who they exploit and encourage them to absorb their anguish without complaining. This reality therefore places Fela's music and revolutionary agitation in a unique position to articulate the identity of marginalized Nigerians. Such conclusion validates Fela's Marxist orientation which other researches have ascribed to him and his music. His strategy for the identity structuration of the yearning of the Nigerian masses is achieved through his active representation of their aspirations in his works. He did this by substituting the masses voices for his own. This enables him to shoulder the courageous assignment of challenging the authorities for their deliberately orchestration of mis-governance that characterizes the Nigerian leadership system. For the record, Fela belongs to a social class that ranks high (or first) in the economic scale of the society and as such enjoys a level of privilege that is enough to distract him from taking up such revolutionary actions. But it seems he was driven by the need for an equal opportunity than he was convinced of benefiting from the system that denies such arrangements.

Ajayi therefore crystallizes the impact and input of Fela to the re-engineering of a better society through his musical activism. He considers the Nigerian society as being a product of stratification between the haves and have-nots, the rich and the poor, the high and the low, and this leads to the realization that such Manichean principles and structures are outrageous impediment to growth. In other words, when the society is notably seen from the lens of those who have power and those who do not, it leads to uneven development where the efforts of the have-nots are enduringly frustrated. A number of Fela's music became a viable signal of this lopsided treatment and arrangement, and few of these are x-rayed by Ajayi. The significance of his works is realizable in the reality that they give credence to the concerns of the masses and place them at the zenith of his yearnings, showing the relationship between their unwarranted helplessness and the government indifference to the consequences of their political inactions to the people. In essence, the words *I* and *We* in Fela's songs are interchangeable, with a constant message that he is representing the masses and not the capitalist community that feast on the people for their euphoria pleasures. One example that Ajayi draws is sufficient for analysis here:

Well well, na true I wan talk again o	Well, I want to say the truth again
Na true I wan talk again o	I want to say the truth again
If I dey lie o	If I am lying
Make Orisa punish me	Orisa should punish me
Make Ifa punish me	Ifa should punish me
Make Edumare punish me	Edumare should punish me
Make the land dey punish me	The land should punish me
I read am for book ee-oo	I read it in books
I see so myself ee-oo...	I observed it myself
I read about one of them inside book like that	I read about one of them in a book
Dem call him name na ITT	He is by the name ITT (International Thief Thief)[19]

Here, Fela uses his identity as a reference point to contrast the behavior of the Nigerian political elite who automatically involve themselves in activities that are morally reprehensible in the society. This is easily revealed by the ascription of roles to identity because of the *Otherness* involved in it. Having drawn the line that the society is structured along the binary side of the good and the bad, the political class does not therefore prioritize the interests of common people as they are either considered as insignificant or are eternally condemned to servitude in which they consider every act of injustice against them as justified. Since the identity of Fela remains with the masses, he therefore exonerates them from the deplorable conditions of the society which, he believed, were the products of the leaders' ineptitude or outright mental incapacity to drive the society to a new level. Beyond what Ajayi termed as the demonstration of individualism, the adoption of pronoun *I* is meant to emphasize the veracity of his claims, and not to absolve the masses of any act of financial misappropriation. However, using *them* as a pronominal element in the song shows that he generalizes the target (the political class) as sharing a familiar characteristic of greed, kleptomania and avarice.

The point being made therefore is that the ideological representation of Fela spreads notably in the domain of activism and revolution that places him between the haves and the have-nots of the society. His allegations of the political class are built from the experience of master-subordinate relationship that has dominated the Nigerian space from the colonial time and that still lingers on. It is apparent that his formulation of an ideology therefore was definitely complementing masses' yearnings to the appropriate authority. Without having a voice like Fela, there is some tendency that the government would eternally consider the interests of the masses as a secondary affair which can be discarded at will. This conclusion is cemented by the understanding that Fela's deliberate identification with the masses was in class defiance, for he chose to abandon class superiority to invest in the struggles of the common people. Contrary to the observation of Ajayi, had Fela been individualistic in his social activism, he would have betrayed his ideological ground when confronted with expensive challenges in the form of tribulations, threats, repression and other expressions of violence that he underwent. However, the fact that he remained committed to his course of action influenced his courage and determination.

"Political Messages in African Music: Assessing Fela Anikulapo-Kuti, Lucky Dube and Alpha Blondy" by Uche Onyebadi

Uche Onyebadi examines the musical productions of three leading African musicians and their different genres. Onyebadi, unlike Ajayi, evaluates not only the musical ingenuity of Fela but more importantly the political messages that Afrobeat delivers. Onyebadi considers music in Africa as an engagement that surpasses mere entertainment. On the contrary, music fulfills a deeper socio-spiritual function. He argues that "the history of colonialism and independence in the continent will be incomplete without adequate attention to the music and songs that were used to mobilize people to agitate for political freedom."[20] For Fela, music is a vital and potent instrument of change that can be used to provoke social modifications of condemnable attitudes, underhand behavior, and political ills—all negative social patterns and attitudes that militate against the progress of the people.

Onyebadi places Fela and his musical activism against the dysfunctional governance and systems that continue to sabotage the country even after independence.[21] It was apparent that the political elites who were then ascending the political stage were camouflaged imperialists who found another conduit for the exploitation of the masses. By their deliberate refusal to initiate policies that would improve the lives of the common people that have been grounded for years because of the callous colonialism they underwent, the post-independence Nigerian leaders identified with their erstwhile despots who were unconcerned by the welfare of the Nigerian people. This thus prepared the ground for revolutionary actions as people inflicted by this leadership challenges would definitely react. This prompted the sudden emergence of Fela.

A number of Fela's songs are clear indicators that the most notorious enemy of Nigerian progress is corruption. For this very reason, quite a large number of his songs are concentrated on decrying corruption and calling out those that are the primary accomplices to its existence. Fela bemoaned the idea that a large section of the Nigerian population suffers financial and economic torture because the political elite is needlessly callous. He believed that the road to good governance, right leadership, and distributive development is by enabling responsible leadership that is accountable and responsive; and this is achievable by constantly calling out the government and his policies. When government abandons these fundamental principles that are conducive to the citizens' well-being, the people become easily vulnerable and susceptible to bad governance.

Onyebadi therefore deployed and analyzed some of Flea's songs that lament the fact that the Nigerian government is indifferent to the travails of the people. One example suffices from Fela's "Vagabond in Power" (VIP):

Him take am	He (head of state) uses it (power)
Steal money	To steal money
Ha ha, why?	Ha ha, why?
I don't know! I don't know	I don't know! I don't know (someone replied)
You don't know anything at all	You don't know anything at all
You just my brother, ha ha	You are just my (ignorant) brother, ha ha
Try this one:	Try this one:
Him no know hungry people	He doesn't know hungry people...
Him no know jobless people	He doesn't know that people are jobless
Him no know homeless people	He doesn't know that people are homeless
Him no know suffering people	He doesn't know that people are suffering
Him go dey ride best car	He will ride the best car
Him go dey chop best food	He will eat the best food
Him go dey live best house	He will live in the best house

Him go dey waka for road	If he walks along the road
You go dey commot for road for am	You will get off the road for him to pass
Him go dey steal money	He will steal (people's) money
Na "Vagabond in Power"!	He is a Vagabond in Power...[22]

Never before has any music activist captured the crudeness of the Nigerian political elite the way Fela did in this VIP track, which parodies the acronym VIP ("Very Important Persons") as Vagabond In Power. Without mincing words, he was able to project how African leaders court corruption and consider the opportunity to lead the people as a lifetime opportunity to loot the treasury. Onyebadi argues that there is an undeniable possibility between the retrogression of the Nigerian people and their leaders' extravagant behavior.[23]

"No Agreement Today, No Agreement Tomorrow: Fela Anikulapo-Kuti and Human Right Activism in Nigeria" by Shina Alimi and Iroju Opeyemi Anthony

Shina Alimi and Iroju Opeyemi Anthony investigate the human rights activism of Fela as expressed in his fiery songs, most of which defend the Nigerian masses against the undemocratic and inhumane policies of successive governments. According to them, "Fela's greatness was rooted in his indefatigable interactions with the ordinary person in society and untiring effort to revolutionize it."[24] Drawing from the historical trajectory of Fela's upbringing, the authors connect his activism with his fearless character while growing up. Fela grew up with a sense of an Afrocentric interpretation of events around him. This led him to eventually connect his surname, Ransome, with the colonial context of his upbringing, and an indication of the continuation of slavery, despite Nigeria's ceremonial independence. The singular action of rejecting his given surname and replacing it with another (Anikulapo), the authors note, signals the nonconformist nature of Fela.[25] And this nonconformism would eventually define the direction and content of Afrobeat as an instrument of protest and resistance against the predatory agenda of successive governments in Nigeria.

Despite the end to official colonization, colonial mentality persisted in the behavior and governance policies of African governments. Just like many Africans protested the horrible conditions under the colonial government, a number of activists sprang up to also protest the failures of the postcolonial African states. And Fela and his music were at the forefront of this activism. In "Colonial Mentality," Fela sang:

E be say you be colonial man	It seems you are a colonial man
You don be slave man before	You were a slave before
Them don release you now	You have been released
But you never release yourself	But you refused to liberate yourself.

In referring to this lyric, Alimi and Iroju stressed the significance of Fela's music in the displacement of colonial mentality and its destructive influences on the African people. The lyrics are indicative of the self-affliction of the African people on themselves. They have been "released," to use Fela's word (meaning Africans have been given freedom), yet they continue to enslave themselves in their slavish attachment to European practices and values.[26] Unfortunately, however, Fela insisted that this slavish attachment would always sabotage the capacity of African states to make sense of their own development.

It was therefore the corrupted trajectory of African development, facilitated by corrupt politicians, that became the focus of Fela's activism. Constant detention was not sufficient to detract Fela from lamenting the extractive mentality of an average African government and the political elite. In another song, Fela called political corruption "Authority Stealing":

Authority people them go dey steal/	People in authority are stealing
Public contribute plenty money/	When common people contribute money (e.g. tax)
Na authority people dey steal/	People in authority steal
Authority man no dey pickpocket/	A man in authority does not pickpocket
Na plentty cash him go dey pick/	He is interested in plenty cash
Armed robber him need gun/	An armed robber needs gun
Authority man him need pen/	A man in authority needs pen
Authority man in charge of money/	Authority man in charge of money
Him no need gun, him need pen/	He does not need gun, but he needs pen
Pen got power gun no get/	Pen has power but gun does not
If gun steal eighty thousand naira/	If gun steals eighty thousand naira
Pen go steal two billion naira/	Pen will steal two billion naira

Fela contrasted stealing between the poor and the elite. While the common people usually steal to eat, the people in authority steal in large quantity for luxury. Regrettably, the money stolen by the government officials are the accumulated sweat of the masses who were coerced to contribute, through taxation, supposedly for the betterment of the community. In fact, he draws an irony from the fact that people in authority use pen as their weapon to steal, against the common understanding that the gun is a more effective means of stealing. This means that when armed robbers steal monies from people, politicians are always many steps ahead because of the magnitude of their larceny.[27] This is a very subtle means, by Fela, to get the citizens conscientized about the corruption perpetrated by their political class. Doing this will therefore inspire public outrage and protest against the self-aggrandizement of the political class.

"Highlife Jazz: A Stylistic Analysis of the Music of Felá Anikulapo Kuti" by Albert O. Oikelome

In this study, Oikelome conducts a stylistic analysis of Fela's songs so as to unveil the underlying messages that are not easily come across when doing a surface interpretation of them. According to Oikelome, "Felá incorporated both foreign and local styles in the creation of the highlife jazz. The challenge then is to identify these styles and see how Fela incorporated them into a distinctive genre."[28] This becomes significant not only because a stylistic analysis of African popular music is scarce but also because such an analysis provides an understanding of the music's uniqueness in terms of how its forms and styles generate its unique aesthetic temperament. Oikelome's evaluation reveals that Fela's music are particularly value-laden in terms of form and content. Fela's style is associated with expressive music that enables him to analyze the sociopolitical and sociocultural conditions of the society without losing focus. In an attempt to understand the dynamics of Fela's style, Oikelome uses ethnocultural indexes to project the uniqueness of an individual style because the society is usually the source of the needed materials which allows the individual fashion its own unique stylistic identity. Given the role that identity plays in the development of a person's role in the African society, Oikelome argues that "a strong model of the 'self' is embodied in Felá Aníkúlápò Kútì. The combination of the 'inner' and 'outer' surface of his identity was central to his authority as a musician."[29] Apparently, Fela collapsed the foreign styles, especially of jazz, with the local one to produce his Afrobeat. The admixture of these two different styles in itself has some cultural and political underpinnings. One, it shows the user is deliberately protesting the imposed identity to favor his own. Two, the combination of the styles would be forcefully influential in projecting his grievances to the elite, on the one hand, and the masses who do not have access to the British language, on the other.

The ascension of Fela into music stardom in Nigeria has a lot to do with the style he adopted. To survive in the midst of notable musicians like Bobby Benson, Roy Chicago, Victor Olaiya, Rex Lawson, Eddie Okonta, Victor Uwaifo, as cited by the author, means that he was doing something different from the musical style and forms deployed by these others.[30] Thus, the popularity of Fela is prompted by the fact that he employed something that the lower class could very easily identify with. This led to their ability to adopt him as their unofficial spokesperson because of the musical style of engaging the political class which resonates with them. Fela was a quick observer of event, and he displayed this perspicacity in his ability to evaluate what his audience wanted and therefore switched into it effortlessly. Although Fela had the capacity for being unusually eclectic, the audience interest in his experiment with jazz and highlife led to the emergence of Afrobeat. Audience evaluation therefore was important for Fela and he always considered their taste in his musical production. Beyond the reality that Fela's style was collectively accepted, there was the temptation to step on toes of those who were affected by the style. The elite were continuously targeted and they therefore impeded the spread of Fela's fame by threatening him intermittently.

The fecundity of Fela's style is enhanced by his eclectic experiment with Western and local styles. He readily assorted his messages with different items that make for a hybridity of different musical contexts and forms. In language, Fela's deployment of pidgin English is considered pragmatic as it appeals to the sensitivity of the people. Quoting Omojola (1995), Oikelome further notes that Fela's style "included the use of short simple, repetitive melody based on Western tonal system. The harmonic pattern was based on Western harmonic form of the tonic, subdominant, and dominant chord with an extensive application of syncopation rhythm."[31]

Oikelome identified four different stages of Fela's stylistic evolution. According to him, there are four different stages in Fela's stylistic evolution. These involve the first period that covers the time when Fela was first coming into highlife performance. This is chiefly between 1962 and 1969. The second phase unraveled the following decade, a time when he rose to the zenith of his musical career. Interestingly, Fela entered into his third phase even in the 1970s at the height of his constant confrontation with the Nigerian military that to several and severe human rights violations against him and his properties. This therefore became an epochal era in his stylistic evolution as he undertook a different and more demanding assignment of calling out the military.[32]

"Behavioural Approach to Political Protest: An Analysis of Fela Anikulapo Kuti, 1970–1997" by Olukayode Segun Eesuola

Although different scholars have examined the protest culture embedded in Fela's songs, Eesuola takes a different research dimension that extends our knowledge about the radical personality and music of the Afrobeat maestro. The author establishes the various dimensions of protest and justifies reasons for protest actions in a society. Among many other things, protests are not expected to instantly bring about the predetermined results because those against which a protest is directed are aware of their excesses but are unwilling to revamp the system or structure because of the benefits and advantages accruing from the status quo. Nonetheless, this does not prevent citizens from protesting the hardship that such an oppressive status quo inflicts on them. The author then presses home his argument about how a single individual can become the arrowhead of protest in a society:

> grievances of "one" individual towards the political regime snowballing into "self-designed" protest actions, drawing thousands others to move en-mass against regimes, attracting local and international attention, as well as leading to changes in policies. Some form of curiosity then ensues: from where do such individuals come who take delight in protest and rebellious behaviour? What explains the type of protest action they exhibit towards their polities and how does our understanding of these issues and others assist in explaining political behavior in general and political protest in particular?[33]

And to concretize his unique radical protest, Fela created a multidimensional protest action: he created Afrobeat as his unique popular protest music; established an organization—the Young African Pioneers—to focus his social movement; formed a political association, Movement of the People (MOP) to contest political election; and went as far as creating a "state"—the Kalakuta Republic—within the Nigerian state to signal his rebellion to the Nigerian government and its laws.[34]

Eesuola's unique approach therefore is to de-emphasize the macro approach to the study of protest music, in favor of a behavioral focus on the individual as the locus of protest. To the extent that group behavior is significant to our understanding of all forms of protest, we must not in a way submerge the individual role and impact in the dynamics of these protest. It therefore becomes significant to trace the behavioral trajectory that leads from a protesting individual, the individual's perception of social and societal ills and injustices, and the individual's choice of a response to these, to the formation of a group or movement against these ills and injustices. This is the approach that Eesuola takes in his dissertation. Thus, for him,

> if Fela as an individual utilized his own methods: music and deviant behaviour to exhibit stern protest against the interregnum of corruption, nepotism, neocolonialism, imperialism, military repression and misgovernance in Nigeria between 1970 and 1997 to the extent of provoking reactions and attentions even in the international community, and if other individuals continue to exhibit political protest actions that are unique to them in their respective polities as demonstrated in Benzoazi's [Bouazizi] recent self-immolation in Tunisia, it becomes imperative to study what is essentially peculiar about such individuals whose lives appear to be protest embedded; to explore how they acquire their protest behaviour, the factors that trigger their protest actions, the dimensions their protests take and why they take them, as well as the impacts their protests have on their political environments.[35]

Eesuola argues that Fela's music signals contemporary history as the songs usually encapsulate significant sociopolitical and sociocultural trajectory of the country. And this also makes it doubly efficacious in tracking the trajectory of Fela's own music. This is what Eesuola does. He provides the systematic analysis of Fela's songs right from the beginning of 1970 till his demise in 1997. This offers the reader what he calls the logical progression of Fela's music in different temporal phases: "songs of criticism," "songs of confrontation and incitement," "songs of political skepticism," and then "songs of cynicism."[36] In the early 1970s when Fela matured into his music career, he was only critical of government through his detailed analysis of Nigeria and her problems. During this period, even Fela affirmed preaching to government to embrace change and upgrade their administration style to a better one that would accommodate the yearnings and interests of the masses. But since the political class remained intransigent, Fela's songs graduated to being used as an instrument of confrontation. Soon, his music metamorphosed into skepticism and finally to cynicism all because the sociocultural underpinnings are not indicative of any improvement.

Conclusion

Fela Anikulapo-Kuti remains an enigma, even close to three decades after his unfortunate death. While alive, there were several interviews and researches conducted on his person and his music. The more Fela became a global phenomenon, the more his persona became more intriguing. This is especially so given the fact that his personality and his Afrobeat were formed at the juncture of social anomie and social change within the Nigerian postcolony. Through his saxophone, Fela blared a liberation call that jarred the earlobes of authoritarian governments in Nigeria. He sang about corruption, religious obscurantism, governance failure, followership apathy, infrastructural rot, mental enslavement, and ideological backwardness.

After his death, what we can call the Fela industry blossomed into multiple levels of intellectual inquiries about Fela's personality, identity, politics, ideology, philosophy, behavior, social deviance, and countercultural dynamics. Some other studies focused on his family background, his family (and specifically mother), his women (and specifically his wives), Sandra Isidore, his journeys, and the evolution of Afrobeat. Each of the authors considered in this chapter approaches Fela and his music from a perspective that enables us to further distillate the relationship between Fela, Afrobeat, and the postcolonial Nigerian state and society.

2

Fela in Historical Perspectives

The world moves forward, not by mere coincidence of nature, or through some magical intervention of unknown spirits. It moves forward by the efforts and influence of certain people that are committed to ensuring a change. This is partly because change requires that humans engage in giving conscious determination that is implicit in the activities they embark upon to bring about a change in the usual methods by which society conducts itself. However, the population profile of every known human society remains the single obstacle for an easy harvesting of ideas which would send the society to the top of the development ladder, or reposition it generally on the map of growth. This, therefore, makes it somewhat a challenging exercise for change to occur in every human society. Regardless of this reality, there are some individuals who, through their commitment to provoking changes, compel their societies to confront the need for transformation through their unceasing physical, social and intellectual struggles. and this is sometimes achieved against the will of the minority benefiting from the status quo. In most cases, these outstanding individuals usually make costly sacrifices which may include their freedom at the best, and their lives at worst. The musician Fela Anikulapo-Kuti belongs to this category.

For Fela, the collateral sacrifices for the change he foresaw in the society were both his freedom and then his life. Born on October 15, 1938,[1] the Nigerian music aficionado was an outstanding star in the sociopolitical atmosphere of his country of birth. Being part of the upper-middle-class in the society, Fela explored all the opportunities he had to register his name in the history books of Nigeria and Africa. Coming at the time when Nigeria was still under the grip of colonialism, and growing up in such an environment, served as the needed armory to arm his arsenal of philosophy. He gave constant social education to people with whom he believed shared genetic and cultural bonds, and upon whose survival depended the social engagement of the people at the helm of affairs: leaders. Growing up, he maintained his voice and would show a clear sense of purpose by outlining the things he wanted and the ways by which he would get them. For instance, Fela went to pursue a career in music against the plans of his parents, who had wanted him to study medicine in London.[2] Such level of exactitude in decision making shows a man who has definite targets with his life, and will not bow to pressures around him.

Fela was a figure whose entire life epitomized originality. He was a constant reminder to the society of their need to wake up from generational slumber. Apart from representing his cultural background through his music to the world, Fela used the medium of music to teach the general populace a lesson that not only would later be regarded as valuable to their own growth but also would later be understood as a call for freedom. His unrelenting nature in the quest for a better environment made it possible for him to write his name in gold, and be celebrated as a clairvoyance who predicted the future of the country in his evangelical music, even by those who did not believe in him during his life crusade. So, the dearth of his message in the current dispensation of sociopolitical affairs of the country cannot but be noticed. For Fela, paying hefty prices for freedom and collective emancipation was the only thing through which his message could be heard, and so he sacrificed without any iota of regret. Tactful, calculative, and proactive, he came across as a brave warrior who salvaged his people and his beloved ideology from the notorious hands of mis-governance, maladministration, and provincial malady of the Nigerian society. Therefore, when talking about Anikulapo, we are on a journey to talking talk about a man whose gospel of truth rings a generational bell.

Fela and His Life's Philosophy

Every man is driven by certain convictions after attaining a particular height in the society. Through the various accumulated experiences, man overtakes the issues that concern his life with confidence; he does so with a form of loyalty to tested ideologies, through which he navigates his existence in life. Man, as a social and spiritual being, cannot avoid being exposed to different challenges in life that will test his abilities in some respect, unless he does not make any human effort to transform the world around him, which is difficult in most cases. The nature of man necessitates that he relates with the immediate world around him in an effort to upgrade his thinking, or compliment his progress. Therefore, it is usually given that man would have attracted different experiences while doing this, which would enhance his ability to think wide and far, depending on the depth of his experience. In some cases, his experience is blown active by the recorded history with which he was raised and nurtured. When this is the case, man tries to consult remote and immediate history with a view to formulating ideas which would help in the area of making reliably helpful decisions as regarding his existence. For example, a man whose family has been attacked by invaders in times past would forever be wary of taking in strangers without putting into place appropriate measures to curb future potential misdemeanors.

This leads to everyone creating and following certain ideologies that would guide them throughout the race of life. For a man who spent his whole life following certain ideologies uncompromisingly, Fela could be seen as an icon with outstanding philosophy to life. In our quest to understanding this man that still has the image of a social engineer, we would take into consideration the philosophical constructs behind the sturdy wall of Anikulapo. The prevalent inequality that pervades the social and political lifestyle of many African countries are testimonies to the class consciousness of the Western world, whose philosophy is hinged on a master-subordinate attitude when dealing with people of different colors. The fact that the erstwhile colonized people inherited this attitude in their eventual political dispensation birthed a form of stunted growth in the profession of life of the people in general. This is actually because the capitalist mentality of the postcolonial African leaders invited a sequence of disasters on the general outlook of the formerly colonized African people. The government, which was supposed to be a safe haven for the defenseless common man, becomes the rallying point for maltreatment.

Such circumstances enhanced jaundiced development, and inactive performance became the watchword of government officials who are determined to use their political power for personal achievement at a time when collective progress should occupy their primary concerns. Thus, many people became mute and would rather endure a life full of agony than call out the government body that was practically responsible for such outrageously poor leadership. It is situations like this that bring out the courageous ones who would defy all odds and stand fearlessly to put the perpetrators of such disastrous political stances into their appropriate positions. Fela belongs to this category, and in him was an energy that invigorated the world around him with his crusade for equality, despite standing at variance with vested authorities. For a man who understood the politics of identity and the covert Euro-Western gimmicks to under develop the continent, he lent his voice to speak against the despicable issues of misgovernance, and earned himself an increased number of enemies. Therefore, the actor in Fela, by taking the risk of standing against the government whenever there is a foul play, sandwiched himself between difficult conditions and challenging situations most of the time.

Aware that this would bring along unfortunate damages to his career and reputation, the man did not back down from the focus he set for himself. Overtime, he was found making his voice heard loudly by spreading the message of emancipation through his music. All these and many more undertakings by him won him the image of an outlaw to the constituted authority, and made him a leader of the marginalized majority. This mainly explains why he had a widespread popularity across his cultural and geographical boundaries both during and after his time. The popularity of Anikulapo outlives him decades after his death to the present moment. His songs speak to power, and encourage egalitarian society to find a workable solution to the plights confronting the people. At every moment, Fela understood and campaigned very harshly against misappropriation of public funds, informing the unassuming majority that it leads to a way of weaponizing poverty where the public will have limited access to education, which in turn makes them incapable of defending themselves and understanding how they are ruled, and by who. No man or woman on the lower rungs of the financial hierarchy would be able to lead a life of fulfillment because their lives have been mesmerized by the compulsive greed of the leaders in power. Therefore, espousing such bravery at a time when the major political machinations in the African continent were by-products of military rule, Fela's music and messages resulted in many untold havocs deliberately orchestrated against him.

Projecting the likely effects of government's spendthrift attitude and their lackadaisical behavior toward the welfare of the common man makes Fela appears more like a soothsayer than an ordinary musical character. In fact, many years after his passing, the things he projected came into reality with so much exactitude that one wonders if he was saying those things as no ordinary being. In contemporary society, the Nigerian music industry features many disciples of Fela, some of which were toddlers when the icon was alive. This happens because his legacy speaks to the prevailing realities of the African people in the postcolonial environment. Africa, despite her claims to numerous natural and human resources, remains the headquarters of pestilence in the world today because of the mindless spending of past leaders and their outright inability to plan for the future. All across the world, the political class is known to throw their weight against anyone who desires to wash their dirty linen in public just like Fela did, and it therefore came as no surprise to see that Fela underwent those torturous moments in an effort to speak the unclothed truth about the authorities. Many a time, Fela went down hard on them in Nigeria and his actions would always provoke their reactions.

On the occasion of one of his songs, "ITT," Fela decries how the international community aided and abetted the power structures of the country. In fact, the song challenges the moral rectitude of the colonial powers who were inconsiderate in milking the country dry, and eventually serving as conduit pipes for the neocolonial power hunters. As a result, in 1977 a battalion of soldiers stomped on Fela's abode, giving him a historical denigration, and bullying him unabashedly to the satisfaction of the power bloc of the nation. Having released a track that pointedly called notable names into question, "ITT" provoked such warring reactions from the government of the day.[3] The song titled "International Thief Thief" seized the political atmosphere and attracted untold battles to him which dealt a severe blow to the things he had worked for and the legacy he struggled hard to establish. Despite this, the man came out unruffled and gave the impression of resilience, of not backing down from the target he had already set for himself. This, among many other things, helped to shape the philosophy of Fela and brought him the popularity he enjoyed during and after his lifetime. Anikulapo-Kuti was such a fierce individual whose choice of weapon in the battleground of life was not guns; he chose music and won ferocious battles.

Fela and Nigeria's Political Struggles

Inclusive in the heartrending struggles of Fela Anikulapo is his uncompromising stance on the political actors of the country. Sequestered from the radical lifestyle that he was popular with, Fela comes across as a man who understood the political dynamics of the world and his immediate environment. He was an apostle of a solid conviction that the progress of every society is particularly dependent on the forms of leadership put in place. In other words, visionless leaders are dangerous to the common progress of the people they lead. Apart from constituting distractions where unexpected, they literally dedicate their efforts to sending people back centuries away, because of their losing touch with reality. Therefore, the usual victims are the innocent majority who either depend on luck to salvage their situations from getting moribund or resort to violence whereby anarchy would rule supreme. Such clairvoyant foresight into the future led to Fela's self-acceptance of the role of a maverick who would hold the people in power into account and demand for fairness in their running of collective affairs. It is not unexpected, therefore, that he was placed at variance with the power blocs of the society during his existence, more so for the fact that the country had not evolved to use diplomatic approaches to solve social problems.

As an important voice when the country still had dictators at the seat of power, all that was needed for Fela to feel the heat of power was a mere pronouncement, which would instantaneously become a game that the power brokers would hungrily feast on. This placed the undaunted figure, Fela, at disadvantage and made him suffer protracted abuse by the people who become threatened by his verbal whips, dished out carefully and intelligently through his music. Gaining inspiration from the kind of support he got from the masses, Fela felt the sympathy of the public was more of a compensation to his brutal experience from the draconian neocolonialists than getting cowed into silence, where these brutish treatments of the powerless would go on unchecked. Apparently, weighing on these two options explains why he would go on to produce more nerve-wracking critical appraisals of the government almost immediately after being treated unfairly by them. It appears, therefore, that Fela showing such a level of resilience became more infuriating to the government representatives, the targets of his criticism, and they would in turn show more aggression in handling cases that bear the tag of Fela. Thus, Fela could be understood better as a powerhouse for political issues and collective affairs of the country during his lifetime. Furthermore, he had been a victim of power mismanagement for more times than can be counted.

On the international scene, Fela collaborated with Roy Meyers in 1989 to produce a very incredible masterpiece titled "2000 Blacks Got To Be Free."[4] This music encapsulates the general worldview of Fela Anikulapo-Kuti and espouses his beliefs. Freedom has been the center of crusade for this music genius, which he dedicated most of his life to. In this particular work, Fela along with his amazing collaborator Meyers delved into the murky waters of political and economic slavery under which the Africans and their African American counterparts struggled to survive. Their constriction, which followed their generational enslavement on both the economic and political fronts, remains a powerful clog in the wheel of progress of the black family. The fact that their sympathetic condition does not attract global attention or provoke reactions makes some brave Africans, such as Fela, occupy the global climate with their message of freedom for the victims: Africans. As such, the focus of the music giant has forever been to ensure a level ground for the financially and politically weak of the society, with a view to giving them a great sense of belonging and to serve as an energy boost to their dying morale. Succinctly, Fela is an individual whose blood is boiled for altruism.

"I have a dream, like many of you, that by the year 2000, Africans would be free." This line from the track described above puts plainly the selfless attitude of the man in question, Fela. The record must be set straight that Anikulapo-Kuti was not of a lowly background where it would be difficult to afford the necessities of life. In fact, he belonged to a family of economically buoyant individuals who were apparently doing well in the country, able to give him all he needed. But from the philosophy of his, it becomes apparent that he prefers identifying with the masses and takes it upon himself to fight for them in places where they are bluntly denied of their human rights. Music is an important medium, and its inherent ability to reach out to audiences very fast makes it more fitting for messages such as the ones that Fela spread in his work. For anyone who understands the hot political terrain of Nigeria following her independence, they would see the context of Fela's struggles more clearly than could be described in words. Coupled with the disconcerting attitude of the political class to social criticisms, many individuals who lent their voices to the harsh sociocultural realities bore the brunt of the government's response with their own freedom, and sometimes with their lives.

When Fela produced "ITT" (International Thief Thief), which grabbed the public's attention by the jugular, he targeted the ruling class. The musical track decries the glaring misappropriation of public wealth by the insignificant few who deployed public offices to garner personal benefits. As expected, such actions would be considered an affront to those who benefited from this lopsided equality and would even deploy the statutory power under their command to combat anyone who stood in their way of "progress." This unavoidably led to the many public harassments that Fela underwent under the government's impervious rulings. In the track that spans through almost twenty-five minutes of recording, Fela's choir of singers injected through the background all the woes that were bedeviling the country at the time. This is a deliberate confrontation with the government for their flagrant abuse of the political offices they hold and the gross inability to establish a connection between their undeserved affluence and the masses' indigence. There is therefore no logical base to not expect reactions from such power blocs.

Understanding that the African people have a tenuous belief in their traditional religious heads, Fela explored this method very artistically and realistically. Before going on to spread the thematic concerns of the musical track, which specifically center on greed as seen from those in power, he opened the floor by invoking the gods of the African lands as the adjudication of what he was about to say—the glutinous character of the average Nigerian politician. The mention features Ogun, Edumare, Sango, among many other Yoruba deities, and these are well-respected celestial characters in the pantheon of the Yoruba people. Their cultural and spiritual powers make them fearful and earn them great positions of exaltation among the adherents of the faith and the Yoruba people in its entirety. So, when Fela invoked them in the track, he was using traditional Yoruba religion as a leverage to get the attention of the listeners and then secure their trust in the message he brought. For the audience, they understand very well the thin line of difference between making unfounded claims and using alien Gods as witnesses, and doing the same thing with native Gods. They know that the latter carries weight and as such would give their entire trust to the messages Fela brought rather than discarding his performance as a mere public stunt.

It is instructive to state that the track under analysis is an indictment of the European world for their role in seeing Africa plunged into war and pestilence. When Fela talks about "shit," a corruption of the word "feces," he was addressing the life history of the Europeans prior to their coming into the African continent. This is done in an effort to play out the glaring irony that the Africans who have attained a certain level of development, particularly of disposing their "shit" appropriately, now suddenly become victims of colonization by their supposed inferiors in the angle of development. This therefore sets the pace for another indictment to be made on the Europeans. In the same track, Fela reiterated how the European world now had many companies in Africa after plunging their former colonies into untold hardship and outrageous retrogression; these companies now served as conduit pipes to milk the African countries dry of their hard-earned commonwealth. This point can be understood as a way of informing the people of the heinous crimes that their political office holders perpetrate using their offices, and this is done in an effort to provoke the reactions of the masses to the government that has taken their silence for an acceptance of the situation. The creative genius Fela reiterated this by saying he read it from a book.

The way the misappropriation of public funds is painted by this outstanding musician shows his in-depth understanding of the situations of African societies. The sinister actions that enhanced the connivance of Europeans interests with African political power hunters make it difficult for Africans to flush out political outlaws and proffer lasting solutions to their ravaging problems. Fela enunciated how the European world would engage in the systematic imposition of candidates on most African countries after they have attracted and make them loyal stooges who would always return favor to their owner. Therefore, when things get excessively bad in governance, the masses either resign to fate by blaming their stars for their grinding misfortune or become silent in the face of outright oppression. This system leads to the weaponization of poverty, and the people lose their dignity at the sight of the little financial help rendered by those who are obviously stealing from them. Therefore, the European interests, in collaboration with their moles in the African political space, hold the continent in ransom where nothing seems promising for their prey in the grand scheme of things. The "thieves" referred to by Fela are able to steal successfully because their foreign accomplices provide safe havens for them.

It is indubitable that in a country where there is widespread miseducation, revolutionaries must make very stringent efforts to educate the sleeping masses so as to plan successfully any struggle that will help secure the attention of the indifferent public officials. Throughout the world, the lack of education of the masses is always an unsolicited opportunity for visionless leaders to exploit the state's commonwealth without reproach. It therefore appears that some leaders with an unbearable amount of greed always will deliberately engage in activities that will take the people far away from the current happenings in the society; in other words, invest heavily in their lack of education. This breeds a docile citizenry and thus makes them an easy target of every political predator. With this horrible development, there are still individuals who take the arduous task of educating the masses upon themselves so as to ensure that they can decide the fate of the leaders prevailing on their affairs. Fela obviously falls within this sublime category. In order for the people to become aware of the sociopolitical realities around them, he went to unimaginable lengths just so that he could draw the downtrodden to the knowledge of the things around them. Such commitment earned him the most precarious identity upon whom the wrath of the state's leadership descended on at will.

Therefore, Fela Anikulapo-Kuti was a man who modeled his political ideology around African socialism and was a strong advocate for it while alive. To him, the extreme capitalism that the African countries were tending to was systematically eroding African cultures, making their identity more vulnerable to their Euro-American counterparts. Rather than taking the masses through insufferable hardships in an effort to amass public wealth, he believed the political power holders should devise ways by which resources would be sufficient for every individual. Committing oneself to an ideology that seems to have become a gradually fading legacy cannot but have fetched the kind of treatment that Kuti endured in the hands of the political despots of his time. In 1983, Fela announced his lovely ambition to contest for the position of president under the political umbrella of his political party MOP (Movement Of the People), a satiric attempt to fumigate the seemingly unkempt political structure of the country.[5] His increased popularity was sending waves of despair through the Nigerian political elites, and their best bet was to deploy all their might in fighting a man they already considered a potential threat to their political survival. This attracted another series of molestations of Fela under the succeeding military government. However, though his body might have been fatally abused, his spirit was unbending.

It was the mere declaration of this lofty ambition that won him more treatments that would instigate further severity of his social image and outlook. For an ambitious man like Fela, popular with the people, formulating criminal justice allegations around him or cooking unfounded claims that would soil his name were the easiest to do. It was the overtaking of the government leadership by the military juggernaut after his candidature that saw to another implosive and brutally orchestrated arrest of him which lasted for about two years, based upon an allegation that he flouted the country's financial rules.[6] His case thus became the proverbial dog who was marked for death by his owner; for the time being, there would be no escaping of name-calling. All these and many more are the costly prices that Anikulapo had to pay for his dogged political ideology. Following this, his treatment attracted another form of toughness to his musical career, and Fela toed the line with unmatched commitment.

Fela and His Protest Orature

In the world of literary discussion, there are different categories that are occupied by various literary giants. This has been a lifelong heritage passed down from one generation to another. Works of art, regardless of the form they take, usually have their utilitarian purposes that they are bound to serve society, which essentially situate their importance within the context of societal usefulness. When they are devoid of this, it becomes readily difficult to attract the attention of the masses. Thus, when a work of art can comfortably entertain the audience as well exhibit important messages to a section of the society, such work is usually said to have a utilitarian purpose. The literary icons who are behind the production of works like this are seen as the compasses of society that direct the concentration of the majority toward a common target. When the leadership of a country strays from the statutory duties that they are primarily expected to undertake, these souls rise to their own feet despite the assumed difficulties they are bound to face and resist any perceived injustice that the power blocs have masterminded again with their misuse of power. Therefore, protest literatures are a common ground in many nations, including Nigeria. During colonial times, many literary productions were particularly made to question the moral superiority claimed by the European world.

In Nigeria's case, Fela protested many activities of the government which had personal or collective negative impacts. At the climax of his popularity, it became a social duty for him to naturally undertake this daunting task of calling the government out, both colonial and neocolonial bandits, because the masses had already accepted him as a man they could expect to confront the actors at the helm of affairs for their deliberate political sadism. Therefore, the combination of forces produced within the literary circle and the music industry during the hot neocolonialist era continued to birth an informed citizenry which became conscious of the activities of their leaders. Although the level of updates they had about their environment did not translate into good governance by the leaders automatically, the new knowledge gave them a voice which would be duly considered before they went about with their stout disregard for moral issues. Thus, it is possible to see the declaration of war against the power custodians in the society as a personal battle for Fela. On many occasions, he was harshly trampled upon and his human rights violated, in a show of muscle between him and the power blocs of Nigeria. Like every individual with blood in their veins, Fela would always show his own reactions through music tracks that sent shivers up the spine of power.

In one of his protest songs, "Zombie," Fela dragged the military into his criticism. The inclusion of this arm of the Nigerian security system into his attack was in an attempt to show to the whole world his awareness of the external political interests in dealing ruthlessly with him. He highlighted the activities of the soldiers in the country and linked their nature of duty to a powered robot that lives only on instruction. Attacking them this way duly attracted the annoyance of the men in khaki and made them show their angst toward their accuser in the subsequent raiding of his house in 1977. While doing that, more than a thousand soldiers descended on Fela's home to destroy his properties and harass the people who associated themselves with him.[6] In a show of power against a helpless Fela, the conflict did not actually end well for him as the lives of the people dear to him had to become an inevitable collateral in his existing war against the authority. In fact, his mother was fatally injured from the ignoble attack by the military. This sort of molestation characterized Fela's life, and his explicit acceptance of fate gave him the public love and sympathy he received during and after his existence on earth. On many instances, Fela enjoyed so much overwhelming love, which can be understood as his source of inspiration when calling out the government's misrule.

"Zombie" is a music track that explicates the involvement of the European world in silencing his voice for black emancipation. It is therefore resident in the metaphoric reference made to the men in uniform about their inability to consider a cause of action before execution. This attribute confines them to a minimal level and makes mockery of their status as humans. Everyone with blood in their veins is expected to consider things logically and emotionally before carrying out certain actions, but for the military men—all they need is a mere order from supreme power and they are on their way to execute another without giving it any further consideration. Coincidentally, the Nigerian government is peopled by agents of imperialism who became informants and stooges to the European world in post-independence African countries, with a view to extending the rule of their colonial masters beyond the time of actual freedom. As a result of challenging this use of force against the comfort of the majority, Fela won more than enough political and economic detractors. Undaunted by this seemingly foreboding nepotistic leadership, the musical icon underwent a series of personal attacks for his philosophical obstinacy.

Known for the consistency in his protest songs, Fela convincingly educated, and still educates, members of the public about the perpetual conflicts that the government cause the people through their own excessive greed and lack of proper planning. Apart from sensitizing the public about these inglorious social and financial acts of desecration done at the corridor of power, Fela's life was modeled on sacrifice that many people would not dare to undertake, even if given an assurance of payback in any form. On many occasions he had trumpeted about the people's deliberate avoidance of speaking truth to power under the excuse for the preservation of their lives, and alleged that such was an attribute of cowardice with nonexistent fear which had been planted into the heart of the people, or through their own incapability to take the bull by the horn. To the voiceless majority, thus, Fela represented a model who they looked up to whenever there existed any perceived injustice. For anyone who understands the sociopolitical climate of Nigerian society, it is easy to predict that government officials usually escape the people's wrath even after making obvious missteps. Rather than call out the people in power, the Nigeria citizenry prefers expressing their discomfort in solitude or relegating their voices into a silent hum where their resignation emboldens these leaders to blow more on the embers of anarchy.

In one of his protest songs produced in 1976 by the name "Upside Down,"[7] Anikulapo-Kuti yet again hit the nail on the head regarding an issue that had become an almost indispensable part of African life, even after independence: the erosion of African culture. The European world did not discard their cultural heritages and maintained their identities despite their social and cultural miscegenation with people from other cultural backgrounds. However, this reality eludes Africans, who seem to have watched their minds eroded with colonialism. Many Africans would take satisfactory pleasure in dislodging their own cultural values in preference over the foreign customs, which have a history of taking them through generations of outright human degeneration. Their indifference to this sometimes provokes insight into the assumption that there may have existed not just the physical colonization of the people but their psychological kidnap as well. The fact that Africans view their own heritages with negative interpretations remains a source of genuine concern to those who care for the survival of the black cultures. Without outside coercion, Africans of the postcolonial environment tried in every way to severe ties with their cultural backgrounds.

Expectedly, this leads to dispossession of valuable heritages and the gradual abandonment of their legacies. In every facet, Africans now become aliens to their own cultural productions so much so that it becomes more and more difficult to see patriots of traditional African cultures. It requires someone who is particularly informed and understands global politics predominantly centered on identity to come out with fearful force to speak out about this without fear or favor. In order for the audience to understand the gravity of his message, Fela placed the cultures of the colonial West side-by-side with African customs and reiterated how the European man does not let go of his cultural heritage regardless of his diverse experiences. He pontificated that the Western people who brought them certain cultures from an alien environment did so in consternation of the black folks, who thought that Western superiority in technology automatically translate to superiority in every other thing. To Fela, there was no single convincing reason why Africans would refuse to model their own growth based on local knowledge databases, rather than foreign ones.

At the forefront of the protestation shown in Fela's music is an American woman who had found intricate attraction in Fela's music while he was away and decided to pitch her tent with the man whose voice remained loud even in the face of threat. Therefore, the metaphoric reference to the contemporary African dealings amplifies the reality that Africans do their things in an anticlockwise direction. Instead of appreciating their own legacies, they have become spectators in the general scheme of things because they have abandoned what rightfully belongs to them. Fela mentions all the important areas where Africans are becoming passive in issues where they should have become unapologetically loud. Thus, their renunciation of traditional names and their sudden abandonment of valuable customs and other traditions have made them incapable of measuring to the standard of the Europeans, who they have implicitly considered as their moral compass, rather than the competitors, which they actually are. It was alluded in the song that everything concerning the black man has been disorganized, and thus they have been sadly relegated to the margins and rendered impotent where it matters. The song protests the African mind of his inability to acknowledge his ignorance.

Fela and Yoruba Epistemology

Epistemology in philosophy is a branch that studies the validity or otherwise of a knowledge by placing it within the truth test, as particularly systematized by the early philosophy and researchers of similar interests. By this understanding, we can come to a very subtle conclusion that knowledge production is exclusive to every group of people with track records of survivalist ideology in their environment. This therefore situates everyone within the actual philosophical construct of the society that produces them. In the situation where a man adopts some strange philosophy to govern his life, he is susceptible to becoming a follower of the new found ideology, and as a result exorcising his traditional body of knowledge in exchange for the new one. Thus, before and after his birth, his epistemology is helplessly subsumed under an imagined superior knowledge base, on whose shoulders rest the gradual erosion of values which are native to him: Yoruba ontology. The Yoruba people of the southwest part of Nigeria had a glorious history with a full-fledged knowledge economy before the incursion of the colonial masters, when their native knowledge was relegated to the background by the European imperial powers who were uncompromisingly on a voyage to efface every local database they came upon.

Therefore, the Yoruba epistemology, now a prey in the jungle of the cultural war masterminded by the European lords, became the powerhouse of Fela Anikulapo-Kuti. Fela found an unusual love for his native knowledge production and would hold no peace in excavating the native resources through his songs. This therefore confirms Fela's music as much more than the mere knitting together of words, to be accomplished by impressive rhythm delivered by his musical instruments. Instead, his music remains an evocation of cultural belonging that already has a shared identity with the potential audience or admirers. With his amazing skills of using the appropriate lexicons to deliver his message in a heterogeneous society where multiple tongues are the given realities, Fela perfectly injected many doses of Yoruba cultural knowledge into his musical products, which would later become the consumables of his local and international fans. Far above the anticipation of the known critics and different detractors alike, Fela raised up all the standards upon which the people could view and evaluate the Yoruba customs and values. From the bold step of naming his center of performance *African Shrine*[8] to eventually conducting some religious-like activities there, Fela was indirectly raising awareness of his Yoruba customs.

This epistemic identity is shown in one of his tracks titled "Gentleman"[9] a song that was characteristically rejecting the form of Western identity which the colonizers believed was a suitable way to make Africans detach themselves from their own natural identity. The concealed vicious intentions of the Western minds by selling the idea of a man with courtesy in their own analysis is specifically, Fela notes, to launch a greater and more diabolical attack on the unassuming folk in Africa, who would accept the idea of a gentleman and in the long run become mute and unable to express their dissatisfaction. In Africa, there is an existential belief in an arrangement where each action deserves appropriate reactions: a cultural understanding that gives credence to a cause and effect theory. Therefore, when someone has deliberately undertaken an action against anyone, he or she must expect a complementary reaction from them. This philosophy has thus mandated the Africans to do things they would accept to their fellow beings. Failure in this regard is an invitation to violence and anarchy that disrupts the organizational flow of society. As such, there is a principle of equity and justice that prevails in African societies. But, the narrative of "gentleman" as espoused by Fela is a concept that was introduced by the Europeans who invaded the African space uninvited with sinister objectives.

After understanding that such actions would attract equal and opposite reactions from the people who were victims of this, the concept of a gentleman was necessary as a way to make them erase the pernicious tragedy that befell them and embrace their part of the dialogue. In such a way, the deeds of the West would be cast into oblivion and Africans would move on like everything is good. But to negate this inherently diabolical aim, Fela rejected the concept on the ground that he would not advise gentleman Africans who would turn mute to the historical evils perpetrated against them by their European visitors. By saying he is a typical African man, Fela diplomatically rejected the idea of a Western "gentleman" and would not encourage his African kinsmen to embrace it either. By making a comical reference to the culture of the West, which the unassuming Africans with tropical climates have adopted, Fela is showing the inherently contrasting and naturally different two worlds which do not require the adoption of one culture in the other environment, since each is distinct and should be appreciated in their given characteristics. Therefore, the African man who has decided to put on the Western dress code, not minding the factor of differing weather conditions between the Western environment and African environment, has actually done an injury to himself because he would personally bear the brunt of such actions alone.

Fela: A Force of Creation

The rugged life of this music icon would almost make one conclude that he led an uncouth life. Such assertions are made based on the numerous occasions of him sticking his hands into the fearful eyes of the authority. However, this is not the case. Drastic measures are usually the best prescriptions when the situation remains endlessly tough. The ideal thing to do by any purposeful leadership is to commit enough attention and resources toward organizing the activities of the state so that there would arise a course of action that would engender all-round development and economic prosperity for all to enjoy, as well as a conducive atmosphere where everyone would have equal opportunity to grow. However, the situation of the Nigerian leadership has forever been exclusively different. The lives of the people became especially more uncomfortable from the ones they experienced under the colonial leadership. Popular expectations of the people would have been to experience an El Dorado under the new political stalwarts piloting the affairs of the country during postcolonial times, but the situation of things sent a signal of imminent danger to every discerning person of the country. It is upon this premise that Anikulapo rose to occupy the position of a compass for the helpless masses with which they navigated their own existential reality.

It is no coincidence, therefore, that many disciples of Fela are found after his demise, a development that sprang from their valuation of his musical legacies and the context that surrounded them. There is a collective acknowledgment of his bravery for speaking at a time when the most courageous kinds would falter easily under the excuse that their lives should not become the sacrificial lamb on the road to Nigeria's emancipation. Aligning his own philosophy with cosmological figures, particularly Ogun (the god of creation), Fela became another force to reckon with in the creative market of Nigerian music. At the peak of his popularity, Fela became essentially unique in the ways he produced content. This, among many other reasons, has given him the deserved position of reverence that he has today. Music from time immemorial has been used judiciously to enhance orderliness in society, especially among the Yoruba folks. Satires are usually sung for people misusing their public positions, invectives hurled on countless individuals with shallow moral values. That Fela excelled in this style and became a point of reverence to many members of the younger generation alludes to the potency of his creative powerhouse. It has thus become apparent that the battlefield of Fela was the soul of the general public. He chose this place because he wanted the people to become alive to the issues that concerned their lives and would determine their altitude in life.

The resounding genre of Afrobeat that Fela introduced to Africa testifies to his ingenious ability to make things happen. One of the admirable qualities he had was the staunch ability to organize his supporters despite the numbers that are swelling in incredible folds. Of course, it was a social responsibility he had accepted to carry upon himself, having found a romance in calling the government out for an inability to organize events in smooth order. Someone of this critical position must ensure that he is not found wanting when there is a need to organize themselves. Appropriately, the sort of leadership acuity Fela exuded spoke volumes of his truthful nature, to himself and to the course of action that he had chosen its part. Often, in response to the heavy criticism they were exposed to by Fela, the government did not spare any moment to smear his personhood by also orchestrating image-denting campaigns against him, either through arrest or outright character assassination. From his dancers and musical instrumentalists to other figures whose presence in the band contributed significantly to the success of his artistry, Fela showed a level of control and an uncommon dexterity in their journey together. His personal life was a good line for freedom, for anyone who cared to toe the line of a sage, which he was.

By marrying off the women who worked with him, Fela was showing the society his unyielding commitment to ensure their safety, after they had been rumored to constitute his sexual prey upon whom he feasted at will. When it became a public question about the moral rectitude of a man that inhales marijuana to front the fight against injustice, corruption, and inefficiency, the music icon was greatly misunderstood for his adoption and rationality of such formula used to conduct his public criticism. To him, the personages who misruled the people seemed not to have done so without the unbending determination to milk the people dry and treat them badly. Therefore, such determination, to Fela, needed to be matched with equal zeal without which the perpetrators of unruly behaviors would record unfettered success in their prodigious actions. The real point however is that it took Fela, after his return from America, to fully adopt his deviant lifestyle which further fueled his muse.[10] Therefore, the resolution to employ a distinct pattern of music and a strategically effective method to trumpet his message attracted mixed reactions from Nigerian society—admiration from people upon whose behalf Fela had undertaken that role of a warrior and an enemy to be crushed in a rootless manner by the people at the receiving end of his criticism. As a result, the man became a victim of timeless angst from the people in the latter category.

Conclusion

In all, efforts have been made to explain Fela in historical perspective. The music icon was birthed by Nigerian parents who belonged to the elite in the Nigerian postcolonial political space. The Afrobeat star was a strong personality who wielded local and international popularity for his social and philosophical underpinnings, which earned him the position he has been recognized with in the immediate and remote society. Like everyone who desires a better sociopolitical condition for his people and who would not compromise their goal to ensure this for cheap financial or economic gains they might be tempted with, Fela singled himself out from the multitude with these outstanding qualities. Finding his romance in a genre of African musical methods garnished with international spices, his work became a taste that is known even far from the geographical boundaries of his home. Fela remains a man that speaks the truth to the African leaders or anyone who stands in the way of the continent's greatness. With this altruism, he bagged himself the masses' love because of his constant struggle to ensure their safety and wellness, at the risk of receiving severe consequences for undertaking such a daunting task.

To talk about the constant reminder of the African people of their need to convert the anger felt through the unsavory experience of colonialism and slavery, without the fear of contradiction to the imperialist West, Fela remains unmatched in his artistic prowess for mounting pressure on the seemingly impenetrable power bloc of the world. Knowing beforehand that such a daring stand against the world powers had the potential to require his freedom as collateral, and yet not backing down in that battle, makes him characteristically different from many people of his type. Education gave him the ability to predict the future having considered the great clouds that have surrounded the African future because of their leaders' greed, lack of a visionary road map in their political assignments and responsibilities, and their obvious redundancy at the corridor of power informed by their minimal understanding of how things work in global politics. This therefore made him an automatic enemy of the power holders in the country and beyond, who assuredly felt threatened by the man's uncompromising checks and balances on the people with the statutory duties of ensuring normalcy, development, and surplus, but who obviously were not going in the right direction.

Fela always came down hard on the corrupt African leaders who violated the public trust and confidence reposed in them by their unassuming followers. In fact, he did so without preference for tribe or ethnic concern. This would explain the reason why he pointedly accused General Olusegun Obasanjo and Moshood Abiola, two of which are his Yoruba kinsmen, calling them enemies of public progress because of their perceived self-aggrandizement at the expense of the collective growth of the society. This would later enrage the personalities who in turn used their social and political positions to inflict aggressive damage on the innocent man. Thus, the life of Fela is a conglomerate of many scars sustained in his bid to ensure a working society where everyone would have access to the basic things of life. Therefore, calling Fela the lone soldier who spoke fearlessly to the world and contributed his artistic ingenuity to the total development of the society is to say the least of the African legend. More than an individual with irreducible interest of the country at heart, Fela carried the African issues upon himself and did a whole lot to enforce a change as long as he had access to oxygen.

We have seen it clearly through Fela's actions and engagements that he had no patience for even a shred of imbecility displayed in the corridor of power, and he would protest every uncivil action of leaders who acted against the interests of the common man. The number of such protests he led during his time makes his appearance in public dealings synonymous with activism. There is no better way to describe the music icon than by referring to him as a man with an absolute commitment to the people's progress and welfare. Exuding such levels of confidence in an environment strictly hostile to truth-telling availed him of any shortcomings which were peddled by detractors to diminish his personality and reduce his philosophical essence to an insignificant minimum. A lesson learned through his persistent amplification of the scourges in society with a view to bringing about changes is that the Nigerian sociopolitical space still has a dearth of progress and a wealth of assignments that must be completed so as to match up with other countries of the world that are growing at an exponential speed. Greed, ethnic consideration, and other debilitating factors are the lingering enemies of progress for Nigerian and African society. The inability to forge a common ground by which the people can carry out their national assignment remains a clog in their wheel of progress.

Part A

History and Culture

3

Natal Tales: Fela and His Family

Olufela Oludotun Ransome-Kuti came squealing into the world, on a fateful day, the 15th of October, in 1938, born to a Christian Egba family in Abeokuta, south-western Nigeria. The Ransome-Kutis were a prominent family in the social, religious, and cultural Yoruba community of the 1930s and 1940s, with the family's "Christian" and "Egba" attributes heavy with historical connotations and achievements, which would play crucial roles in Olufela's maturation into adulthood. They were middle-class family, with strong roots in the Anglican Christian tradition, and they were simultaneously infused with an ethnic political component, resulting from the Egba society's colonial and postcolonial nationalist ferment.

Olufela's paternal grandfather, the Reverend Canon Josiah Jesse Ransome-Kuti, was one of the frontline pioneers of Anglican Christianity in Yorubaland. Reverend J. J. Ransome-Kuti's priestly vocation commenced at the Church Missionary Society Training School in Abeokuta, and he was ordained in 1897. Part of his duties included the translation of Christian hymns into Yoruba, as well as the composition of new Christian Yoruba songs. He was musically talented, and in his hands, music became an evangelical instrument that drew people to church. Reverend J. J. Ransome-Kuti eventually became the first Nigerian to record an album, and he recorded several indigenous Yoruba gospel songs for Zonophone Records in the UK. However, he was not only a Christian elite but also an Egba who understood the political dynamics of his communal context. During his time as a district judge in Egba, in Ogun state, he developed a critical sense of fairness that served his priestly responsibilities and earned him local respect. This sense of justice came to the fore in the early twentieth century, which was a period of great tension between the colonialists and the local Egba people. In 1918, there was an urgent need for his intervention and mediation in an issue over taxation. This issue would later become the source of deep troubles in which Fela's mother would play a leading role.

Israel Oludotun, the last of Reverend Ransome-Kuti's children, definitely carried his father's genes. The senior Ransome-Kuti, "the Singing Minister," bequeathed an aesthetic sense for music, a love for teaching and religious service, and a strong sense of social justice to his son. Israel was born on April 30, 1891, and attended Fourah Bay College at Freetown, Sierra Leone. He went on to become a charismatic educationist with a passion for the arts, discipline, and activism. At his second posting in Ijebu Ode, Israel spent fourteen years as the principal of the Ijebu Ode Grammar School, developing his innovativeness and establishing his nationalist credentials. Within the divisive logic of Nigeria's incipient plurality, no one initially believed that an Egba schoolmaster could have the capacity to shun ethnic rivalry, especially between the Ijebu and the Egba, and to become the champion of an ethnic community other than his own, but the younger Reverend Ransome-Kuti became the spokesman of the Ijebu in the colonial court. Beginning in 1932, when he left Ijebu Ode for Abeokuta, he dedicated the next twenty-two years to sustaining the educational glory of his alma mater, Abeokuta Grammar School, as its principal.

Abeokuta Grammar School was "a source of local pride and subtle resistance against the colonial authorities"; it had been built entirely by the local populace.[1] The school therefore served as the platform for not only the strict mentoring regimen of "Daudu" (as Reverend Ransome-Kuti was fondly known) but also nurturing nationalist activism on behalf of the people. In May 1926, Reverend Ransome-Kuti established the Association of the Headmasters of Ijebu Schools. A similar establishment, the Lagos Union of Teachers, had been formed by the Reverend J. O. Lucas in May 1925. By July 1931, the idea of a single national body representing all Nigerian teachers culminated in the Nigerian Union of Teachers. Reverend Ransome-Kuti was its founding president, and he held the post for successive terms until his retirement in 1953. Ransome-Kuti's forceful and charismatic character, using the Abeokuta Grammar School as his base to pursue national unionism, served to help leverage the union to fight for and win improved conditions of service for all Nigerian teachers and, most importantly, to oppose the colonial educational policy. It was an almost inevitable result when he became a member of the 1943 Elliott Commission for the Institutionalization of University Education in Nigeria.

The Reverend Israel Oludotun Ransome-Kuti married Funmilayo Abigail Thomas in 1925. She had been one of the first graduates of Abeokuta Grammar School, and she became principal of Ijebu Grammar School. Her affectionate nickname, *Béère*, used to denote the first-born daughter of the Yoruba people, also speaks to the pioneering achievements of Funmilayo Ransome-Kuti's life. She was not only the first daughter in the Thomas family, she was also the first female student of Abeokuta Grammar School, the first Nigerian woman to ride in a car, the first woman to attempt to depose a king during the colonial period in Nigeria, and the first Nigerian woman activist to be globally recognized by the socialist community. Funmilayo Ransome-Kuti had a strong Christian and educational legacy on both her maternal and paternal sides. Her mother, Lucretia Thomas, was educated at the Church Missionary Society (CMS) school, Ikija, where she trained as a seamstress. Her father, Daniel Olumeyuwa Thomas, attended the Araromi Mission School in Lagos, where he became a tailor. They met and got married at St. Jude's Church, Ikija, in Abeokuta, where they later became highly active in Anglican Christian circles. After the tragic demise of their first two children, their third child came on October 25, 1900. They named her Olufunmilayo Olufela Abigail Folorunsho Thomas.

Funmilayo Abigail Thomas grew up within the context of the growing ferment of colonial and anticolonial pressures and tensions, which would first emerge within the church and its relationship with its African converts. A contentious debate was taking place over the possible incompatibility between conversion and polygyny. The larger context of this dispute was tied with the colonial church's relationship with its African converts, as well as the racial denigration of African cultures and traditions. European church missionaries spurned "heathen" practices, and their "spiritual" analysis forbade polygyny as a Christian practice for those already converted. A man who was already married to many wives would be expected to forsake all of them except one, on the pain of excommunication. These religious tensions created a veritable groundswell of nationalist fervor, culminating in the establishment of separatist African churches that held that polygyny was just a harmless cultural practice that did not violate the laws of God. Funmilayo's parents were caught in this maelstrom of nationalism; Daniel Thomas had two wives, Lucretia and Rebecca. He was pressured by the church to abandon polygyny, but Daniel Thomas retained his Yoruba cultural practices.

Like the Ransome-Kutis, Funmilayo Thomas also had the best Christian education and upbringing. In 1919, her parents sent her to England to continue her studies. She returned in 1922 to take up an appointment at the Abeokuta Grammar School as the head teacher. When Funmilayo became Mrs. Ransome-Kuti in 1925, she entered the marriage already armed with an anticolonial and anti-authority temperament that would find a complement in the Reverend Ransome-Kuti's own nationalist unionism efforts on behalf of Nigerian teachers. She had dropped her two foreign Christian names—Frances and Abigail—on her return from Britain. Gradually, she picked up the tenor of anticolonial activism that saw her championing women's rights, access to education, and substantive representation in the political process. In 1944, and at the height of her husband's unionism activities with the Nigerian Union of Teachers, Funmilayo Ransome-Kuti founded the Abeokuta Ladies' Club (ALC), which later became the Abeokuta Women's Union (AWU), and then the Nigerian Women's Union (NWU). She gained prominence as a fiery activist, visiting China, Yugoslavia, Poland, USSR, and Hungary, along with other socialist states. She met Mao Tse-tung and became an intimate friend with Kwame Nkrumah.

Like her husband, Funmilayo Ransome-Kuti would soon emerge from the Abeokuta Women's Union and its local political focus into the national limelight. To achieve this feat, a reigning king to abdicate his throne, and the legend of the "Lioness of Lisabi" needed to be born. The AWU platform was not only a movement to secure women's rights but also an opportunity to make a cultural statement. It had specific rules for the language and dress of its members; Yoruba culture became a touchstone of cultural affirmation for women drawn from the markets. The literate and illiterate converged around Funmilayo Ransome-Kuti's charismatic leadership. This movement of Egba women had its defining moment when a discriminatory tax law came into effect in 1918 and became the visible representation of colonial aggression in Abeokuta. This was a gender-differentiated approach targeted specifically at Egba women. Women who could not pay the direct tax were harassed, beaten, stripped naked, and jailed. This colonial assault went against everything that the AWU stood for, and Funmilayo Ransome-Kuti rose to the occasion. Between 1947 and 1948, three huge demonstrations and protests, led by Funmilayo Ransome-Kuti, rocked Abeokuta. The protests rejected the harassment and arrests of women, as well as the inherent injustice of the colonial legal system, and called for the abdication of the Alake of Egbaland. Direct taxation of Egba women was finally suspended in April 1948, and the women achieved an increased level of political representation. Oba Samuel Ladapo Ademola II, the Alake of Egbaland, abdicated the throne by January 3, 1949. In the wake of this success, the fame of Funmilayo Ransome-Kuti, the Lioness of Lisabi, spread across Nigeria. The AWU became the NWU, with branches across the country.

These familial, sociocultural, and political dramas played out against the background of a strong provincial identity. Abeokuta stood out as a distinct Yoruba town at the intersection of several historical and cultural events. The Ransome-Kuti and Thomas families embodied the insurmountable Egba spirit, which bred cultural pride, fierce loyalty, and rebellion and accommodation, especially within the context of nineteenth-century Yoruba politics and colonial adventures. Abeokuta and the Egba were situated at the nexus of multiple incursions and interventions in the arenas of politics, religion, culture, rebellion, and social change. There was a symbiotic dynamic that ensured that the Ransome-Kuti not only gained the genealogical restlessness and rebellious spirit of the Egba people but that the Abeokuta community of the Egba people also served as the starting point for the agitations of the Ransome-Kuti for reform. Funmilayo Ransome-Kuti was compared to Lisabi Agbongbo-Akala, the legendary Egba warrior-hero who withstood the might of the Oyo Empire to liberate the Egba people. She was also seen as the modern version of the historical Egba heroine, Madam Efunroye Tinubu (1810–87), who was the scourge of patriarchy in nineteenth-century Yorubaland.

The nineteenth century was a period of intense cultural and political upheavals throughout all Yorubaland, and Abeokuta played a significant role in these events. The Old Oyo Empire's expansionist predilection, and its eventual fall, caused political and demographic shockwaves that devastated Yorubaland. For Atanda, the breakdown of the Old Oyo Empire's constitutional dynamics "was not so much as a result of any inherent weakness in the constitution, but as a result of the inordinate ambition of the functionaries of the central government."[2] A major source of internal disequilibrium came from the hostile political relationship between Aláàfin Aólè and Afònjá, the Are Ona Kakanfo (generalissimo of the Oyo army). Afònjá's was driven by ambition to seek out the support of Sheikh al-Salih, also known as Alimi, a Fulani Muslim preacher at Ilorin. Alimi betrayed Afònjá, and the Oyo Empire subsequently faced a series of wars culminating in its eventual dissolution. One of the consequences of this dissolution was demographic dynamics of confusion, expansion, and regrouping. For instance, Oyo refugees who had been displaced due to these wars became a terror group on their own, and one of their targets were Egba towns that had supported Owu in the Owu-Ife war. The residents of these towns fled and found refuge around the Olumo Rock between 1829 and 1830.[3] Their settlement led to the growth of Abeokuta. Displaced Egba people became a military presence themselves in search of political power. They were confronted with the necessity of addressing problems of unity, as well as the need to consolidate their political significance. This became more urgent due to the emerging danger of colonial encroachment into Yorubaland.

The 1840s and 1850s were also periods of religious incursions into Yorubaland. Islam came to Yorubaland early, especially through Alimi's jihad. Christianity came much later, through the missionary efforts of Methodist and CMS missions—Abeokuta was their major entry point. When the first mission school was established in 1841, Abeokuta became a vibrant, modern center of diverse cultural and political influences that revolved around Christianity, Western education, Islam, and a strong traditional elite bound together by their shared Egba cultural identity. Egba politics, centered in Abeokuta, became one of the most volatile in the region as a result of the actions, reactions, and interactions of all these elements with an encroaching colonial modernity. Christianity brought its own contradictions, which added to the confusion. On the one hand, Western missionary education led to the emergence of a new Yoruba elites, like the Ransome-Kuti and the Thomas. On the other hand, Christianity led to growing nationalist ferment around the missionaries' rejection of the new Yoruba elites' cultural affirmation. This cultural affirmation was aggravated by Yorubaland's experience under colonial rule. When Funmilayo Ransome-Kuti was born in 1900, Yorubaland had come fully under colonial rule, the Egba people in Abeokuta had started asserting their independence, and the Ransome-Kuti family had begun playing its own critical role in undermining the colonial authorities. When Olufela Oludotun Olusegun Ransome-Kuti was born in 1938 into the colonial context of Abeokuta, Reverend and Mrs. Ransome-Kuti had been married for eight years, the Nigerian Union of Teachers was fully operational, and colonialism was in full swing.

Fela became heir to four distinct traditions—a tradition of music, a tradition of discipline, a rebellious tradition of defiance, and a tradition of authority. His life can be summarized as a search for freedom within the interstices of these traditions. The search began from Fela's longing for freedom within an oppressive home run by two stern disciplinarians.

> Nobody was more in a hurry than I to become an adult. Adulthood meant freedom, man! Freedom at last to do whatever I felt like. And what I felt like doing most was having fun, enjoying myself. So the older I got, the happier I got. At least outside of my house. I was glad to finish primary school and be

> somewhat outside of my father's reach. I began feeling like a different person in secondary school. a total extrovert. I was in the forefront of entertainment in school. I'd run around, always joking, laughing, making others laugh. I was easily the most popular boy in the school.[4]

Contrary to their individual and collective activism against colonialism and patriarchy, the Ransome-Kuti family's home was a model of respectability, self-assertion, accountability, authority, educational awareness, and discipline. Both Oludotun and Funmilayo brought different family backgrounds and parental upbringings to the marriage but nevertheless had some common denominators which assisted them in raising their own children: education, cultural assertion, duty, and service. The middle-class echelon to which the Ransome-Kutis belong enabled them some leeway to provide their children a measure good training. Their marriage was considered atypical for that period "in that the partners operated from a sense of equality and were highly supportive of each other's public activities … the Ransome-Kutis did not have the typical male-dominated marriage of their time."[5]

However, despite their home's egalitarian basis and openness, it was essentially oppressive for someone of Fela's character. It was too organized, too punctilious, too strict, too pious, too tough, and too perfectionist. As educationists, they had reputations for domesticating unruly students that refused to heed the rules, and one can only imagine what that implied for their children. It was inevitable that the educational principles of the Ransome-Kutis would require that their children be held up as the very example of what they taught and wanted other children to embody. "Home" and "school" merged into a grueling template of discipline and studiousness. Dolupo, Olikoye, Olufela, and Bekolari were caught in a kaleidoscope of mixed emotions toward their parents: pride and hatred, admiration and revulsion, excitement and exasperation, and attachment and detachment.

Fela would stand out as the most rebellious of the four children. He was allegedly his mother's favorite, but Fela testified that he got the most beatings for his rascality, rebellion, and stubborn restlessness. In his parents' eyes, Fela represented the antithesis of all they stood for: the very negation of all virtues. According to Fela:

> I always stole my mother's money. She had a school, so I had a lot of money to steal from her. The more she beats me, the more I stole. Anytime she caught me she must beat the shit out of me but next time I have a chance, I would steal it. So, I stole till I left school from my mother.

His notorious behavior was punished not only by his mother but also by his father and teachers:

> My father was so strange! He was strict, but he was also interesting because he was always jovial … I always wondered how a man who looked so jovial could be so fucking cold when he would flog you …. My mother wasn't any better than my father … she beats the hell outta me, man! My mother was the most wicked woman in life when it came to beating …. My teachers, too. Oh yes, they kicked my ass almost everyday, man![6]

Fela's exaggerated account of the three thousand strokes of the cane received from both parents between the ages of nine and seventeen tells a story of severe discipline.

Fela's father was the target of one of his rebellions. At age sixteen while at school, Fela founded a club that, even at such a young age, represented his carefree philosophy of fun and mischief. He named the club "The Planless Society": "The rule of the club was simple: we had no plans. You could be called upon to disobey orders at any time. Disobedience was our 'law.' We'd take my mother's car, for example."[7] If the Planless Society was a club for mischief, *The Planless Times*, the club's newspaper, crossed the boundary from mischief into open rebellion against authority. The newspaper, for instance, caught wind of a new prefect chosen by the school principal, and Fela and his cohorts reacted by protesting the appointment with a special edition of their newspaper, printing 500 copies. The protest brought the police to the school, and confusion ensued. Fela had taken the fight to his own father!

Olufela Ransome-Kuti incarnated the often overlapping, complex, and contradictory tendencies of his household's different parental temperaments—the difference between discipline and unruliness, talent and mischief, middle-class wealth and Spartan existence, Christianity and cultural traditions, and authoritarianism and defiance. He called himself "a colonial boy," but Fela was a child of multiple conditions and different historical, cultural, ideological, and political circumstances. He was the complex product of an even more complicated fusion of Yoruba protest dynamics, stern Christian upbringing, conflicting patriarchal and anti-patriarchal impulses, social activism, and musical dexterity. Colonialism, and its racial policing of the cultural, became the most significant factor fusing all these influences together into one huge keg of gunpowder, waiting to explode. Even as a young person, the rebel was already waiting to launch himself. First, it was to be against the constraining discipline of his parents, and then the rebellion would be aimed at the conventional limitations of society. The final target of Fela's rebellion would be the ideological confusion of Africa and the Nigerian state. Unlike his father and mother, music was going to take a significant role in Fela's ideological and social activism. He would unleash a new brand of protest music on Africa, far beyond the sanitized musical renditions of his grandfather or the educationally correct musical prowess of his father. It would catapult him into global renown as one of the most ideological composers of all time.

4

The *Performative Rhythm*: From Highlife to Afrobeat

One of the sore points of contention between Fela and his father, the Reverend Oludotun Israel Ransome-Kuti, was Fela's commitment to the rigorous Western musical training that his father saw as a significant and necessary dimension of a proper education. Fela had the benefit of the musical gene that spread far back two generations to his grandfather, the Reverend Josiah Jesse Ransome-Kuti, the Singing Minister, but still was pressed into a stern educational regimen. Beyond the formal and constricted setting of the Reverend Ransome-Kuti's music class and lessons, Fela also had the complement of rich traditional oral and contemporary popular performances at Abeokuta, which provided many opportunities for refreshing cultural and musical experiences he found far more rewarding than the enforced musical lessons from his father. Alongside traditional showcases from the *Egungun* masquerade performance and the *Gelede* ceremonies to the percussion-heavy *apala* music, there was also the alluring musical presence of the Western concert and operatic performances which the Saro returnees brought along from Sierra Leone and which defined the music scene in Abeokuta and Lagos.

One could only imagine the deep influences that Fela must have soaked up from the rich ambience of cultural knowledge that Abeokuta provided, especially in terms of music and traditional cultural dynamics. True, Christianity had a strong presence, but the Egba were equally and solidly rooted in traditions. The festivals of *egungun* and *gelede* would have provided a carnivalesque atmosphere that must have piqued the young Fela's curiosity in a different manner than his father's strict education. No one would ever have suspected—not even Fela himself—that in later life, he would feel the need to re-inscribe his performances with the *gelede*'s spiritual and satirical components in ways that transcended his family's musical tradition. It is in this sense and context that we understand Fela's music as signifying a "performative rhythm"—a musical encoding of the performance aesthetics that bring dance, music, drama, and ritual together into one fused rhythmic performance in the service of a social or ideological function.

Fela's father represented the typical generational blend of stubbornness and talent. It was also prominent in Reverend Josiah Ransome-Kuti. Those who knew him testified to his unwavering commitment to the Christian faith, especially regarding his complete disavowal of "idol worship" in Abeokuta. One nostalgic reminiscence noted that "[Baba J. J.] was a great man. He fought the wizards and the witches of the time. He fought the Ogboni Confraternity. He won the battle."[1] In *Ake*, Soyinka—the Reverend J. J. Ransome-Kuti's grandson—narrated an incident that would have frightened any other man except the Singing Minister:

> One frightening experience occurred in one of the villages in Ijebu. He had been warned not to preach on a particular day, which was the day for an Egungun outing, but he persisted and held a service. The Egungun procession passed while the service was in progress and, using his ancestral voice, called on the preacher to stop at once, disperse the people, and come out and pay obeisance. Rev. J. J. ignored him. The Egungun then left, taking his followers with him but, on passing the main door, he tapped on it with his wand, three times. Hardly had the last member of his procession left the church premises than the building collapsed. The walls simply fell down and the roof disintegrated. Miraculously however, the walls fell outwards while the roof supports fell among the aisles or flew outwards—anywhere but on the congregation itself. Rev. J. J. calmed the worshippers, paused in his preaching to render a thanksgiving prayer, then continued his sermon.[2]

Rev. J. J.'s fanatically ardent faith in God, and his rejection of the Yoruba heritage that he regarded as idolatrous, was single-minded devotion. For some, this zeal made him one of the greatest African composers of the nineteenth century. But music had lost a bit of its religious appeal for his son, Reverend Oludotun Ransome-Kuti. For Fela's father, the aesthetic appreciation of music had become an ideological means of challenging the colonial presence at Abeokuta. The best way to make it more empowering was to insert it into the school curriculum; he compelled the students of Abeokuta Grammar School, including Fela, to become musically literate. In this context, Reverend Oludotun Ransome-Kuti's subversive ideological intent for musical instruction intersected his wife's ardent campaign on behalf of the Egba women. A prominent dimension of the Funmilayo Ransome-Kuti-led protests was the many chants and songs which enhanced the protest performance calling out the colonial leadership and their local collaborators for anti-people policies and practices. With the fierce engagement necessary to deliver these satirical and abusive songs, Funmilayo Ransome-Kuti—like her husband—had found function for music out of the realm of aesthetic appeal. Music meant more than dancing! When in 1948, Funmilayo Ransome-Kuti's women marched on the Alake's palace in Abeokuta, they were dancing, chanting, and singing:

> If he dares, let him come;
> if he does not dare do so, let him come
> We have written our letter to someone else
> if he comes let him be disgraced.
>
> ***
>
> We gave you a crown and you indulged in excesses
> Ademola piled crown upon crown
>
> ***
>
> If your hand should catch Ajibodu (Ademola)
> Kill him, do not spare him
> demolish him as you would demolish a good meal of *eba*.[3]

Fela, their rascal son, was privy to all the anti-authority context of his parents' activism. It would eventually define his musical future, around the same themes of defiance, cultural affirmation, within a broad ideological framework overlapping class, status, and education. He would transcend every reservation or affiliation with religion, authority, and social respectability that had kept his parents within the bounds of the conventional despite their willingness to challenge every authority that is oppressive. But first, he needed to find his feet: freedom outside his parents' home, away from their influence, beckoned. And he needed the perfect musical framework within which he would unleash war against all forms of authority.

When Fela left for England to study music, he was embarking on what we can consider to be the most significant journey of his ideological life. He expected he had finally escaped the clutches of his parents; it was time to expand his horizon, testing the boundaries of what it meant to be free. This journey would take him through an ideological wilderness that attempted to make sense of black, white, and every racial hue in between. From Abeokuta to Lagos, then London, back to Lagos, and then on to the United States, Fela searched for the right revolutionary tone to provide a stentorian strain for his radical engagement with music. The journey took him from the Koola Lobitos to Egypt 80, from highlife and jazz to Afrobeat, and finally from the Black Power movement to blackism.

In keeping with their middle-class expectations, medicine was a respectable discipline for the children of the equally respectable Ransome-Kuti family of Abeokuta. Fela's parents may have hoped that going to England, and being subjected to the rigor of studying to become a medical doctor, would work a miracle and temper Fela's rebellious spirit. Unfortunately, Fela's sojourn would take him far beyond his parents' expectations. It was the second disappointment for the family, after their first daughter, Dolupo, lost interest in her studies, entered into a nursing program, and got pregnant out of wedlock. Fela's parents could be blamed, in terms of children upbringing, for failing on several fronts. They were too preoccupied and too demanding and, worse, they failed to understand how their children's temperaments, and especially Fela's, and their own genetic input would shape how they developed. There is evidence that Reverend Ransome-Kuti saw himself in Fela's restlessness and musical talent, yet he worked to cultivate the latter and constrain the former. The Ransome-Kuti may have been like most parents, but like most parents, they failed with regard to the expectations they had for their children. It was not that their expectations were so extremely off base but both the husband and the wife were too distant from their children to nurture them with love and intimacy. They were both too engrossed in their series of crusades for social justice. Fela's mother was not only a local organizer but a national and global agitator. She and her husband were always involved in one cause or the other, and were always traveling. When Fela eventually chose to be a musician, and a radical one at that, one can imagine the initial reservations and ultimate resignation of his mother. One can imagine further that the late Reverend Oludotun Israel Ransome-Kuti would have turned in his grave!

Before traveling to England in 1958, some of Fela's impetus to go first required him to meet Jimo Kombi Braimah (J. K.) in secondary school. They would strike up a lifelong relationship, which was an integral part of Fela's search for meaning and freedom. In fact, J. K. played a singularly significant part in Fela's bounds toward freedom in secondary school. As Fela's "partner-in-crime," J. K.'s role in his life was not only ironic but definitive. J. K., from Fela's own description, had a respectable mien—good-natured, jovial, calm. And he was also born to a respectable family, who would not want him to have anything to do with the "rascal" Fela. Yet, J. K. and Fela were kindred spirits—both anti-study, both anti-discipline. Indeed, it was J. K. that gave Fela most of the push to travel from secondary school in Abeokuta to London, which would redirect his focus along the path he found there. J. K. served as a significant juncture in Fela's search for release. Being three years older than Fela and having more freedom from his parents than what the Ransome-Kutis afforded, J. K. became a kind of model for Fela—the very embodiment of freedom and autonomous individuality. J. K. got into highlife long before Fela. He schooled in Ghana, and so was already knowledgeable about not only the highlife hits of the time but also the great highlife stars, especially E. T. Mensah and The Tempos, Victor Olaiya and the Cool Cats, Bobby Benson and the Jam Session Orchestra, and many others from Cardinal Rex Lawson to Zeal Onyia.

Reverend Ransome-Kuti had died in 1955, Fela was seventeen and restless, and in stepped J. K., the free spirit:

> [J. K.] … wasn't a Christian, so he was just doing as he liked. He wasn't from a Christian home. He was a different man from me completely. He was all so free. The girls always liked J. K. He was a nice guy with a fucking nice voice. He used to be a guest artist to several local bands, like Victor Olaiya's. Actually, he was the steady singer for the Cool Cats. Since he had lived for a while in Ghana, J. K. became popular singing Ghanaian tunes. At that time, man, there was nothing more popular in Nigeria than Ghanaian highlife. Women everywhere would be shouting, "J. K.," "J. K.," "J. K." That's how I got my first break in singing. J. K. introduced me to Victor Olaiya and the Cool Cats and I began singing with them. J. K. got a *Kumba* band together—with people like Godrich Khan, who is now a doctor, Femi Williams, and some other boys—and we would go on the air. We were playing highlife and some jazz on the radio, man! Oh, those were such beautiful days![4]

Together, they explored the highlife circuit in Lagos, and J. K. led the way from highlife to nightlife. They were ready for the dance-band highlife and the technical proficiency that it required from them. The late Reverend Ransome-Kuti had taught them the basics of European music very well, and Abeokuta had prepared them for the fundamentals of concert music. By the 1940s and 1950s, when Fela and J. K. were hitting Lagos, E. T. Mensah had commenced his deep experimentation that fused indigenous African musical elements with Afro-Cuban and Afro-Caribbean dances, like the rumbas and the mambos. All the great Nigerian highlife maestros situated in Lagos, with Victor Olaiya as the primary star among them, already learned a great deal from E. T. Mensah and the best of Ghanaian highlife innovation. At the time, J. K. was also a rising vocalist with Olaiya's Cool Cats. Fela, the son of a middle-class Christian family playing bourgeoisie "high life" music in Lagos, was situated right in the middle of the highlife scene, performing as a backup vocalist to Victor Olaiya, the grandfather of Nigerian highlife.

Highlife, despite its middle-upper-class context, was suited to the emerging ideological texture of Fela's steadily growing philosophical groping. The rhythmic structures of highlife were essentially a secular music form, gaining popularity in West Africa because of its capacity to divest itself of ethnic and religious contexts, although it also had the flexibility to draw from those contexts. Its melodic rhythms originated from traditional Akan music, but it went on to adroitly incorporate and synthesize other European, African American, and Afro-Caribbean aesthetic sensibilities to achieve a pan-national and pan-ethnic template; it appealed to upper-class circles and audiences in colonial Lagos. The combination of an asymmetrical rhythm, drawn from the Yoruba drumming pattern, together with the displaced-accent guitar melodies that accompany the songs gave highlife a large following in Lagos.

In 1958, with serious experience with highlife music and social life in his pocket, it was time for Fela to leave for England. His destination was the Trinity College of Music, and more Western art music training. Trinity College of Music offered another opportunity for Fela to conform to the Establishment, after he rejected his parents' middle-class expectations for him. They had hoped he would become a medical doctor, like his brothers Olikoye and Bekolari. European music schools like Trinity College of Music had produced many great African composers—Ato Turkson and Kwabena Nketia, from Ghana; Anthony Okelo and Solomon Mbabi-Kayana, from Uganda; Fela Sowande, Akin Euba, and Sam Akpabot from Nigeria; and Kevin Volans from South Africa. But it is certainly very difficult to imagine Fela as a respectable Western art composer, like Fela Sowande, staying faithful to the tenets of Western classical music and composition, leading a symphony orchestra in Nigeria, and developing a reputation through hoary established music. Neither could we imagine him as a medical doctor, or a properly suited office employee working for the government at the Federal Ministry of Commerce and Industries. Fela had his eyes set on a goal beyond Trinity College of Music and any Establishment respectability. That was not freedom for him, in any meaningful sense of the word.

London gave him the opportunity, outside of the education in theory and practice of music composition and performance, to pursue his curiosity about jazz. Fela wanted to *play* jazz music and not just study music theory, and the multicultural London of the early 1960s was just the setting for the cross-cultural interactions, ideas, and experiences necessary for nurturing the kind of musical experimentation that was taking shape in Fela's mind at the time. With J. K., Fela's extracurricular musical preoccupations would find many interesting subjects in the melting point of many cultures present in the London of the 1960s. Subjects from Britain's far-flung and proximate colonies all came to London, and it exploded with a burst of cultural heritage on display, especially in music. Musical innovations from all these colonies—rhumba, calypso, mamba, highlife, and jazz—combined to form a formidable experimental tapestry that further encouraged Fela's reluctance to dedicate himself to the Western art music that the Trinity College only offered a restless musical soul like Fela.

By this time, Fela was already growing weary of highlife. It simply was no longer creative for his restless artistic sensibility. It was not long before the name of the band he formed with J. K. changed from the "Highlife Rakers" to "Koola Lobitos." London also presented him with early premonitions about culture and its identity imperatives. With this growing awareness, Fela's experimental spirit had to innovate: "He had always wanted not only to play African music but also to explore the African origins of jazz. Highlife, he thought, had the beat, but not the depth; whereas jazz had depth but no beat. So, he explored the rhythm and beat in highlife and with jazz embellishment came up with an innovation he called highlife-jazz."[5] The years 1958 to 1966 were Fela's experimental years with the Koola Lobitos and highlife jazz. Afrobeat would not surface until later, after his restless spirit spent years searching for a suitable musical receptacle.

Soul music, from James Brown to Geraldo Pino, gave Fela a mighty creative jolt that disrupted his complacency with highlife jazz and the Koola Lobitos. Geraldo Pino took over the Lagos music scene in 1966, and took Fela's musical self-esteem as well after he encountered Pino and soul music in 1966 in Lagos, and again in Ghana in 1968. Fela was depressed, seeing his highlife jazz displaced by Pino and soul music, but it led to an epiphany:

> "You OK, man?" [Raymond Aziz, a Nigerian-Ghanaian] asked.
> I said: "Raymond, you see that my music. I must give it a name-o, a real African name that is catchy. I've been looking for names to give it. And I've been thinking of calling it Afro-beat."
> He said: "Yehhhhhh! That's a good name."
> I said: "Thank you."[6]

Thus, Afrobeat was born in 1968, but it was lacking its true soul; Fela still needed to encounter black ideology. The first intimation of that had already happened in London. There, in spite of all his carefree *joi de vivre*, he had to relearn all the subconscious lessons in activism and anti-authoritarianism he had received from his mother. The first intimations happened in London, with the Koola Lobitos bringing Fela and J. K. into contact with politicized students and expatriates. Fela engaged with the racism and pan-Africanism, which had always been present at the periphery of his ideological consciousness, through his relationship with his mother and later during his stays in England and the United States. He had met Nkrumah earlier in 1957 and visited East Berlin, behind the Iron Curtain, in 1958.

Soul music is essentially popular black music, different from rhythm and blues, which evolved from the 1950s to the 1970s in the United States. Sam Cooke, Ray Charles, and James Brown are some of soul music's most prominent precursors. It dug firmly into the very root of black music in blues and gospel as one of the distinct markers of the black experience. Unlike the highlife that Fela had been introduced to in Lagos, soul was a unique synthesis of the sacred and the profane. It is founded on a highly charged emotional delivery, accompanied by a large instrumental ensemble that includes all kinds of horns, from saxophones to trombones and trumpets, keyboards, electric guitars, basses, percussions, drums, and male and female vocalists. Soul music is supported by rhythmic off-beat bass lines, chordal parts on the guitar and piano, a very brisk tempo, melodies based on pentatonic scales, and call-and-response vocals.

The soul ensemble that Fela saw with Geraldo Pino laid the foundation for Afrobeat. Between 1969 and 1970, when he left for the United States and the Nigeria Civil War happened, Fela (re)discovered marijuana, and the Koola Lobitos experimented with jazz. Fela rebounded and claimed a portion of the Lagos nightlife, recording some albums. From 1965 to 1969, the Koola Lobitos highlife music introduced significant jazz elements, then Afro-Latin styles, especially from the Cuban salsa, and finally rhythm and blues. The Koola Lobitos became more prominent, with a more strident and complex mood and harmony resulting from the band's "blaring horns, aggressive jazz solos, and dense arrangements."[7] According to his own bemused testimony, Fela was "singing love songs, songs about rain, about people": "Onidodo," "Bonfo," "Alagbara," "Oritshe," "Laise, Lairo," "Wa Dele," "Se E Tunde," "Ajo," "My Baby Don't Love Me," and so on. But all these were still done under the auspices of the fast-fading reputation of Fela's highlife jazz genre, which was under intense siege from soul music's invasion of the Lagos scene.

As Geraldo Pino incarnated James Brown as the face of soul in Ghana and Nigeria, disrupting Fela's rising prominence, it gave him a reason to "split to America." The Lagos years, from 1963 to 1969, were filled with an intense search for a musical identity—a span in which Fela had to compete strenuously with foreign styles while attempting to cobble together a distinct musical identity. Afrobeat had been named, but it still lacked the stylistic and aesthetic identity making it the fully formed protest music that Fela would later use to become the scourge of authority in Africa and Nigeria. From Lagos to the United States, Fela's "jaye-jaye" (happy-go-lucky) understanding of freedom was undergoing a qualitative transformation. In Lagos, he had been outside of J. K.'s orbit of influence, who had stayed back in London when Fela returned in 1963, and whom he missed tremendously. All through the Lagos phase, Fela had confronted critical existential challenges. He had met Remilekun Taylor while in London in 1959; he married her in 1961, and three children followed in rapid succession—Yeni, the eldest daughter (1961); Femi, the son (1962); and Sola, another daughter (1963). Then the changing music environment of Lagos challenged Fela's musical dexterity, and he was faced with the possibility of not making ends meet but also of being forced to totally abandon music! Life was tough in Lagos, and Fela's simplistic desire to just escape his childhood home and "enjoy life" disappeared within the complexities of life outside of Abeokuta and his parents' influence. Freedom now meant something entirely different.

In America, Fela immediately experienced the same kind of cultural awareness that he had encountered in London. The American Civil Rights Movement was in full swing, and the figures of Martin Luther King, Jr.; Malcolm X; Kwame Ture, born Stokely Carmichael; Elijah Muhammed and the Nation of Islam; and the Black Panther Party were all over the news. They were all at the frenetic core of the already consolidating black consciousness around black nationalism, black power, and pan-Africanism. Fela's trip to America became his ultimate initiation into politics, ideological consciousness, and cultural reorientation. He met Sandra Smith, a former Black Panther member, and read *The Autobiography of Malcolm X* at her prompting.[8] Malcolm X represented half of the forces—with Martin Luther King, Jr., representing the other half—that challenged the ideological foundations of American society from two opposing perspectives. Fela witnessed these powerful events unfolding, but they were also powerfully unraveled for him by Sandra's tutelage. The deep historicity of the American black experience began to draw Fela's own thinking back to Africa and the vast ideological baggage that he had carried subconsciously. From his adolescent years until his trip to postcolonial London, Fela had been influenced by his mother's anti-authoritarianism with its Marxist elements, Nkrumah's pan-Africanism, and Marcus Garvey. In developmental terms, he could see that postcolonial Nigeria compared badly with America's technological progress.

With *The Autobiography of Malcolm X*, Sandra's lessons on Africa and black history, and his own resolve, Fela set out to write the real African music. In Sandra's living room, using her piano, paying tribute to her support for him, and his band, Fela wrote "My Lady's Frustration" (1969). Finally, after his long search, Fela was able to achieve the musical artistry and find the inspiration that enabled him to properly fuse jazz, rhythm and blues, and highlife into a sustained style founded on an increased use of modal harmony:

> Built upon a mid-tempo highlife groove, the song begins with a dominant fifth chord vamp in which the soul-styled rhythm guitar is prominent. This is followed by the entrance of a three-part horn theme, over which Fela sings.... Following Fela's soul band exhortation to the soloists ("Now blow, man!") there are three horn solos, each supported by a horn background derived from the song's main theme. Following the solos, the main theme returns and the ensemble drops out as Fela offers some a capella vocalizing before the song ends on a sustained dominant chord.[9]

Fela called "My Lady's Frustration" his first African tune. It was indeed Afrobeat's first entry, and the beginning of Fela's revolutionary emergence. Under Sandra's prompting, the Koola Lobitos became the "Nigeria 70," and the lyrical lightness that had suffused their work would not return.

From 1971 to 1972, Fela launched into his new discovery with a profusion of iconic titles that strengthened and consolidated Afrobeat's ascendance—"Why Black Man Dey Suffer" (1971), "Open & Close" (1971), "Shakara" (1972), "Roforofo Fight" (1972), "Gentleman" (1973), "Expensive Shit" (1975), "Confusion" (1975), "Alagbon Close" (1975), "Yellow Fever" (1976), "Sorrow, Tears and Blood" (1977), "Zombie" (1977), "Shuffering and Shmiling" (1977), "VIP (Vagabond in Power)" (1979), "ITT (International Thief Thief)" (1980), "Authority Stealing" (1980), "Coffin for Head of State" (1981), "Black President" (1981), "Original Suffer Head" (1982), "Perambulator" (1983), and more. Afrobeat's stylistics would be refined and improved over the years. The ensemble would come to include rhythm guitars, trombone, bass guitar, drums, saxophones, trumpets, keyboards, rhythm congas, *sekere*, lead solo conga, *Akuba* conga, claves, chorus vocals, and lead vocals. But the musical movement was still defined by the call-and-response, improvisation, and repetition. The use of Pidgin English, another key characteristic, would be introduced with "Lady" in 1972.

Afrobeat represented the artistic culmination of Fela's search for relevance. It eventually became the vehicle for the simmering defiance and anti-authoritarian temperament that had laid dormant in Fela since his protests against his father at Abeokuta Grammar School. Afrobeat is a performative rhythm that projects action and protest and dissent. It is "culture and politics aesthetically realized in music. The performance is characterized by the creation of a liberal cultural space that allows for free discourse about society's fears, doubts, and inhibitions, be they governance, sex or the general feelings of restive youth."[10] In terms of politics and social change, Afrobeat is far beyond what highlife is lyrically programmed to do. It marshals protest music with the radical vision of a revolutionary, projected into a postcolonial context of Africa.

In "Zombie" (1977), and at the very height of his crusading experience, Fela had the military, and its mindless regimentation, right in his sights. The military struck and seized power in 1966 in Nigeria, and its misplaced political adventurism only ended in 1999. A major part of Nigeria's political history is therefore ascribable to the military and the various juntas in its postcolonial experience. "Zombie" is a hard-hitting, derisive commentary on the dislocated governance dynamics of the Nigerian socioeconomic condition. It is a musical characterization of the military's command structure, and by implication, its effects on the governance of a country. In Nigeria's case, the country had barely managed to get its developmental and political acts together before its "mindless" rulers surfaced.

Zombie o, zombie (Zombie o, zombie)
Zombie o, zombie (Zombie o, zombie)

Zombie no go go unless you tell am to go
[*Zombie will not go unless it is told to go*]
Zombie no go stop unless you tell am to stop
[*Zombie will not stop unless it is told to stop*]
Zombie no go turn unless you tell am to turn
[*Zombie will not turn unless it is told to turn*]
Zombie no go think unless you tell am to think
[*Zombie will not think unless it is told to think*]

Zombie o, zombie (Zombie o, zombie)
Zombie o, zombie (Zombie o, zombie)

Tell them to go straight
A joro, jara, joro
No break, no job, no sense
A joro, jara, joro
Tell them to go kill A joro, jara, joro
No break, no job, no sense
A joro, jara, joro
Tell them to go quench
A joro, jara, joro
No break, no job, no sense
A joro, jara, joro

Go and kill! (Joro, jaro, joro)
Go and die! (Joro, jaro, joro)
Go and quench! (Joro, jaro, joro)
Put am for reverse! (Joro, jaro, joro)

Joro, jara, joro, zombie wey na one way
Joro, jara, joro, zombie wey na one way
Joro, jara, joro, zombie wey na one way
Joro, jara, joro

[Outro]
Attention! (Zombie)
Quick march!
Slow march! (Zombie)
Left turn!
Right turn! (Zombie)
About turn!
Double up! (Zombie)
Salute!
Open your hat! (Zombie)
Stand at ease!
Fall in! (Zombie)
Fall out!
Fall down! (Zombie)
Get ready!
{2x}

Conclusion

In this chapter, we have traced the historical trajectory of what we call Fela's "performative rhythm." This unique performance aesthetic is an attempt to balance Fela's Western musical sensibility with the traditional African musical imperatives. This attempt is historically demonstrated in Fela's coming of age and the struggle that led to the birth and evolution of Afrobeat from jazz and highlife. Afrobeat represents the musical culmination of a restless artistic spirit that succeeded in fusing Fela's cultural background, musical training, and the ideological context of his upbringing into a highly charged performative aesthetics. This transformed an ordinary saxophone into an Afrocentric instrument that blared into authoritarianism on the continent and imperialism abroad. It is in this sense that Afrobeat becomes the source for a philosophical framework tied to a specific continental and national suffering.

5

The "Woman Question": Fela and His Women

Apart from music, women played a central role in the evolution of Fela's complex persona. In his entire life, Fela was inseparable from the influence of the women around him and the issues of sex and sexuality. Considerations of his life and persona generate a "woman question" that is complicated and difficult to resolve. Fela's search for freedom, from Abeokuta to the United States and back to Lagos, was facilitated by a large retinue of women who played one significant role or another in illuminating what Fela really is and what he was looking for. Grappling with the woman question becomes all the more interesting because it can only be unraveled at the intersection of tradition, culture, ideology, and the personality of Fela himself. Two contending narratives offer definitive answers to the question: on the one hand, textual references throughout Fela's songs and interviews that speak to women, and his women in particular, in unflattering terms; and on the other, the objective significance of these women in his evolution as a revolutionary musician.

First, there is a need for an unraveling of the historical and political context around women, polygamy (or polygyny), and sexuality in Africa and especially within the Yoruba culture. This serves the purpose of contextualizing Fela's gender attitude within a specific dispensation of cultural philosophy in order to be able to better appreciate it within his overall political philosophy. Most African cultures are patriarchal in nature. The Yoruba precolonial societies were. And monogamy and polygyny were certainly marital practices that coexisted. Polygyny was necessitated especially by the social, moral, and economic factors. At the moral level, polygyny (and surprisingly, not polyandry, which was not as prevalent and was even frowned at) allowed a man to have as many wives as could enable him satisfied his sexual urge and limit his capacity for extra-marital relationships. But this is not to say that the latter was totally absent in the traditional Yoruba societies. It was just the case that those societies did not consider criminalizing polygyny; it was a pragmatic marital arrangement through and through. It was expected that the rich, the chiefs, and monarchs would be polygynous as a mark of status and wealth. But even more so, the agrarian nature of the traditional Yoruba societies, like most precolonial African societies, required a pragmatic economic consideration. Polygyny ensured the availability of many wives and many children as the labor hands to assist in farm work and inevitably increase the material wealth of the family.

The criminalization of polygyny came with Christianity, and definitely not with Islam, which made an inroad into the Yoruba societies far earlier before the coming of the Christian missionaries. Islam theologically permitted polygyny as part of its religious practices, and this was one of the reasons for its spread in Yorubaland. It is interesting to note that Islam spread through the agency of kings who had obvious reasons to accept it. On its part, Christianity, according to Wiredu, conflated "good conduct" with "moral uprightness" with regard to its treatment of polygyny. In other words, for the Christian missionaries, polygyny was at variance with their own norm of good moral conduct, and therefore, it was "condemned … as immoral" and hence something to eradicate with force.[1] However, argues Wiredu, the success which Christianity has had with eradicating polygyny has been countered by a measure of superficiality

> which has been responsible for a kind of ethical schizophrenia in the consciousness of many of our people. However sincere the African convert has been in his avowal of the foreign faith, he has too often not been able to erase from all the recesses of his consciousness a predisposition to many of the cultural habits ingrained in him in the course of his domestic and community socialization. As a result, many of the noble and pious Africans have been known to operate a subtle compromise of an official monogamy supplemented with informal but quite stable and demographically significant amorous relationships. Needless to say, the "pagan" sections of our populations have been able to view this dual system of behavior as anything but a somewhat amusing form of emergency pragmatism.[2]

It is within this context that we can insert Fela's political philosophy and gender agenda. Did he understand the complexities of gender and sexuality in Africa? If yes, how then do we reconcile the apparent contradiction between his political radicalism and his patriarchal attitude? Or, does it make more sense to argue that gender was a subordinate item on his hierarchy of political and social issues? This indeed has some precedent which Fela would have been familiar with. The radical activism of the Black Panther Party, and indeed of Rastafarianism, seemed to subordinate gender equality to the larger quest for liberation.[3] We can say, for instance, that there was no "woman question" in Rastafarianism since it accepted the power and authority that comes with the heightened power of the male that is projected in the Bible. On its part, the Black Panther Party projected an ideology of liberation that was fundamentally masculine. The possibility of liberation, that is, was hinged on a politics of virile manhood that has the capacity to snatch the initiative from the white oppressors. However, there is a strong ongoing debate as to whether the Black Panther Party's masculine politics translates into a submissive womanhood.[4]

The war between the two gender narratives about Fela's women is further complicated by the attempts in the Fela scholarship to rate and compare the relative level of importance of these women in his life. The dominant perspective in the analysis of Fela's women says that Funmilayo Ransome-Kuti, Fela's mother, was the most important woman in his life. In terms of chronology, and not discounting the significance of biology, we can concede this significance to Fela's mother. But it seems that this illustrates the limits on how far one can go in creating this type hierarchy of impact. Saying Funmilayo Ransome-Kuti was the most important projects a reading that fails to adequately interpret the complex tapestry of Fela's life and the dynamic roles each of the women within it played in his search for self-realization and musical significance.

Previous work on Fela charts five different types of women and four correlative levels of relationship which Fela had with all the women in his life—Fela's mother; Remilekun, his first and only legal wife; Sandra Smith, his ideological catalyst; Fela's "queens"; and the surplus retinue of women in the concubinage that Fela kept throughout his life. What this scholarship fails to take into account is that all these levels overlapped and interacted to such an extent that they undermine the assumption of any hierarchy of significance. In chronological order, Funmilayo Ransome-Kuti comes first as Fela's mother and he had a love-hate relationship with her:

> My mother was a motherfucker, you know. She would flog you like a man. You know how? She'd say: "Touch your toes. Bend down." And it was *batabatabatabatabatabatabatabata*...! She and my father wanted their son to be an example. So any time there was punishment, I would get the most. Man, my mother and father were so honest with their discipline, their child had to be flogged. They were the baddest parents I ever met in my life. It was systematic flogging. There was no week I didn't take sometimes three, sometimes six floggings. Any time my mother flogged me, it was rough flogging-o: *chagachagachagachagachagacha*...! If I tried getting away, she would say in a severe, commanding voice: "Come back here." And I'd have to come back.[5]

Between his father and his mother, Fela estimated that he must have received some 3,000 strokes of the cane; his admiration for his mother was constantly mixed with revulsion. Fela's childhood and adolescent years followed a long trajectory of discipline that instilled a lifelong dread. In 1958, while barely settled in London, his mother notified him that arrangements had been made for him to visit East Berlin, behind the Iron Curtain:

> And I don't want to travel nowhere. I didn't even have money to travel. But my mother wanted to arrange a holiday for me. Why … East Berlin? …. It was said that if you went into communist countries you would never come out; … So I was scared to go, man. I didn't want to go. *But how could I disobey my mother?*[6]

At the height of his confusion about the creative form that his music would take, Fela similarly testified again: "In '66 I was playing highlife jazz with my Koola Lobitos band. Eventually I dropped that name too. *'Cause my mother had told me*: 'Start playing music your people understand, not jazz.'"[7] Yet Funmilayo Ransome-Kuti also occupied an iconic place in Fela's heart. She was consciously deified in Fela's spiritual pantheon of heroes and contemporary divinities, alongside Malcolm X, Kwame Nkrumah, and Patrice Lumumba. This demonstrates how far Funmilayo Ransome-Kuti succeeded in impacting her son's life as a mother.

Fela's unconscious introduction to politics correlated with the increasing involvement of her mother in protest movements and the decreasing frequency of her punishment. That fascinated the young Fela; if his mother deferred punishment, then what was distracting her must be interesting! He met Kwame Nkrumah at one of his mother's frequent political meetings with significant political personalities of her period. Eventually, his parents' anticolonial resistance temperament, and their involvement with the NUT and the ALC-AWS-NWU, would rub off on the concretization of Fela's restless and radical character. But we have Fela's mother to thank for his early, if unconscious, introduction to the ideological tendencies that would later manifest in his musical intervention on behalf of Nigeria and Africa. According to Veal, "The Marxist influence provided a blueprint for the use of art as a means of shaping political consciousness; the nationalist influence led Fela to use his art to uplift his nation; and the Pan-Africanist influence led him to define his art within a theoretically unified Afro-Atlantic cultural sphere."[8] Another key influence was the informal introduction to Yoruba cultural dynamics and spirituality; Funmilayo deployed them in her activism against the colonial authorities and their collaborators.

Funmilayo Ransome-Kuti stayed with Fela throughout his musical and ideological maturation, changing her last name to "Anikulapo-Kuti," as well as moving in with her son. In the process, she bore the brunt of the Nigerian state's attacks on them both. A particularly brutal encounter with the military establishment in Nigeria, on February 17, 1977, precipitated the demise of Fela's mother. On that fateful day, soldiers stormed the Kalakuta Republic home of Fela and brutalized its inhabitants. Funmilayo Ransome-Kuti, now seventy-seven years old, was thrown out of a window with killed. On April 13, 1978, Frances Abigail Olufunmilayo Thomas Ransome-Kuti also died due to a combination of complications from the attack, old age, and the acute shock and depression from the recent events. Fela and Funmilayo's time together till her death, as well as the later support she gave to his protest philosophy, also enables us to chart a timeline of the unrelenting authoritarianism that bound their activism together, from the colonial authorities she dedicated her life to fighting to the postcolonial authorities that her son continued to battle until his own death.

Remilekun Taylor arrived next into Fela's life in chronological order and she had the distinct honor of being Fela's first and only legal wife. They met in 1959 in London and were married in 1961. Remilekun gave Fela three children—Yeni, Femi, and Sola—in rapid succession between 1961 and 1963. She was certainly the most silent but still a significant feminine force in Fela's life, a refuge of quiet solidity in the midst of the turbulence that marked Fela's search for self-realization. She was also probably the most sinned against, as far as the status of Fela's "first wife" permitted transgressions. Remilekun stayed with Fela from 1959 when they met until 2002, when she died, and the period of forty-three years that she was married to Fela was a span that would have tasked anyone's patience, despite their prenuptial agreement that all the other women—the concubinage—would not, could not, disappear. But it seemed that Remilekun bore those years relatively well, with a grace that came from understanding her reluctant husband[9] and accepting both his authoritarian dominance and predilection for philandering.

In February of 1978, Fela would take his cultural beliefs about relationships and marriage to an extreme end by simultaneously marrying twenty-seven female members of his Africa '70 band in Lagos:

Fela's QUEENS

Funmilayo Onile, Alake Adedipe, Kevwe Oghomienor, Tejumade Adebiyi, Ngozi Olisa, Najite Mukoro, Adejunwon Williams, Adeola Williams, Fehintola

Kayode, Ihase Obotu, Emaruagheru Osawe, Bose James, Kikelomo Oseni, Aduni Idowu, Olaide Babalaiye, Tokunbo Sholeye, Ibe Agwu, Orode Olowu, Iyabo Chibueze, Omowunmi Adesumi, Omolara Shosanya, Oluremi Akinola, Dupe Oloye, Folake Orosun, Omowunmi Oyedele, Chinyere Ibe, and Idiat Kasumu.

This act offended the delicate sensibilities of Christian middle-class society in the 1970s. It was the ultimate projection of supposed social excesses that had occurred within the confines of Fela's Kalakuta Republic home before the "wedding." And the act was an affront that ought to have outraged Fela's first and only legally married wife, Remilekun, who had already put a solid seventeen years into their marriage. Fittingly, "Remilekun" is a Yoruba name that means "Let someone wipe my tears." Such a blatant disregard for their legally contracted and officially sanctified relationship could have made tears flow freely in aggrieved outrage. But Remilekun accepted it with stoic resignation. According to her, what mattered was the mutual respect shared between them and the fact that she loved him. For her, being authoritarian was "how I think a husband should be."[10] Yet, it would seem that it is not only the Yoruba name that Remilekun owes a culture that is deeply patriarchal; Remilekun seemed to fully accept her husband's cultural attitude of masculinity. This comes with the cultural dynamics of being the first wife in an African context.

All these women, Fela's "Queens," ranging from seventeen to thirty years old, were drawn to Fela from various social perspectives and deprivations. Most came from polygamous homes, while some others were propelled by an adolescent spirit of adventure. Fela became a larger-than-life figure that they could relate with. In fact, for most, he was the very image of freedom that had been denied them in their homes, and by the constricting norms of society (as will be discussed in more details in Chapter 14). Fela justified his act of excess in two ways. First, it was for him an authentic act of African polygamy. How else could he have behaved as an African man? Monogamy was un-African, even unnatural. There is more on this later. Second, the "wedding" also served for him as an act of gratitude for these women who had stood by him through thick and thin, and had endured the enormous existential pressure of establishing the Afrobeat brand, especially when Kalakuta Republic was stormed by the Nigerian military. Marrying them all legitimized their social standing and is just reward for their loyalty.

But beyond these two justifications, each of these women had one thing or another they contributed to Kalakuta Republic and the Afrika Shrine. They were not only essential to the administration of Fela's music organization, they also contributed to the creative artistry behind Afrobeat, as part of Fela's stage act. They cannot therefore be relegated to the lower rungs on the hierarchy of significance. It is doubtful to conceive of an Afrobeat *performance* that did not include the Queens' mesmerizing presence on stage. They were not just there to satisfy the leering gaze of the basically male audience; they constituted an integral part of the Afrobeat ensemble. It would be strange to consider Afrobeat without their gyrating sensual energies on stage, and beside Fela himself. They essentially defined a unique aesthetic presence, adding vitality to Afrobeat's entertainment and political dimensions.

Specifically, Fela's Queens are significant to the emergence of what Olorunyomi calls "Afrobeat dance": a "semantics of dance" that fuses different African dance forms into an energetic and "anarchic display of femininity, an open challenge to contemporary definition of 'proper' female gender posture in patriarchal Nigeria."[11] Fela's Queens imposed their performance imprimatur on the performance space between the "Lady Dance" and the "Fire Dance." In "Lady," the song that allows Fela to define the cultural boundary of African femininity, Fela sings:

Call am for dance	[*Invite the Lady for a dance*]
She go dance lady dance	[*She dances the Lady dance*]
Call am for dance	
She go dance lady dance	
African woman go dance	[*When the African woman dances*]
She go dance the fire dance	[*She dances the fire dance*]
African woman go dance	
She go dance the fire dance	
She know him man na master	[*She knows the man is the master*]
She go cook for am	[*So she cooks for him*]
She go do anything he say	[*and she does anything he says*]
But lady, no be so	[*But the Lady is not so*]
But lady, no be so	
But lady, no be so	
But lady, no be so	
Lady na master	[*The Lady is the master*]
Lady na master	

In Fela's ideological song, the "Lady Dance" corresponds to the stylized Western dance steps of the educated Africans, and the "Fire Dance" defines the athletic dance expression of the Africans. Since the fire dance is fundamental a female dance domain, Fela's Afrobeat, and especially the dance-instrument call dynamics (or metaphrasing), provided the context within which the Afrobeat dance is perfected as a unique choreography of African story-telling with the body and with music. And in choreographing the dance, the Queens creatively achieved a blend that established the collective dance tapestry through the infusion of the individual and local dance styles. The rhythmic and ideological vocabulary of the Afrobeat dance of Fela's Queens generates a sufficiently rich performance template that could serve as the starting point of a genuine and deep study of African dance.

Fela's Queens also defined a boundary of cultural functionality that is not easily squared either with Fela's traditional perception of women or his struggle to free society's disenfranchised. The fact that the Queens represented one of the administrative backbones of Fela's success constitutes one of the great paradoxes of his sexist traditionalism. It raises the question whether Fela's presentation of masculinity could have been possible without the functional dynamics of his Queens.

One woman who would seem most likely to occupy the topmost rung of Fela's relationship hierarchy, if there is one, is Sandra Smith. She was a former member of the Black Panther Party and the woman who provided the ideological education to jumpstart Fela's awareness and the musical identity of Afrobeat. Sandra was Fela's last link to self-realization:

> Sandra gave me the education I wanted to know. She was the one who opened my eyes. I swear, man! She's the one who spoke to me about … Africa! For the first time I heard things I'd never heard before about Africa! Sandra was my adviser. She talked to me about politics, history. She taught me what she knew and what she knew was enough for me to start on. Yeah, Sandra taught me a lot, man. She blew my mind really. She's beautiful. Too much. Nothing about my life is complete without her. Sandra was the woman … I swear.[12]

Sandra, in a sense, was the conscious catalyst of all the unconscious ideological equations that had lain somnolent in Fela since he began observing his mother's political activism. His American experience with Sandra, especially his reading *The Autobiography of Malcolm X* and his direct observation of the Civil Rights Movement's historical dynamics, enabled the initial fusion of ideology with his music. It was through Sandra's prodding that Fela finally found a deeper understanding of what freedom meant in ideological terms. After this point,

Fela was ready to step into what Foltz calls the "freedom within the African state" through the combative creativity of Afrobeat. The crucial lyrical content of Afrobeat music was born in Sandra's room, and at her piano. In fact, the first Afrobeat tune that Sandra's ideological prompting brought forth—"My Lady's Frustration"—was a dedication to her resilience, though this was a titular concession Fela was reluctant to make:

> Oh, this woman, she has helped me in America-o. She has fed me for five months. There are telephone bills I've run up; they've even cut one telephone line of their house .... I've almost made her family bankrupt .... I've spoiled their cars .... This was what was going on in my head, you know. *So I said to myself, if I'm gonna sing about any one woman, I would sing about this one. At least to clear my conscience.* That's how low I was at that time, man. *I hated to give women any fucking credit, man. Everybody was singing about women. How could I sing about a woman in my tune? I didn't want to start singing about women.*[13]

Despite her tough background and strong grounding in black feminist ideals, Sandra complied with Fela's patriarchal, authoritarian directives. When they met at a bar in Los Angeles, Fela went to her and said, "You're going with me."[14] And Sandra went with him.

The last set of women around Fela was the string of girlfriends and mistresses that he kept at all time and everywhere he went. According to him, he had about seventy of them at times at Kalakuta Republic. These other women all met his need for sex and companionship at one time or the other. They were the sensuous juices that kept Afrobeat's creativity turning and spinning.

Afrobeat enabled Fela to open space up for discourse in a variety of domains. And one of those themes that intersected his activism and projection of Africanity was that of women and sexuality. Fela never hid his sexual proclivity. He wanted women and, for him, that was as African as his sexual orientation would allow him. His first marriage happened only because he was still struggling to define his "African" persona, but that marriage would ultimately not stop him. Fela had a most demeaning and devaluing view about women, according to his supposedly traditional African worldview, even though he grudgingly recognized all the roles they had played in his formation. According to his own testimony, the common denominator for all the women in his life, minus his mother, was sex:

> What attracted me to each of them? Sex! I thought they were sexy and fuckable. That's what attracts me to a woman first. Some came to my house on their own.

> Others, I had come. Why? 'Cause I wanted to fuck them. That was all. I wanted a house where I could be fucking and I had it. It grew into something else after though. Something special. But it started just with sex. The desire to fuck.[15]

All through his life, Fela objectified the female body into an article of pleasure. A woman is *a thing* that should be domesticated and dominated for the sole pleasure of men. For instance, it was Renilekun's beautiful face that attracted Fela, which invoked an uncontrollable yearning to possess her, to subject her body to his orgiastic whims. The same sexual attraction drove the first point of contact with Sandra, though Sandra was an exception in the sense that she had an ideological aspect that subordinated sex to ideas. They were equals of sort. There was something to her more than her body. But Sandra was just that: an exception.

Fela's fascination with Yoruba traditional cultural dynamics also has contributing to the contradicting strain of authoritarianism he inherited from both his parents. What role did the sexual allusions and innuendoes in Funmilayo Ransome-Kuti's protest songs play in Fela's construction of a woman? How was that construction helped by his dedication to Yoruba culture and its deeply patriarchal context? Whatever the answer to these questions, Fela's libidinal objectification of women derived from his patriarchal interpretation of gender and cultural roles. These are the basis of Fela's assured understanding of women:

> What do I understand about women? First, that they like to be slept with. They like you to make them do things for you. They're like Satan in that stupid book, the Bible: they like to test you, so that they can get away with something. If you let them get away with it once, you're in trouble. But if you stop them from getting away with it, then they'll stop .... Men and women are on two different levels. You can say different wavelengths. Man. Woman. Two points that can never meet. Women have different feelings than men. It's as simple as that. You can't compare them. Equality between male and female? No! Never! Impossible! Can never be! It seems the man must dominate. I don't want to say so, but it seems so .... Do I see man as being naturally superior to women? Naturally. Why? Well, I wouldn't say superior. I'd say *dominant*. Yes, dominant. Dominant is the word I want, not superior. Dominant means that there must be a master. Men are the masters, not women. When you say the "master of the house", you mean the head of the household: the father, not the woman, man. That's life, man. Natural life. Life is based on nature .... It's part of the natural order for women to be submissive to man .... What's the woman's role? To keep the home

> smooth, the children happy, the husband happy. To make the husband happy, that's a woman's job. Women got no other work than making the man happy.[16]

It is easy to relate this libidinous "philosophy" with the excessive masculinity projected by Fela, which even suffused his musical ensemble. Indeed, jazz has been discussed in feminist literature as a "hegemonic masculine discourse."[17] In other words, it participates in the larger problematic by which the semiotic dynamics of music itself construct gender and sexuality. Jazz and other types of music are not neutral forms of entertainment; jazz not only "serves as a public forum within which various models of gender organization (along with many other aspects of social life) are asserted, adopted, contested, and negotiated [but] Music is also very often concerned with the arousing and channeling of desire, with mapping patterns through the medium of sound that resemble those of sexuality."[18]

We can further argue that Afrobeat, despite its protest credentials, successfully provides a context that connects music, bodies, and gender. In the hand of Fela, Afrobeat explored sexuality as a cultural practice that undermines women as legitimate members of the society that Afrobeat hopes to reform. There are two iconic songs that construct the "woman" according to Fela's understanding of traditional Africa cultural values—"Lady" (1972) and "Mattress" (1975). These songs not only projected Fela's thoughts but simultaneously also constructed him as a "Big African Man." "Mattress" transforms the symbol of sleeping into a sexual metaphor that semiotically becomes the image of a woman's body:

> The thing wey we dey sleep on top, call am for me
> Mattress mattress
> The thing wey we dey sleep on, call am for me
> Mattress mattress
>
> If e be mat, wey e dey cold for ground
> Mattress mattress
> If e be plank, wey e dey hard for back
> Mattress mattress
> If e be spring wey you bounce like ball
> Mattress mattress
> If e be cushion wey e dey soft like wool
> Mattress mattress
>
> E be mat, e be plank, e be spring, e be cushion
> Mattress mattress

So when I say woman na mattress I no lie
You no lie my friend

What we lay on top, call it for me
Mattress

If it is a mat, so cold on the ground
Mattress
If it is a plank, so hard on the back
Mattress
If it is a spring that bounces
Mattress
If it is a cushion soft as wool
Mattress

So, when I say a woman is a mattress, I am not lying
You're not lying, my friend

The mattress becomes a metaphor for a woman's body sexualized for pleasure, whether on the mat, plank, spring, or cushion.

With "Lady," as with its counterpart "Gentleman," Fela attempted to construct a binary opposite between tradition and modernity; or more precisely between the modern Westernized constructions of lady and gentleman as opposed to the "authentic" African understanding of a man and a woman. The so-called modern lady affects sophistication and calls for equality:

She go say him equal to man
She go say him get power like man
She go say anything man do himself fit do

***

She go want take cigar before anybody
She go want make you open door for am
She go want make man wash plate
For am, for kitchen

She says she is equal to a man
She says she has power like a man
She says she can do what a man can do

***

She wants to have a cigar before anyone
She wants the door to be opened for her
She wants the man to wash the plates

On the contrary, the authentic African woman, according to Fela, knows her place in the natural and social order of things:

She know him man na master
She go cook for am
She go do anything he say

She knows the man is the master
And so she must do the cooking
And she must do anything he says

In line with this cultural understanding of who and what a woman is, Fela had constructed all his women as objects of desire for his masculine domination. This cultural construction seems to blind him from perceiving the critical significance of these women in his search for self-realization.[19] Here, it is not Sandra that serves as the emblem of significance but his Queens. These women have been characterized by various social perceptions, seen mainly as prostitutes, ne'er-do-wells, and societal rejects who had nowhere else to go; some saw Fela's marriage as an attempt to buy respectability for them. However, contrary to Fela's construction of women as mere bodies and subjects waiting to fulfill male desires, these women were "unconscious feminists" that redefined the tenets of sexual politics in his own home![20] By their aestheticization of the erotic, the Afrobeat Queens enabled a rethinking of the sphere of the respectable and the acceptable within the bounds of social expectations. Unknown to Fela himself, they could actually be considered the true ambassadors of Afrobeat and its dissent activism.

Part B

Fela, Art, and Politics

6

Fela and Postcolonial Political Economy of Nigeria

The immediate post-independence period in Nigeria of the 1960s and 1970s was a period of acute sociopolitical and development pressures, tensions, and crises. The implementation of the 1914 Amalgamation policy integrating the Northern and the Southern Protectorates into a single state called Nigeria immediately began showing signs of its terrible consequences, including the pre-independence tensions that the young Fela had become aware of growing up under a politically active mother and an activist father. Since the political involvement of Reverend Ransome-Kuti did not go beyond the occasional confrontation with the colonial authority, as well as the massive commitment to winning better working conditions for the Nigerian teachers, it was with Funmilayo Ransome-Kuti that Fela was first intimated with his infantile understanding of Nigerian pre-independence politics.

The 1940s and 1950s were already a turbulent period of political maneuverings, interactions, and negotiations due to the amalgamation and the politics of ownership which had made ethnic mobilization a potent instrument in the power politics that was already fermenting during the build up to independence in 1960. The three major political parties—Action Group (AG), led by Chief Obafemi Awolowo in the Southwest; the Northern Peoples' Congress (NPC) of Sir Ahmadu Belo, the Sardauna of Sokoto; and the National Council of Nigeria and the Cameroons (NCNC), led by Nnamdi Azikiwe—were motivated by ethnic consideration in the pursuit of independence. The NCNC's initial, broad-based nationalism apparently drew Funmilayo Ransome-Kuti and appealed to the young Fela. He was, however, incensed that Awolowo had facilitated the Alake of Egbaland's reinstatement—the king who had abdicated due to the taxation protests led by Funmilayo. With the success of her women's movement in contributing to the eventual abdication, it became inevitable Mrs. Ransome-Kuti's focus would turn national; the plight of Abeokuta women was similar to what Nigerian women faced everywhere in the country. The NCNC, with its conglomeration of diverse parties and groups from across Nigeria, was the only party with a spread that appealed to Mrs. Ransome-Kuti's ambition for a truly national platform to push her agenda for women's rights.

As the date of independence drew closer, several national and political events led to the disintegration of the NCNC into an ethnic party servicing the interest of the Igbo, including the critical carpet-crossing saga in the Western region involving Awolowo's Action Group and the NCNC. The results of the 1951 general elections put both the NCNC and the Action Group in precarious political position. The NCNC won the majority of votes in the Eastern region, while the NPC captured the majority in the North. The Western region then became the final test over who would produce the outright winner to form the Western Regional Government. The NCNC could not count on the support of the Ibadan People's Party and the AG could not win a majority vote itself. Charges of carpet-crossing were leveled to explain the AG's eventual victory in the election, rendering Zik, as Dr. Nnamdi Azikiwe was popularly called, and his party into the ethnic enclave of the Eastern region. It cost Zik his nationalist credentials and the NCNC lost its reputation as a national party. Mrs. Ransome-Kuti was one of those who suffered as a fallout of the political palaver, expelled from the NCNC because she was unable to win a seat in the Western regional House of Assembly, and her bid for a second candidacy was rejected in 1959. She went on to campaign as an independent candidate and split the NCNC vote.

The young Fela was privy to these political tensions, and the negotiations his mother was involved in during this period. It was his first glimpse into national politics at the intersection of the colonial and the postcolonial. His recollection:

> I liked the way she took on those old politicians, all those dishonest rogues. She wouldn't have anything to do with them. None of them. Except Nnamdi Azikiwe ("Zik"), for whom she had a little sympathy. But she was against all the others, all those politicians like the Obafemi Awolowo ("Awo") type. She even finished with Zik later on because he began playing a double game with her. It happened when she went to London with Zik for a press conference. When she returned, she said that Zik was sabotaging her. She said that Zik didn't want progress for her at all. Awolowo? To her, he was the biggest crook. She could tolerate Zik, but not Awolowo. At the time—in 1949—I was one of those encouraging her to join NCNC, the National Council of Nigeria-Cameroons, Zik's party. Everybody loved Zik, because he was a nationalist. I wanted my mother to be in his party.

> I wanted her to win the elections. She was so popular, man! Oh, those politicians of that time destroyed the country, man.[1]

The seamless transition from the violence of the colonial government to the various postcolonial and post-independence political shortcomings, blind turns, and blunders eventually transformed Nigerian into an authoritarian postcolonial political context that subverted the will of Nigerians in the same way the colonial authority did. From the colonial Nigeria of Funmilayo Ransome-Kuti to the post-independence Nigeria of Fela Anikulapo-Kuti, there was hardly any significant and qualitative political difference in the freedom the citizens had to activate their capacities for meaningful existence. By the time independence came for Nigeria in 1960, Fela was well within the grip of the historical processes that pushed him toward self-realization through the emergence of an ideologically charged and politically active Afrobeat.

At independence, the three significant issues of administration, politics, and the economy became the focal points for the Nigerian leadership who supervised the lowering of the Union Jack and replaced it with Nigeria's Green-White-Green national flag. The Nigerian leadership was immediately confronted with the administrative challenge of determining the principle by which appointment to crucial positions vacated by the colonialists would be filled. Choosing between merit and representativeness, the leadership gave a nod to representativeness as a concession to Nigeria's pluralistic status, but that plurality would eventually polarize the Nigerian state into warring political and ethnic factions competing in zero-sum agitations for political power. The pre-independence political contestations were transposed into independent Nigeria with even more brutal energy and the political shenanigans characteristic of Nigeria's First Republic (1960 to 1966) inevitably led to the Nigerian Civil War (alternatively called the Biafra War or the Nigeria-Biafra war).

Fela still remained apolitical at the time Nigeria went to war with itself. The search for self-realization was much more demanding to him at the time than any political intervention in Nigeria's problems. And even if he were to be political, there was nothing about him, no status or platform, that could ever give him a voice. In fact, when the exigencies of living in the United States became too stifling due to legal complications involving visas and contracts, Fela and his Ghanaian record promoter, Duke Lumumba, made the opportunistic decision to sing a pro-government song that could transform their economic situation if the Nigeria government were to endorse it. The result was a recitation over an instrumental version of one of Koola Lobitos' tracks, "Wakawaka." It was titled "Viva Nigeria" (1969):

> This is brother Fela Ransome Kuti
> This is one time I would like to say a few things
> Men are born, Kings are made
> Treaties are signed, Wars are fought
> Every country has its own problems
> So has Nigeria, so has Africa
> Let us bind our wounds and live together in peace
> Nigeria, one nation indivisible
> Long live Nigeria, Viva Africa
> The history of mankind
> Is full of obvious turning points and significant events
> Though tongue and tribe may differ,
> We are all Africans, War is not the answer
> It has never been the answer
> And it will never be the answer fighting amongst each other
> Let's live together in peace
> Nigeria, one Nation Indivisible
> Long live Nigeria, Viva Africa
> Let's eat together like we used to eat
> Let's plan together like we used to plan
> Sing together like we used to sing
> Dance together like we used to dance
> United we stand, divided we fall
> You know what I mean
> I hope you do
> Let us bind our wounds and live together in peace
> Nigeria, one nation indivisible
> Long live Nigeria, Viva Africa
> Brothers and Sisters in Africa
> Never should we learn to wage war against each other
> Let Nigeria be a lesson to all
> We have more to learn towards building than destroying
> Our people can't afford any more sufferings
> Let's join hands Africa
> We have nothing to lose
> But a lot to gain
> War is not the answer

War has never been the answer
And it will never be the answer
Fighting amongst each other
One nation indivisible
Long live Nigeria
Viva Africa

Apart from the fact that the song did not succeed in making a blip on anybody's radar, it shows that not only had Fela not yet arrived at Afrobeat and political radicalization but the song's simplistic lyrics betrayed political ignorance about the complex dynamics of a postcolonial state like Nigeria. General Yakubu Gowon, Nigeria's war-time military head of state, was, for Fela, "a foolish man," and in his "political assessment," "The Biafrans were fucking right to secede, man."[2] In retrospect, Fela regretted the release of "Viva Nigeria," and we can accept the blunder as part of Fela's apolitical years. While the war raged, he was busy playing his highlife jazz in Lagos, standing far outside on its fringes.

While Fela was playing highlife music in Nigeria between 1963 and 1968, at the height of the civil war, and enjoying the bliss of political ignorance, the foundations for Nigeria's postcolonial economy were being laid in a way that would eventually fuel the musical creativity of him and his Afrobeat band. Eleven years before the first gunshot kick-started the civil war, Shell D'Arcy discovered oil in Nigeria on January 15, 1956, at the Oloibiri Oilfield in present-day Bayelsa state. This find not only transformed Nigeria's economic status into a wealthy state sustained by petrodollar, oil also set in motion the dynamics of development that would eventually cripple the Nigerian state in a manner contrary to the optimism and expectations that postcolonial Nigeria was about to be launched into an era of developmental well-being. But by the time the civil war was underway, the truth of the resource curse theory was already being demonstrated in Nigeria; first, the discovery of oil wiped out the growing status of agriculture as a crucial catalyst for economic growth, and second, crude oil became the sole source of revenue for the Nigerian government and the economic basis of Nigeria's lopsided federalism. In fact, the discovery of oil transformed control over the Nigerian state into a prized aim—a National Cake—that had to be captured at all cost in a zero-sum political game.

What has been called the opacity of the Nigerian oil industry—the practice of deliberately obfuscating the data related to oil production, accounting, and operations—was a key cause of the Nigerian civil war, shaping the "structures, policies, and political relations" that led to the resource curse and Nigeria's development impasse.[3] The oil boom—and the influx of the oil dollar—certainly aggravated the possibility of war. With a burst in crude output from 84,000 barrels per day in 1964 to 301,352 in 1965, and the correlative increase in revenue from 20 million to 60 million pounds, Nigeria became the thirteenth largest producer of oil in the world, and the oil boom was ushered in. The tension that this created arose from the revenue allocation then in place, which gave 50 percent of the oil revenue to the region of origin, 30 percent into the general pool for allocation to other regions in Nigeria, and 20 percent to the coffers of the federal government. Since the Eastern region serviced a large percentage of Nigerian oil production in the 1960s, it was inevitable that the other regions, especially the North, would nurse the fear of ethnic domination.

Opacity, the practice of deliberately obfuscating the data related to oil production, accounting, and operations, became a critical matter contributing to the escalation of the prospects for war. While the various oil companies involved in the Nigerian oil industry pursued the strategy of opacity, Ojukwu also could not avoid strategizing around oil since the Eastern region was Nigeria's oil base. The Revenue Collection Edict of 1967 in particular insisted that oil companies operating in the region had to pay their taxes to the Eastern regional government. After the war, the revenue formula changed immediately: first, there was a distinction between "on-shore" and "off-shore" oil revenue, with the postwar allocation regime giving 100 percent of the off-shore revenue to the federal government; and second, the regional revenue allocation came down to 45 percent, while the distributed pool was increased to 50 percent.

The end of the war brought untold hardship to Nigerians. The economy was suffused with an enormous cash flow, but it was not impacting economic growth. This was worsened by the authoritarian command structure of the military and an economic strategy that placed the state at the "commanding height" of the economy. Several developmental plans failed to transform the Nigerian economy. The oil curse had finally taken hold! When Fela returned to Nigeria in 1970, the military was fully in charge, supervising an underdeveloping Nigerian state. Nation building had become fraught with many landmines; the escalation of ethnic tension was directly proportional to Nigeria's move up the ladder as the tenth largest oil-producing state in the world. The socioeconomic, political, and cultural situation that Fela returned to was one that was ready for a revolutionary renaissance and a takeover. The economy, on the one hand, was coasting with lots of petrodollar but without any significant noneconomic objectives to supervise its dynamics. The oil boom was driving a significant inequality gap that was already creating national disaffection from a growing army of the poor. On the other hand, the sociocultural scene was going through some experimentation that had still not produced any definitive outcome.

When Fela arrived, several things happened immediately. He changed the band name from Nigeria 70 to Africa 70 and the Afro-Spot, his former entertainment site, was renamed The African Shrine. He produced the track "Jeun Ko Ku" (Eat and Die), in 1973, which became an instant hit and brought Fela finally into renown that made Afrobeat a commercial success. His Surulere residence in Lagos gradually became a large communal compound, as Fela's nod to his extreme individualistic ethos. Still, between arriving back at Lagos and the release of "Jeun Ko Ku," Fela had to go through another phase that included further experimentation on his new Afrobeat style, the gradual emergence and honing of his political sensibility, and the inevitable harassment from the Nigerian government:

> Who was I? It was in America I saw I was making a mistake. I didn't know myself. I realized that neither me nor my music was going in the right direction. I came back home with the intent to change the whole system. I didn't know I was going to have … such horrors! I didn't know they were gonna give me such opposition because of my new Africanism. How could I have known? As soon as I got back home I started to preach. I had decided to change my music. And my music did start changing according to how I experienced the life and culture of my people.[4]

The resistance to Fela's new ideological sensibilities came from many quarters. His Nigerian audience was not familiar, or even comfortable, with the new political tone. The clenched fist salute did not make sense to anyone! It did not follow the musical norms the audience was used to. But gradually, and with more instrumental experiments, Fela started assembling a political profile that was assisted by the presence of abject inequality all around him. With tracks like "Buy Africa," "Black Man's Cry," "Why Black Man Dey Suffer," and especially "Beggar's Lament," all released in 1971, Fela gradually became a radical and political musician. "Jeun Ko Ku" was the final step in the chain of events that would not only solidify Fela's profile as a radical musician but would also bring him into series of hostile encounters with the Nigerian government. As a first sign of the bad times to come, "Jeun Ko Ku" was banned by the Nigerian Broadcasting Corporation (NBC) for its sexual references.

Fela's newfound political activism not only disrupted the apolitical dynamics of Nigeria's music scene, it also was at cross purposes with the regimental authority of the military government in Nigeria. The sarcastic and critical humor which was finally manifested in "Jeun Ko Ku" became the lyrical modus operandi to be found in Fela post-1970 works. Afrobeat, in line with Fela's resolve to remain faithful to the cultural and national template, started deriving its lyrical materials from Nigeria's development crisis. His decision to live among Nigeria's poor was a strategic one that not only was coterminous with his desire to reenact the spirit of African communalism but also gave him artistic benefits through partaking in the developmental deficiencies that plagued Nigeria firsthand. The slums and the streets gave Fela lyrical insights into concepts, slogans, terms, and ideas which were emanating from the people's lived experience. The antagonism engendered by the suffering and trauma of the people was refracted through Fela's dissident tunes directed at the government. As we shall see in Chapter 14, the communal compound he decided to create—alongside the African Shrine—became the grounds for the cultivation of the countercultural practices that further promoted his profile as a social deviant and an iconoclast.

The impending confrontation finally happened on April 30, 1974, when a heavily armed contingent of the Nigerian police force came charging into Fela's Surulere home. Fela and more than fifty other occupants of the house were arrested and taken to Alagbon Close, the notorious Police Central Intelligence Division headquarters in Lagos. The cited offenses were drug peddling and addiction, as well as the presence of underage girls in Fela's compound. After his release on bail after eight days in captivity, the police returned and produced trumped-up evidence sure to earn Fela not less than ten years in prison. The dramatic incident of how Fela snatched the wrap of marijuana (that the police planted and suddenly "discovered" in his house), chumped on it, and swallowed it down with a dose of whisky became a colorful part of the lore that defined Fela's radical engagement with the Nigerian state. The police, no less dramatically, insisted that Fela must excrete the "evidence." He was locked up in a special room, with instruction to those monitoring him to ensure that the wrap of marijuana was retrieved. That first jail experience confronted Fela with a real-life experience of injustice. He reminisced:

> But after they put me in that cell with the people they call "criminals", I started thinking: "Who the fuck is Society? Who jails Society when it does horrors to people? Why Society does nothing to help beggars; to provide jobs and keep people from having to steal just to chop? Why don't Society fight against corruption, punish the powerful ...?" I concluded to myself: "Fuck society, man. It's unjust!"[5]

It was precisely this injustice of social relations that he sang about in the track "Alagbon Close" (1974): the bureaucratic blindness of deliberate incarceration and the loss of dignity and self-esteem. The track has a plaintive rhythmic evocation that seems to bewail not only the indignity visited on the jailed but also the loss of the humanity within the jailer. The refrain of "Never mind, I dey play my part; I be human being like you (never mind, I play my part; I am a human being just like you)" tells the story all by itself:

For Alagbon,
Dem no get respect for human being,
Dem no know say you get blood like them,
Dem go send dem dogs to bite bite you,
Dem go point dem guns for your face,
The gun wey dem take your money to buy,
Dem don butt my head with dem gun
The gun wey dem take my money to buy,
Dem go torture you and take your statement from you … for Alagbon,
Dem go lock you for months and months and months … dem dey call am investigation

At Alagbon
There's no respect for human beings
They are not aware you have blood like them
They send their dogs to bite you
They point their guns right in your face
The very guns they bought with taxpayers' money
They butted my head with these very guns
The very guns they bought with taxpayers' money
They torture you and then demand for a statement … at Alagbon
They locked you up for months on end, and call it "investigation"

The prison experience only served to increase Fela's stature as a rebel, with the Nigerian state's banality set before his lyrical crosshairs. In fact, Fela's prison experience served as further instigation for creative experimentation. "Akunakuna" was composed in the Maiduguri prison, while the inspiration for the introduction of the second bass guitar into the Afrobeat ensemble came while he was at the Benin prison. When he was released after his third jail experience on November 23, 1974, Fela renamed his compound "Kalakuta Republic," after the name of the cell in which he was incarcerated at the Central Intelligence Division (CID) Headquarters in Lagos. Kalakuta Republic was an act of defiance tinted with some hubris about the inviolacy and invincibility of his cause. His change of name from Ransome-Kuti to "Anikulapo Kuti" in 1975 was not only an ideological act but was as if Fela was saying, "You can keep trying to cow me, but I have death under my control!" as "Anikulapo" literally means "He who has death in his quiver" and "Kuti" means "He that cannot be killed." Unfortunately for Fela, Kalakuta Republic only succeeded in infuriating the establishment further. The harassment picked up from 1974 until 1976, when it was further aggravated by "Upside Down," which Fela made with Sandra. Everything culminated in 1977, when Kalakuta Republic was sacked once again and the fallout led to the death of Fela's mother, Funmilayo Ransome-Kuti.

The year 1977 was also the year of the Second World Black and African Festival of Arts and Culture (FESTAC) in Nigeria, supervised by the Obasanjo regime. Of course, Fela was at the height of Afrobeat radicalism at this period, but the federal military government recognized his relevance as a significant cultural figure that could be deployed to legitimize the entire event. It is not certain whether anyone was under any illusion whether this unusual "collaboration" between the government and Fela could ever work, from the first moment the idea was conceived. Considered an anathema to political scientists because it undermined the country's democratic aspirations, the military government of Obasanjo needed all the legitimate acceptance it could get from the over fifty delegate countries arriving from across Africa and the African diasporas in the Americas, Europe, the Caribbean, and Asia. Fela obviously played a critical part in the government's play for validity, yet it was inevitable that the relationship would be doomed to fail before it even commenced.

At the first meeting of the Nigerian National Participation Committee, held in Kano in 1976 under the chairmanship of Major-General I. B. M. Haruna, the federal commissioner for Information and Culture, the conflict points became immediately obvious. Fela became grossly uncomfortable immediately with the appointment of a military man as the head of a committee preparing for a major *cultural* program.[6] Much more substantive disagreement came from Fela's recommendation that Nigeria make the cultural event more inclusive, facilitating the participation of Nigerians from all walks of life. He made a nine-point proposal to the committee:

- The aim of the festival as a whole should be to redirect the thinking of the common man;

- Specifically, the festival should attempt to re-educate the common man in Nigeria and Africa about the role of colonization on African history and religion;
- The festival should aim to rid the present generation of the imposed influence of foreign cultures. The festival should provide African history books that are written from an African (rather than colonial) perspective, and which, due to imperialist maneuver, are not easily available in Africa;
- To achieve a solid unity among the black race, based on a strong foundation of African unity, an effective communication system should emerge from the festival;
- Efforts must be made to encourage all Nigerians to participate in the festival. Financial incentives and encouragement should be given to artists to encourage them to participate and perform at their best;
- All directors responsible for various sections of events should be given opportunities to use their positions to bring about policies that will enhance the future development of cultural institutions in the country, that is, theatres for film, performance space and art galleries;
- The activities of the festival and the ideas behind them should be channeled through the educational curriculum in the country to benefit future generations;
- Mini-festivals should be held all over the country to select the types of artists to represent the country, and those selected should be provided with necessary instruments and equipment to perform. In view of this, the sum of 5 million Naira (approximately $7 million in 1977) voted is inadequate to support meaningful participation;
- The composition of the committee itself, drawn from outside the circle of working artists, makes Nigeria's participation in a festival of this nature a huge joke.[7]

It is easy to see how these proposals would irk Major-General Haruna and the Obasanjo regime. On the one hand, Fela raised issues that were serious and cogent; no one can fault the ninth recommendation on the committee's composition, which was surely the basis of Haruna's anger. The eighth recommendation for mini-festivals, which was ultimately accepted, was equally critical, except that the source of funding, the petro-dollar of the 1970s, was already laying the foundation for the corruption that would ravage Nigeria and was also something that Fela himself later railed against among his general criticism of

FESTAC. The sixth recommendation, for developing cultural infrastructure, was a genuine policy proposal that could have cemented the gains of the festival for Nigeria's cultural renaissance, as could the other recommendations. Still, Fela was attempting to turn FESTAC into a cultural revolution, an agenda that went far beyond the event's purview. The first three populist and Africanist proposals seem too farfetched for the festival to achieve.

Fela's presence on the committee eventually got under the skin of Major-General Haruna, while the command structure of the military grated on Fela's nerve in turn. The partnership degenerated into a media war, with Fela resuming his musical diatribe against military highhandedness. He led nation-wide criticisms of the government's handling of the cultural event and the blatant corruption that attended its organization. Fela not only boycotted the FESTAC but his absence became the impetus for an alternative event at the Afrika Shrine that Fela called a "counter-FESTAC." Since Fela was at the height of his musical prowess and his Afrobeat was already globally recognized, he was the central Nigerian cultural icon that all the international visitors wanted to see. Fela rose to the occasion for another moment of *yabis*, delivering firsthand information on the government's insincerity and incompetence. Fela not only stole the show but equally undermined the overall integrity and legitimacy of the FESTAC event. As he himself acknowledged, the military government never forgave him for his "treasonable" act, and one of the truly tragic prices he had to pay for his intransigent rebellion was the death of his mother in a most terrible manner.

The simmering "war" between the Obasanjo regime and Fela would escalate into the bloodiest and most tragic of all the raids that had been visited on him. On February 18, 1977—just six days after the conclusion of the FESTAC event—as the narrative goes, one of Fela's drivers was arrested by a soldier at Ojuelegba, a few meters from Fela's Kalakuta home. The driver was beaten and left for dead, later rushed to the hospital on the orders of Fela, who was at home on that day, resting. While the soldier responsible for manhandling the driver was not found at the scene of the incident, it later became obvious that he had gone to mobilize reinforcements from a nearby barrack. An army captain arrived with a contingent of soldiers to ask that Fela release the driver into his custody. Fela refused, with the argument that the driver desperately needed medical care. Things would take a turn for the worse from that point, when the captain left and asked his soldiers to stand guard with the order that no one was to be allowed out of the Kalakuta compound, and it became obvious that some form of calculated intent and official authorization was involved in the execution of the raid.

More soldiers arrived to join the considerable number that had already laid siege to Fela's house. But they all stood waiting for two more hours until an official looking Mercedes Benz arrived, around which the soldiers converged. When they seemed to have received their approval for the raid from the vehicle, the tragic action commenced. First, the soldiers had to ensure that the power supply to the community was cut off and one of the soldiers had to go to the nearby National Electricity Power Authority to achieve this. It was only after this that the mayhem was unleashed on Kalakuta Republic. Incidences of rape and looting were reported. Bekolari Ransome-Kuti, Fela's younger brother—who had insisted on being let into the compound at the beginning of the siege—was seriously wounded when he was thrown from a window. Even Fela's dogs were burnt alive. Of course, Fela was the focus of the entire raid, and he came out of it bruised, battered, and fractured. According to him, "And me? Oh, man, I could hear my own bones being broken by the blows!"[8] The tragedy was compounded by the unfortunate presence of his mother, Funmilayo Ransome-Kuti, at Kalakuta that day. The seventy-seven-year-old woman was bodily thrown from the first floor of the house by the soldiers. Kalakuta was not only totally destroyed and ransacked; it was torched.

Fela never fully recovered from this tragic attack on everything he held dear, especially the assault of his mother. After being hospitalized and in acute shock and depression, Fela's mother died a year and two months later, on April 13, 1978. Fela's political ideology had finally been accepted by his mother in her later days, and this had brought them extremely close. And there was his mother, being thrown to her death. To worsen matters, the Nigerian state manufactured a judicial "victory" that not only saw the dismissal of Fela's suit against the government but blamed "unknown soldiers" for the recklessness of the assault on Kalakuta and for the inferno that razed it to the ground. It was as if the Afrobeat muse equally tasted the brutality of the Nigerian state on that fateful day, and had enough. From 1978 to 1992, Fela released just a paltry sixteen albums, compared to the period between 1970 and 1977, when he produced more than thirty.

Yet, Fela would not back down. In 1978, he formed a political party he called Movement of the People. Of course, Fela had no illusion that the political party would cause any serious disruption in the political establishment; it was just a further act of defiance. The politico-economic structure of post-independence Nigeria was large and combined the self-aggrandizing acts of so many actors, from politicians to the military, and the business class: "Fela's bitter opponents were people like Ibrahim Babangida, Olusegun Obasanjo, MKO Abiola, Margaret Thatcher, Ronald Reagan, zombie soldiers, and generally people and institutional structures that held social, political, religious, and economic power over the progress of the masses."[9] But it is a testament to Fela's obdurate spirit and expansive vision that he was able to keep going, and to keep singing Afrobeat.

7

The Politics of Fela's Music

Music, Society, and Politics

Music is the arrangement of sounds and tones to produce a composition of melody, harmony, and rhythm. It embodies and transfers culture and values from one generation to another, and its functions are multifaceted in every culture. Music is a powerful instrument in the transmission and preservation of values. In every culture of the world, music is an integral part of society, and especially in Africa, there are songs for every festival, ritual, activity, profession or craft, and so on.

Music has impacted politics, and politics has profound impacts on the music of a certain era. From political mobilization to social sensitization of the masses, music is imbued with the power to address several anomalies in society and also calm ruffled nerves and tension from marginalized people. Music deals with the emotions, feelings, and experiences of people which often reveal the inner turmoil, fear, ambition, and projection of personal or collective dreams and aspirations. It reflects what is happening at a particular time in history; the history of a place can be understood from the music it produces. Histories are told in the music of that society; music is an instrument of edification and historical preservation. Music shapes society, and society, in like manner, determines the tone and content of any music.

Music is an instrument for the effective expression and exploration of any political ideology. It pervades almost every sphere of life with far-reaching results. To understand a nation's policy and ideology, the appraisal of their music is essential and paramount. Musicians use their craft to address the sociopolitical issues in their milieu. Music is embedded in every activity of the primordial African life; it permeates every aspect of existence, to the extent that music is incorporated in every religious activity. Music offers a grand platform where issues, especially unfavorable conditions in the society, can reach a wider audience and speak to the people who need to be mobilized to demand for a change in the status quo. It is a constant feature in the history of politics; on the international stage, it unites oppressed nations of people and brings them together to fight and pursue the same cause. There have been several instances of collaborative works of musicians that speak and sing about world peace in war-ravaged countries with dictators at the helm of affairs.

Politics and music have a long history of influencing each other in Africa, where musicians are at the front of political revolution and mobilization. From the Mau Mau uprising in Kenya, anti-apartheid struggle in South Africa, and the rebellion against the regime of Mugabe in Zimbabwe, music remains one of the most powerful tools for political emancipation from colonial and post-independence dictatorship. Politics and music have an inseparable relationship; music has always been a powerful tool for political expression. Independence from colonial rule came with several postcolonial problems in terms of governance and administration, unity and social integration, economic independence and stability, and so on. Fela Anikulapo-Kuti's music was an instrument of political resistance during the period of military dictatorship in postcolonial Nigeria. His music pierced the fabric of state violence, raised political awareness, and sensitized the people about socioeconomic inequalities, suppression, and gross infringement of human rights present in their society.

Afrobeat: Political and Cultural Development

The emergence of Afrobeat as a style of performance took impetus from Fela's introduction to Pan-Africanism. However, the transition to this stage took a lot of experimentations with several American styles of music and highlife. Fela's pan-Africanist vision and rejection of the colonial style of music led him to evolve an African contemporary style of music. Creating a unique African tune started to seem impossible, as several experiments failed to bring the desired result of an indigenous African music. His increasing interest in black studies and African cultural forms preceded his determination to create a style of music that incorporated African tunes and instrumentation. The term "Afrobeat" as a musical genre is a coinage of two morphemes, "Afro" and "beat"; "Afro" is a derivation of the root word Africa(n), with the cosmopolitan ideology of African ethos and sensibilities denoting the concept of being "Black" or relating "Africanness." The genre Afrobeat is an aphoristic organization of African rhythms and social relations. Many scholars have defined the musical genre, which Oikelome (2013) explored in his essay on the performance practice of the Afrobeat of Fela Anikulapo-Kuti. This study will not dwell on the full trajectory of the musical genre but rather discuss the relevant confluence of the genre in the life and politics of Fela Anikulapo. The definition of the musical genre from the angle of politics will be of importance to this study.

Afrobeat is a musical genre that can be defined from different areas of scholarship, having a web of interconnectedness with history, ethnomusicology, literature, theatre and performance, psychology, and so on, due to its forays into the different facets of life.

> Afrobeat music can be described as a unique genre consisting of associations between the sound of the music and extra musical concepts. The different elements interlock to form a synthesis of the arts, with all contributing to the development of the performance. In Afrobeat, the songs do not exist only for their entertainment value, but develop story, mood, theme, communicating the arts through music.[1]

This unique genre is a confluence of sounds and ideas expressed in its performance and aesthetics. History, theme, emotions, and ambience are expressed in the Afrobeat genre, influencing the audience and connecting them to the realities of their societies. Fela used this genre to communicate his ideas and thoughts about the historical, political, and cultural events of his time. His music moved from the traditional themes to engage political and cultural issues which had grievous consequences of torture, witch-hunting, and incarcerations for Fela and his band members. Fela's Afrobeat became a political tool of attack against the oppressive and dictatorial government in Nigeria and Africa at large.

Olorunyomi notes that the transition to Afrobeat was noticeable in Fela's songs "Jeun K'oku" and "Why Blackman Dey Suffer," where the vocals and instrumentation reflect the percussive bass drums, snare drums and cymbals, two tom-tom drums, and a three-membrane drum. This ensemble later included the "gbedu" drum, conga drums, two-a-piece interlocking membrane drums, and a second bass section that intensified the rhythm, after which the chorus and cantor take over.

> The bass drum rhythm has been identified by Steve Rhodes as Egbaesque, with its roots reminiscent of certain rhythms of the Oro cult. What is equally incontrovertible is the choice of most of his simple Egba chants such as "tere kutc" or "joro jara joro," which are built on harmonics based on the

pentatonic scale. It is a format Fela respects and does nor depart from in any fundamental sense.[2]

Fela's cultural background influenced his music to the point that he incorporated cultic codes, African traditional religion and Òrìsà worship, and the African gods and goddesses in his performance at the famous club, Afrika Shrine. His cultural influences were visible through the use of West African patterns of musical ensemble, costume, and props, a combination which reflects the tonality of the African speech pattern. The structuring of the African instruments enhances commentary which Fela incorporated based on the African traditional griot and "chief priest" who makes declarations and comments on the events of the society. The introduction of the all-female dancers with the different African print costumes and aesthetics into the band explored the cultural ideology and education of the Afrobeat composer. The language of his music was initially the Yoruba language and English. However, this gave way to the cultural nationalism ideas propagated by the political influences in his life and the reintroduction to African values in the writings of Kwame Nkrumah, Thomas Sankara, Ahmed Sekou Toure, and Julius Nyerere. The language changed vividly to carry a message of dissidence with the use of Nigeria Pidgin English, which was the lingo of the urban poor.

Of Politics and Lyricism: Afrobeat and the Music of Military Brutality

Fela's music was initially not political in nature. However, this changed dramatically after his introduction into the world of politics and political resistance when he visited the United States of America. From the names of his band, to his commune, to his musical genre, politics radiated throughout his life and music. Politicized music bears the torch of a political ideology and message with the aim of upturning the political hegemony. From the beginning of the nineteenth century, music has been politically charged to fight every form of domination and suppression of a particular class of people. Fela Anikulapo-Kuti infused politics into his music with the aim of attacking the oppressive rule of the military regime and the neocolonial hegemonies in the Nigerian nation. Afrobeat, which originated from the legendary pan-African musician Fela, started with jazz, funk, soul, and the African call-and-response styles. The politics of Fela

Anikulapo's music was discernable from the performance of Afrobeat. In the song "Army Arrangement," the lyrics move beyond the encapsulation of rhythm to the politics of oppression of the masses and embezzlement of public funds.

Man dey suffer him no fit talk na condition
Man dey suffer him fit talk na condition too
Man dey suffer him no fit talk na condition
Man dey suffer him fit talk na condition too
Suffer dey Africa, pa-pa, ra pa
I suffer dey, pa-pa, ra pa
Condition dey e, pa-pa, ra pa
Me I no say you be African man
And we dey suffer, pa-pa, ra pa
Which condition you dey I don't know
The condition me I dey me I know
My condition don reach make I act

Humans are suffering but they cannot talk; that's the condition
There's suffering in Africa
And I am suffering too
There is condition here
I know you are an African man
And we are suffering
I am not sure about the condition you find yourself
I am only sure about my own condition
And that condition has got to a point at which I must act

The third stanza addressed the politicians embezzling the treasury and the inquiry set up to probe the looters. Fela was direct and brutal in his criticism of these public offenders and the irony of setting a body that is also corrupt to investigate the criminals in public office. The organization of a body to investigate the criminals was a perfunctory act to silence the masses. After a while, once arrests had been made with sentences of ten to fifteen years given, the offenders still walked free out of these sentences with little or no results produced in the inquiry of the "missing" public funds. "Army Arrangement" is a highly politically strung song with the message to the people to stand and fight for their rights. The title itself, "Army Arrangement," reveled in the kind of collaborative work and activities of these military officers in the looting of the treasury. The lyrics of the song sung in a strong Nigerian Pidgin pointed accusing fingers to the military head and his caliber of friends in power. The language of Fela's music is thus politicized, giving the aura of an oppressed victim of the dictatorial regime in Nigeria.

In the songs "Beast of No Nation" and "Authority Stealing," Fela revealed the dehumanizing activities going on in the prisons in Nigeria and how the political leaders misappropriate funds for personal use. He talks about nepotism, forgery, embezzlement, mismanagement, and maladministration rampant in these public offices. He sang, in "Authority Stealing":

> authority stealing pass armed robbery
> we Africans we must do something
> about this nonsense
> we say we must do something about
> this nonsense …

As the armed robber uses a gun to steal, the politician in the position of authority steals with his pen, his pen possessing more power than a gun does. The robbery that takes place in the government offices is silenced even before they get out to the public hearing. Fela urged Africans to stand up against these kinds of people in government who steal from the state coffers. The rhetoric of defiance in his music endeared him to the masses that were being oppressed by their leaders.

> Songs like "Government of Crooks" dishonored the corrupt politicians and soldiers who plundered Nigeria's oil money and by extension the natural resources of Africa, while "M.A.S.S. (Music Against Second Slavery)" and "Colonial Mentality" (1977) exposed and evaluated the negative impact of Islam on Nigerian (African) politics and power relations, the effect of slavery and neocolonialism, the looting of African people's wealth by the neocolonial and neo-slavery African leaders, and their international counterparts and multinational companies.[3]

These songs were grand narratives produced by a man with seasoned and skillful knowledge of Yoruba wordplay. This is evident in the use of words of the proletariat class, revised to challenge the bourgeois with music at its core. "M.A.S.S" is synonymous with the term for the oppressed and subaltern, the acronym standing for "Music Against Second Slavery." Fela coined the word "Mass" to subvert the narrative of the "other" and the "self." The song itself is a musical text with the theme of political resistance, neocolonial rejection, and anti-establishment sentiments. The thematic preoccupation, form, style, and aesthetic codes reveled in the politics of self-liberation. Fela fused his music with the experiences of the people and became an instrument the plebeians used in demanding for a better condition, knocking down the colonial and neocolonial structures. The masses' narratives became his muse, pushing the music to the threshold of power to dismember the bodies of government hegemonies.

Fela's music was not only a medium of protesting against the subjugation of the masses, it was also a medium for the politics of words and knowledge encoded in lyrical form to decapitate the African leaders and the colonial bodies in Africa. From the title of his songs to his rhetoric and performances, Fela's politics was of a grand nature and delivery to the oppressive regime. In the song "ITT" (International Thief Thief), political angst and fury were unpacked in the lyrics to criticize the African leaders and foreign multinationals companies conniving to plunder the natural resources in Nigeria and Africa.

International Thief thief
I.T.T
International rogue
Well, well
Ha!
Well, well…
Ha!

Motherfuckers, bastard motherfuckers	
We yab dem, yeah	[*We abuse them*]
Them go be:	[*They are*]
Friend friend to journalist	
Friend friend to Commissioner	
Friend friend to Permanent Secretary	
Friend friend to Minister	
Friend to Head of State	
Then start start to steal money	[*They start to steal money*]
Start start them corruption	[*They indulge in corrupt practice*]
Start start them inflation	[*They instigate inflation*]
Start start them oppression…	[*They oppress others*]
Like Obasanjo and Abiola	

His music was more than the mere production of entertainment; it was a demonstration of a counterdiscourse of political resistance enveloped in comic cynicism. He engaged in open debate with his music on politics, condemning the deplorable state of the economy and the contribution of these African leaders.

The multinational companies were not spared in the politics of his music; he termed their activities in Africa as a neocolonial strategy of slavery and cultural colonialism.

The song "ITT" was directed in particular at M. K. O. Abiola, who was heavily criticized for conniving with foreign companies to loot the Nigerian economy and further promote colonial activities of the West. Fela's music took up the fight for the marginalized class who have not only been silenced but have been cheated in the distribution of wealth which belongs to them. This and several other events led to the creation of Movement of the People (MOP), a political party founded by Fela to further his ambition to run for the presidential position in 1978. This ambition to run for the presidency was not to be fulfilled, as Fela's party was disqualified from the presidential race. Fela's songs "Alagbon Close" (1974), "Expensive Shit" (1975), "Kalakuta Show" (1975), "Zombie" (1976), "Sorrow, Tears and Blood" (1977), and "Unknown Soldier" (1979) are all couched in acerbic lyrics with politics of resistance. In "Alagbon Close," which he sang with his band Africa 70 after he was detained at the police station, Fela criticized the force and brutality employed by the police on poor citizens. Of notable interest is the song "Zombie," with the vitriolic lyrics of satire against the police and the military which the government employed to victimize and repress the people.

> Zombie no go go, unless you tell am to go
> (zombie)
> Zombie no go stop, unless you tell am to stop
> (zombie)
> Zombie no go think, unless you tell am to think
> (zombie)

This is a satirical song targeted at the almost lifeless attitude of the military and police to the order of their leaders to maim, kill, and destroy life. It satirizes the "obey before complain" dictum of the Nigerian Army. Fela sang against the military men who were openly whipping the masses and using brute force on people in the streets, with open disregard for human lives and rights. These songs were a political counterattack on the authoritarian hegemonies in Nigeria and Africa whose activities reduced the people to cower before their leaders. The prevailing preoccupation of the Afrobeat legend was power relations between the state and the marginalized people. Fela's music was deconstructing the power of the state while infusing the people with the knowledge to take the power that is their right as electorates.

Fela and the State: Power, Politics, and Music

One such politics in his music is the creation of "Yabis," an ideological music of lambasting and speaking against the corrupt activities of the government. Yabis were organized like quasi-political scenery referred to as "yabis session," where political issues and public matters were discussed.

> Fela uses the medium of yabis to x-ray the Nigerian political, social and economy scenes for his audience. Fela's objects of criticism are germane to the very existence of the country people and the black race. To get the message across to them, he required a medium that would not be too serious and that would require the least effort.[4]

These sessions took place in Fela's Afrika Shrine, which created an ambience for the masses to listen to the power play between the government and the marginalized. Fela became not only a social critic but also a credible political adversary to the ruling elite and military officers. In 1974, Fela's commune was invaded by the police and arrested for possession of the illegal drug cannabis, using maximum force and brutality on the musician and his followers causing them to sustain multiple injuries. This particular year was not a jolly one for the musical icon, as it marked the beginning of several attacks and clashes with the law agencies in the country. One of the several arrests of the Afrobeat singer served as inspiration behind the production of the song "Kalakuta Show," as his imprisonment triggered the unrepentant criticism of the police force. It is not presumptuous to state that national and continental crises served as Fela's muse, as the man was not one to shy away from political issues in his country.

Kalakuta show	
1974	
Kalakuta show	
Dem make sure dem	[*They ensure that they…*]
Use tear gas, baton & bullet	[*Use tear gas, baton and bullet*]
Dem use them basket	[*They use their basket*]
For protection too	[*also as protection*]
Dem do one thing	[*They did one thing*]
Dem never do before	[*they never did before*]
Dem-o hire … axe-o … dem bring … cutlass …	[*they hired axes and brought cutlass*]

The rhetoric revealed the horror and pandemonium that was unleashed on Fela and his people. These events took place during the era of Gowon's regime, which was undoubtedly repressive and had corruption at the base of the regime. Fela criticized this regime in clear language without any attempt to couch his distaste for the military brutality and corrupt activities in pleasant lyrics.

Fela's anti-establishment and anticolonial music started stirring political awareness in Nigeria and also in Africa. His music addressed the political, cultural, and spiritual issues; the emphasis of this study will be on the politics of his music. Fela's music challenged the military regime and drew his audiences (usually the masses) into the discourse of political instability that incited them to take action against these political problems. His music explored the everyday life of an average Nigerian and reflected the lives of the masses, often making the point that the oppression of these people by their leaders should lead to revolution. For a large percentage of Nigerians in the 1970s, Fela's music provided a new channel of social and political critique. Fela used his music to educate the people of the dictatorship and neocolonialism carried out on the psyche of the people by the government. Afrobeat, a syncopated fusion of jazz, funk, and African beats, formed a backdrop for Fela's caustic social and political commentary and political criticism, framed by lyrics replete with defiance, symbolism, satire, and dry humor. The man, Fela, is described as being synonymous with music and protest.

The year 1976 was another important one in the politics of Fela's music, as it witnessed the installation of another military head, General Olusegun Obasanjo. This era heightened the political engagement of Fela's music and also the persecution of the Afrobeat composer. The political scenario at that time was rife with instability, police and military brutality, the government's siphoning the national treasury, and neocolonial activities of the foreign multinational companies. In his song "Shuffering and Shmiling" (1978), the Afrobeat legend called the African people not only to participate in the song but to take active steps and action in their liberation from the oppression in their country. He proceeded to beckon on non-African listeners and audiences to have an open mind, not just to his music alone but to the politics of his narrative. "Religion is the opium of the masses" was a latent discourse of the song—unraveling the mind games and the contributions of religion to keep the people from revolting against the class and power hierarchies in operation. The Marxist's thesis of dialectical materialism, which espoused the culture of the upper class marked by unbridled access to economic, political, and religious powers and its constant attempt to perpetuate the status quo, was explored in the song. Fela's music became a profoundly powerful tool utilizing Marxist subversion ideology of the toppling of the super ordinate by the subaltern.

Suffer, suffer for world	[*Suffering in the world*]
Enjoy for heaven	[*And enjoyment in heaven*]
Christians go dey yab	[*Christians will be saying*]
"In Spiritum Heavinus"	[*In Spiritum Heavinus*]
Muslims go dey call	[*And the Muslims will be shouting*]
Allahu akbar	[*Allahu Akbar*]
Open your eyes everywhere	
Archbishop na miliki	[*Archbishop is having fun*]
Pope na enjoyment	[*The Pope is having a good time*]
Imam na gbaladun	[*Even the Imam is enjoying himself*]

"Shuffering and Shmiling" sought to jolt the masses from the spell of religious dogma perpetuated by the capitalists who engaged religious institutions with the diversion technique of disengaging the minds of the masses from revolutionary activities through the promise of a tranquil imaginary space. Fela's disdain for these institutions is palpable in the lyrics and performance of the song:

Every day my people dey inside bus	[*My people plies the road daily in a bus*]
(shuffering and shmiling)	[*Suffering and smiling*]
Forty-nine sitting, ninety-nine standing	
(shuffering and shmiling)	
Dem go pack themselves in like sardines	[*They're packed like sardines in cans*]
(shuffering and shmiling)	

The people are oppressed, yet their spirits were not broken; they still smiled in the face of the abject poverty and squalor which engulfed them. The song spoke of the resiliency of the African people's spirit in the midst of daunting sociopolitical problems created by their leaders. "Vagabond in Power," "Tears and Blood," and "Original Suffer Head" were released by Fela at that time to lambast the actions of the government in not improving the standard of living, electricity supply, transportation systems, availability of potable water, and housing policies. Fela graphically illustrated in his lyrics the pitiable conditions of the plebeians living in overcrowded apartments, such as "ten people sleep inside one room" and "my people are packed inside buses like sardines." Fela vehemently proclaimed that "suffer head must go" and "j'eba head must come"; however, this can only be possible if "we must ready to fight for am now." Fela attacked the government with his music, and educated the masses to seek for a better condition and governance.

Two Republics: Federal Republic of Nigeria and the Kalakuta Republic

The Kalakuta Republic was more than a commune for Fela; it was a symbol of his freedom from the Nigerian government that was repressive and domineering. The Kalakuta Republic and the Afrika Shrine were the seats of Fela's political protest and outburst. The origin of the name "kalakuta" was an adaptation of the name of the prison cell he was detained in, which was known to be the place of confinement for notorious criminals. Kalakuta Republic was a place of succor to the oppressed, and free from the government's reach. This structure was seen by Fela as more than a place of communal living, as he declared it a republic separate from the Republic of Nigeria. Thus, Fela's politics moved from mere rhetoric to having a concrete structure of power in the naming of his commune as a republic.

The attack on Kalakuta Republic, which caused a lot of damage on property and injury on persons, also triggered the political song "Coffin for Head of State." The song was preceded by a street protest to the Dodan Barracks, where a replica of Fela's mother's coffin was deposited at the gate as a testament to the injuries she sustained during the invasion, which led to the deterioration of her health and her subsequent death in 1979. The song, "Coffin for Head of State," was a metaphor for the head of state who Fela blamed for the murder of his mother, due to the order that was given to invade and destroy his commune. Many women were also allegedly beaten and raped during the attack, while the men were shipped into prison with many of them sustaining injuries from the maximum force unleashed on them by the armed police and military men. The metaphor Fela employed in "Coffin for Head of State" was not only for the death of his mother but for every man, woman, and child that had been killed through the action and inaction of the government. He uses the corpse of his mother to symbolize the death of students and youth who were killed during the face-off with the dictatorial regime of the General Obasanjo. Fela was also not afraid to criticize the two popular religions, Islam and Christianity, and their spiritual leaders, who lived in affluence while their followers lived in abject poverty. He satirized the corrupt leaders who claimed affinity with these religions and yet did not desist from all corrupt activities. "Coffin for Head of State" is a double-barreled attack on the imported religions and the deplorable activities of the African leaders.

The politics in his music continued after the brief transition from military rule to democracy, which the radical Afrobeat master deemed undemocratic. The government of Alhaji Shehu Shagari was seriously criticized in the music of Fela due to its undemocratic process and activities. The electoral process that oversaw the installation of the head of state was seriously flawed, with many alleged incidences of electoral malpractice. Fela captured this era in the song "Teacher Don't Teach Me Nonsense," which featured words like "democrazy," "demonstration of craze," and "crazy demonstration." The song condemned the acculturation of the Western system of government in Africa, the dependence of Africans on Western knowledge, and the disdain of African epistemology. The effect of the politics in Fela's music caused a political shockwave that shook the very foundations of the military regime, causing an earthquake of reactions from the masses which provoked the government to attempt to silence the musician

Politics in Fela's music was explored in his political ideology, political ambition, and music of political resistance, which was a confrontational counternarrative to the hegemony of the state. The narratives in his music carried political themes, commentary on social and economic disparity, and critiques of public oppression by law enforcement agencies. Fela's music threatened the legitimacy of the government and created space(s) for the people to locate their narratives of economic inequality in the elite-dominated narratives of economic power. In the songs "Ikoyi Blindness" and "Noise for Vendor Mouth," Fela addressed the class divide between the poor and the rich, the mental blindness of the African man, and the hooligan tag given to himself and members of his commune. He subverted the narrative by comparing the masses' dwelling place with the elite abodes in Lagos: the Indian hemp-smoking members of his commune and the "fighting parliamentarians" who were supposedly cultured and symbols of morality. The music of Fela was a narrative space for the renegotiation and re-imagination of the marginalized narrative and identity in Nigerian political discourse. The song "No Buredi" (1976) captured the failure of Gowon's government intervention plan, which was aimed to make Nigeria economically self-reliant and free from foreign aid and intervention.

> You no get-e power to fight [*You have no power to fight*]
> …
> For Africa here e be home… [*Africa is the homeland*]
> Land-e boku boku from north to south [*There are plenty lands from north to south*]
> Food-u e boku boku from top to down [*There is plenty food everywhere*]
> Gold dey underground like water [*There is gold underground like water*]
> Diamond dey underground like san san [*There is diamond like the sands*]
> Oil dey flow underground like river [*Oil flows underground like a river*]
> …
> Everything for overseas, na here e dey go [*Products from elsewhere end up here*]

"Buredi" is the word for bread in Nigerian Pidgin English, which is meant to stand as slang for money; "No Buredi" throve on the economic disparity prevalent during that time. Fela questioned the reasoning and complacency of the masses, as they could not stand up against the oppressive government. He concluded that this complacent attitude was because of the lack of food and sustenance. Hunger and poverty were tools used to suppress the people from revolting against the hegemonic structure; when the people have been decapitated through a scarcity of food and money for sustenance, the spirit of revolution will be quelled. The arrangement of the song with the call-and-response chorus was an expression of the inequality in the distribution of wealth which the Nigerian people and other African countries were experiencing at that particular time. Affluence and poverty operate side-by-side; hence the lyrics of the song had the chorus reflecting abject penury alongside the body of the song. The oil boom should have created better conditions of living for the proletariat; however, the masses experienced inflation in the price of goods and services due to the excessive circulation of the crude oil money within the upper class. There was no even distribution of the means of production in the country; the rich were getting richer from the state coffers, while the poor were getting poorer.

Fela's music spoke of the past, the present, and had a futuristic foreshadowing of the political discourse in Africa. It transcended its era to foresee the future of the Nigerian space where discourses of nepotism, austerity, judicial injustice, parliamentary lawlessness, and subjugation of the masses still persist in extant literature. Despite the independence of Nigeria and many African nations, the West still had control over the economic and political activities in these nations, casting a shadow on the growth of these countries. Britain and the United States of America were the largest investors in these countries, often having the largest share of the economy, therefore dictating the tune which the national leaders had to sway to. "No Buredi" was an acerbic narrative against the culture of Eurocentric importation and consumption of the nouveaux riche which downgraded African products, thereby causing the downward slide of the economy.

Fela's music was a constant thorn in the nether regions of the government, as the newspapers and other mass media had been hijacked by the state. In the song "No Agreement," the Afrobeat founder declared his undying and unrelenting efforts in the pursuit of social and economic equality for the oppressed people.

> I no go agree make my brother hungry
> [*I will not agree with seeing my brother hungry*]
> I no go agree make my brother jobless
> [*I will not agree with seeing my brother jobless*]
> I no go agree make my brother homeless
> [*I will not agree to seeing my brother homeless*]

His music, commune (Kalakuta Republic), and Afrika Shrine were more than just entertainment spaces; they were spaces for the re-imagination of a new nation where their troubles would be solved. Fela's music sought to create a utopian state, where everyone would have equal access to socioeconomic capital in the country; Fela would not allow his brother to go hungry, be homeless, and out of a job, unlike the Nigerian government. The government implemented housing policies that favored the bourgeois elite in the civil service. In 1977, when "No Agreement" was released, it responded to the policy and activities of the government in areas like Ikoyi and Lagos Island, which put many people in those locations out on the streets without shelter. The government trembled at the power and influence of the Afrobeat legend with the political messages in his music influencing the oppressed populace to demand for accountability from their political leaders. The political leaders were terrified of the politics of the musician and took several measures to stamp him out of the limelight via violent attacks, punishment, and imprisonment. The attack on his commune in 1977 by a thousand soldiers who destroyed his albums, musical instruments, and set the building ablaze revealed the agenda of the government to repress the voice of sociopolitical revolution.

> The narratives in Fela's songs challenged those of the Nigerian government by presenting social locations that opposed those of the government. The government declared that it would create an equitable society with ample opportunity for all. The narrative of development obliged the urban poor to be patient. It normalized their poverty while maintaining the idea that economic inequalities would soon be addressed. According to this rhetoric of relation, the poor were included in the national project. Fela's lyrical narratives disagreed with state narratives of an inclusive society.[5]

"Mr. Grammarticalogylisationalism Is The Boss," "Ikoyi Mentality vs Mushin Mentality," and "Alagbon Close" explored the elite space of Nigerian society. Fela narrated the experiences of disparity in the economy, and how social segregation, oppression, and institutional neglect created for the masses a different connection with the government. These new social spaces demanded that the masses identify themselves outside of prevalent imaginings of the Nigerian social order. These imaginings of a Nigerian society by the plebeians are lived in the periphery of the elite narrative. However, through the music of Fela Anikulapo-Kuti, the people could seek for an egalitarian society.

Afrobeat performance has politics at its core with its socioeconomic, cultural, and political critique and re-conception. Other genres of neo-traditional music have reinforced systems of clientele adulation and patronage which valorized the culture of the bourgeoisie. According to Arogundade, the framing of these "traditional" genres promotes the concept of authenticity, continuity, and heritage of the class system. The creation of Fela's Afrobeat negated and criticized the class stratification and valorized the simple and unpretentious lives of the masses. His music genre satirized the bourgeoisie culture of the African leaders and elites, structured in the theory of the "other" and "self," and challenged the legitimacy of the distinction and divide in the African context.

> "Us" and "dem" were diametrically opposed throughout Fela's repertoire. Identifying "us" as his audience, Fela gave new value to their experiences of socioeconomic marginalization. Fela continually positioned "dem" as inauthentic and illegitimate. His structural adaptation of call-and-response patterns (such lyrics are noted in this work through parentheses) beckoned his audience to take an active part in these new narrative spaces. The "response" often was in agreement and confirmation of Fela's prior critique. In this way

Fela invited others to fully situate themselves in the narrative of the song and to rethink their own process of self-understanding with new countercultural narrative locations.[6]

Fela's music was decadently sung in Nigerian Pidgin English, which accentuated the politics in his music. It was the lingo that penetrated the ethnic and social diversity of the multiethnic and multilingual Nigerian society. The choice of this language was deliberate because it invoked an anti-elite sensibility and boycotted the Eurocentric and colonial sensibilities which Fela was so opposed to. The Standard British English (SBE), which was the lingua franca of the country, was elevated above the African languages by the colonial masters and their stooges and became the mark of social mobility.

The better oyinbo you talk	[*The better English you can speak*]
The more bread you go get	[*The more bread you get*]
School start na grade four bread	[*Primary school equals grade four breads*]
B.A. na grade three bread	[*Bachelor's degree equals grade three bread*]
M.A. na grade two bread	[*Masters degree equals grade two bread*]
Ph.D na grade one bread	[*A doctorate degree equals grade one bread*]
The better oyinbo you talk	[*The better English you can speak*]
The more bread you go get	[*The more bread you will get*]
Hear it	
First thing for early morning	[*The first thing early in the morning*]
Na newspaper dem give us read	[*We were given newspaper to read*]
First thing for early morning	
Na newspaper dem give us read	
The oyinbo wey dey inside	[*The English in the newspaper*]
Market woman no fit read to read	[*A market woman will find difficult to read*]
The oyinbo wey dey inside	[*The English in the newspaper*]
Na riddle for laborer man	[*becomes a great riddle for a laborer*]
Inside the paper	
Lambastical dey ...	[*There is "lambastical"*]

In the song "Mr. Grammarticalogylisationalism Is The Boss," Fela claimed that speaking English was an attempt to stamp out and erase the "Africaness" off the African man. Nonliterate people are sidelined in the affairs of the state, as the policies of the government are written and disseminated in SBE to the exclusion of the peasants' understanding. The song was directed to the political leaders who were elected by the people due to their acquisition of "Western education," which was supposedly a mark of intelligence. However, these African leaders have failed to improve the living conditions of their people after the acquisition of Western knowledge, but they philosophize and make impressive speeches about the economic situation in the country which affects the masses the most. Fela argued that the African leaders supported and elevated the colonial system of education as the only means of socioeconomic upward mobility in the rhetoric of developing the nation. Fela's music took the perception of politics from the preserve of the elite group to the people in the grassroots to debate and demand for a significant change in the status quo. His political stance was vividly enunciated in his music and performance, and his legacy will remain evergreen in the history of political activism and contemporary music in Africa and the world.

Conclusion

Music has always been a tool for political emancipation from every form of dehumanization, subjugation, and cultural domination. Beyond its function as entertainment in society, music has always occupied a central role in every form of human activity in different cultures of the world, and Africa is definitely not an exception. Afrobeat, like any kind of musical genre, has enjoyed a central place in the hearts of African people with its multidimensional functions in the Nigerian and African context.

This chapter has explored the life and musical career of the Afrobeat icon, Fela Anikulapo-Kuti, and the politics of his music through the varying lenses of his musical, political, and cultural ideology. The man rose from his privileged pedigree to renounce the social and economic divide prevalent in Nigerian society. Rummaging through Fela's biography, musical education, political awareness and influences, and lastly the messages encoded in his songs, it is apparent that Fela and his music are a bundle of intricate politics. His music carried several politically charged messages directed at the military juntas and government with repressive policies and activities. Fela only commented about the political situation at the time; he also took active steps to subvert the government-orchestrated narrative of economic dominance. This study did not exhaust the impressive discography of Fela Anikulapo-Kuti, but a copious number of his songs have been explored to achieve the aim of unearthing and explicating the dominant political tropes in his music.

More than two decades after the passing of Fela Anikulapo-Kuti in 1997, his music and activism continue to speak of narratives that expose political injustice, oppression, and subjugation of the masses, as well as the socioeconomic disparity in Nigeria and Africa as a continent. Fela's music was more than a musical production; it was (and still is) a space for the narratives of the marginalized to be rewritten and to dictate the rhythm of their socioeconomic freedom. Fela Anikulapo and the politics of his music will continue as a benchmark for the production of epistemology in the nexus between music and politics.

8

Fela's Use of Language

Fela sang in English or pidgin (which some now call "Naija") intentionally, for he knew that he could reach an extensive audience across the world (and especially in Nigeria) by communicating in these two languages. It is likely that Fela often used English because he wanted his voice to reach all continents and because he was more than aware of Nigerian languages being "Europeanized." He also must have been aware of the impact of globalization around the world and how English is a "globalized" language. Indeed, Omoniyi has argued that Nigerian hip-hop artists often use English for this very reason: to communicate with world citizens affected by globalization.[1] While Fela's music is not considered hip-hop, his choice to sing in English does fit into Omoniyi's hypothesis.

As for Fela's choice to sing in pidgin, it was more than appropriate because it represented two worlds—Nigeria and English-speaking nations—coming together. As Olaniyan describes, pidgin is a language "located in the interstitial space where English meets the indigenous language."[2] Certainly, it must have been no coincidence that Fela's increased political alertness and his beginnings of the use of pidgin happened at the same time in the 1970s,[3] for Fela understood how pidgin was a fusion of nativism and globalization. It is also worth noting that pidgin was known and spoken by tens of millions of Nigerians in Fela's lifetime. Therefore, by singing in pidgin, Fela could effectively spread his message across his home country.[4] Truly, when he spoke pidgin, Fela became all the more relatable and in communion with the common Nigerian population. As "one of the people," Fela was able not only to entertain the people with his music but also to defend the people with messages that truly resonated with them.[5]

Using pidgin is also a form of code-switching—"the process of shifting from one linguistic code (a language or dialect) to another, depending on the social context or conversational setting."[6] According to Babalola and Taiwo, Nigerian musicians in the hip-hop industry code-switch from Yoruba to English and vice versa in order to affirm their sense of identity and to show that their identity has power that can be spread across the world.[7] This can apply to Fela because he was, at least outwardly, a self-confident individual who had conviction and was not afraid of who heard his message or who disapproved of it. It seemed, actually, that he welcomed disapproval. His choice to use pidgin, therefore, seems to be in alignment with an argument by Olatunji, who has contended that Nigerian hip-hop musicians have also code-switched from English to Pidgin English so that they could be readily understood by both common people and elites.[8] Indeed, Fela fits into this mold—at least in the Afrobeat universe—because he knew that pidgin could be understood by the elite.[9] Fela did not want his message to reach only poor and desolate audiences worldwide. Rather, he wanted the elites of the world, and especially Nigeria, to also hear his words and feel threatened. Without any doubt, he achieved his goal.

Besides the fact that Fela's language of choice in his music was English or Naija, Fela's language in his songs was also intimidating to leaders and resonant with the public stylistically. His language was filled with "direct irreverence, often with a touch of ridicule and humor and a sharp twist of sarcasm; symbolism and imagery; the use of a communal/collective voice; didactic conversational style; and repetition and emphasis."[10] As Diala-Ogamba argued, Fela served as a social poet. His words and phrases contained "clarity, succinctness, and simplicity,"[11] just as poetry does. Diala-Ogamba also argued that Fela served as a social orator because his language was used to persuade others and bring them into a democratic awareness.[12] As Fela himself said: "I have opened the eyes of the people to oppression in our continent. The people know I did it. I'm honest and consistent. That's enough."[13] Fela certainly never wanted his songs to be misinterpreted or vague; he wanted his art to have a distinctive language that was filled with critique but also humor, because humor amplified the critique's truth.

One of many such examples of Fela's pointed and sardonic language can be seen in "Colonial Mentality":

If you say you be colonial man	[*If you say you are a colonial man*]
You don be slave man before	[*It means you have been enslaved before*]
Dem don release you now	[*And though you have been set free*]
But you never release yourself	[*you have not released yourself*]
…	
Dem judge him go nack wig	[*The judge will put on his wig*]
And jail him brothers	[*And then send his brothers to jail*]

No be so? (E be so!) [*Isn't that so? Yes, it is!*]
...
Dem go proud of dem name [*They are so proud of their European names*]
And put dem slave name for head [*They happily don the slave names*]

In this song, Fela clearly criticizes and satirizes Africans (specifically African officials and leaders) who blindly renounce their African identity by pretending to be European and meanwhile are harming their fellow Africans.[14] Ultimately, as Fela clearly says in his line "but you never release yourself," he sees these people as frauds who are only lying to themselves. Truly, this is a striking line in its brutal honesty and signal toward hypocrisy.

Fela's song that caused the Nigerian military government to attack his club and his mother, "Zombie," is another example of a work with unmistakably direct and sarcastic language. Particular within this song is striking imagery:[15]

Zombie no go go unless you tell am to go
Zombie no go stop unless you tell am to stop
...
Zombie no go think unless you tell am to think

When hearing these words, one cannot help but think of the their aptness; after all, how could any human being with an independent mind proceed with orders—even to kill—without any reservation? The visual is clear: one imagines an army of brainless half dead, half alive men, marching for some useless purpose unknown to them. They are like puppets or automatons—not truly human because they are so unfeeling and mechanical. Their main human faculty—their reason—is gone, and all that they have left is the desperate wait for orders so they know how to move next.

It is also important to mention that in "Zombie," Fela crafted repeatable language so that it could be spoken (or sung) by his audience. The people were encouraged to respond in parts of the refrain of "Zombie" with the phrase "Ojooro jaara jooro."[16] Though this phrase is senseless on the surface, it is onomatopoeic in nature and thus poetic and memorable. It is also "a repeated idea to create pleasure, excitement, surprise, and recognition." It was a way to allow for "musical participation, emphasizing the stages of the story in his poem."[17] It also allowed a way for Fela to be in conversation with his audience. This is most certainly a tool of any master poet or orator, for it can elicit intrigue among audience members and allow them to feel connected with one another.

Perhaps most importantly, this language tool was another way for the common, oppressed people to feel that they had a voice. The "jooro jaara jooro" phrase was not meant for the Nigerian military government or for Nigerian hypocritical leaders. It was meant as somewhat of a "battle cry" of unity for those whom the government and leaders were suppressing.

In Fela's song "Beast of No Nation," released after his time in prison in 1978, his language consists of symbolism, imagery, and sections for an audience response. In this song, Fela describes himself as a "basket mouth" in order to symbolize how he is back on stage and has refused to stay quiet.[18] Perhaps he also called himself "basket mouth" so that he could poke fun at the name "Loud Mouth" that the government had given him.[19] As the lyrics go:[20]

Basket mouth wan start to leak again oh
[*Basket Mouth is about to start leaking again*]
Basket mouth wan open mouth again oh
[*Basket Mouth is about to open his mouth again*]
Abi you don forget say I sing ee-oh
[*Have you forgotten I can sing?*]
Basket mouth wan open mouth again oh
I sing-i say, I go open my mouth like basket ee-oh
[*And I sing: I will open my mouth like a basket*]
ma lanu be apere
[*I will open my mouth like basket*]
Basket mouth wan open mouth again oh

Additionally, the title itself "Beast of No Nation" is significant because it demonstrates how the common people of Africa are treated like homeless animals without any basic human rights.[21] The word "beast" was a wise choice for Fela to use, for it is conceptually scathing: it connotes absolute wildness and savagery. Surely, then, this word would have resonated with the audience as they felt in their very beings that they deserved better and were, contrary to what the government suggested, human beings worthy of dignity.

Of course, not all of Fela's music had a sarcastic edge. Some of his songs served as a lamentation, such as "Shuffering and Shmiling" (or "Suffering and Smiling"). In this song, Fela points to the sadness and suffering on earth that Nigerians feel can be alleviated by the promises of their religion. Even if in this life, though the people lack basic essentials like water, they can still find comfort in going to listen to the pope or bishop or the imams, for these individuals promise even more comfort in the next life.[22] In "Shuffering and Shmiling,"

Fela's words are reminiscent of a priest engaging in a chant-like, religious ritual that informs a congregation of the promises in the next life. To his words, the audience responds (as a congregation does) with "amen":[23]

Suffer suffer for world
Amen (Response)
Enjoy for heaven
Amen (Response)

Undoubtedly, these words are deeply emotional, and they also suggest a great deal of strength for the common Nigerian person and believer: as long as they endure their tremendous suffering on earth, they will be rewarded with tremendous joy in heaven.

It is also no wonder that Fela was so relevant and relatable to the common Nigerian people, because his language often employed collective pronouns like "we," "our," and "us" to demonstrate that he, too, is affected by oppression and that he will fight for all those who are oppressed. By using these pronouns, he allows himself to be not a distant poet or orator but rather a personal one. For example, in "Beast of no Nation":[24]

And, they wan dash us human rights	[*And they want to gift us human rights*]
Animal must talk to human beings	[*Animals talking to humans*]
Give dem human rights	[*"Give them human rights"*]
I beg-I oh, make you hear me well-u well	[*Listen and hear me very well*]
I beg-I oh, make you hear me very well	
Human rights na my property	[*Human rights is my property*]
So therefore, you can't dash me my property	[*You cannot gift me my property*]
Human rights na my property	

Here, not only does Fela associate himself with the common people; he also adds new nuance to the word "animal." No longer does it necessarily refer to the common people's supposed wildness and savagery used by government officials to condemn the common people. Instead, it refers to the government officials themselves—those who are soulless and the true wild savages. Thus, we see how curious it sounds that someone that wild could even understand what human rights means. And government could trample on these rights because, as "animals," they do not understand its implications. Furthermore, when Fela associates himself with "us" (the people), he separates himself from "they" or the "animals."[25] In doing so, he shows the Nigerian people that he can be trusted.

A similar "us versus them" narrative is conveyed in "Original Sufferhead" through the distinction between "we" or "us" and "dem":[26]

Dem go call us third world	[*They called us the third world*]
We must dey craze for head	[*We must have been really crazy*]
To dey sleep inside dust-bin	[*To have been sleeping in the dust bin*]
Dem go call us non-aligned nations	[*They called us the Non-Aligned nations*]
We must dey craze for head	[*We must have been crazy*]
To dey sleep under bridge o	[*To have been sleeping under the bridge*]
…	
Dem turn us to suffer head	[*They have turned us all into sufferers*]
…	
I want to tell you my brother	
One bitter truth	
…	
We must be ready to fight for am now	[*We must be ready to fight back now*]

In this song, unmistakably, Fela gives a clarion call for his audience to join him in the fight for freedom: "We must be ready to fight for am now." This message is all the more poignant, for it is emphasized with imagery that would be relevant to his audience: sleeping under the bridge.

Ultimately, as has been evinced through some of Fela's songs, Fela's Naija and poetic/oratorical language effectively portray major themes of identity, social justice, and political activism. While he may not have been the doctor that his family had imagined, Fela was arguably something more impactful: a rebellious artist with a cause. Luckily, Fela continues to inspire—but not just famous artists and musical adaptations. He continues to inspire the common people of the world. Because of social media and the internet, Fela's music is readily accessible to the global community. Folajimi examined the number of views and public comments on an internet platform that provides much of Fela's music: YouTube. As of May 2016, the video "Fela Kuti—The Greatest Hits" had about 947,700 views.[27] As of July 2019, the video had over 2.4 million views. On this video, one person commented "Fela is God"[28]—seeming quite redolent of other complimentary names given to Fela in his lifetime. Another person commented: "[Fela's] music is revolutionary soul music … Fela didn't die … he is still alive today and will continue to live forever."[29] Indeed, nothing seems to be truer. Fela will live forever and will continue to inspire work for equality and independence.

9

Postcoloniality and Art in Fela and His Afrobeat

Art is what is happening at a particular point of a people's development or underdevelopment. As far as Africa is concerned, music cannot be for enjoyment, music has to be for revolution.

—Fela Anikulapo-Kuti

In a fundamental way, Fela's art and story are a reaction to Nigeria's transformation from colonial rule to independence.

—Banning Eyre

Indeed, if there is one overarching conceptual thread running Fela's music, it is that the postcolonial Nigerian, and African, condition is an incredible one.

—Tejumola Olaniyan

Art, in whatever form of representation, is a form of expression of thoughts, feelings and interpretation of lived experiences. The artist either give this a visual representation in paintings, drawings, sculptures, carvings, drama, and the likes; or oral, as in music, African poetry and others. Moreover, because the production of these works is inspired by the same ambience, all that is represented in paintings, carvings, music, and the rest, are, in one way or the other, carefully weaved in letters of words that are produced by literary scholars and other members of the intelligentsia community of the society.[1] This reality simply explains the insistence of Fela on the harmonization of the artistic thoughts produced by Africans:

> If you're in Europe, music can be an instrument of enjoyment. You can sing about love; you can sing about who you are going to be in bed with next. But in my environment, my society underdeveloped because of an alien system. So, there is nothing like enjoyment .... There is nothing like love, but there is something like

> struggle for human existence. So, as an artist, politically, artistically, the whole idea about your environment must be represented in the music, in the art.[2]

Put differently, the literary scholar, and her other colleagues in the art of intellectual production of knowledge representing the imagery of the environment they reside, cannot be lamenting about the retrogression of Africa and finding ways to rectify this gloomy stigma in their works, while the musician, is representing the same environment in light of romance, love and whatnot; all of which have never been an issue calling for attention in Africa. Originally, the writer and the musician are in the same trade of word-weaving to express their environment. However, the musician takes this a nudge further by way of fashioning such expressions and interpretations into lyrics and soothing rhythms. In all of these, artists share the commonality of interpretation and representation.[3] The theme covered by their thoughts and as expressed in their art might vary and given different degree of attention by the public. By far, however, the musician stands the chance of reaching out to wider audience and, by implication, have a broader base of listeners and be better known for her philosophy and convictions. As Africa began to be liberated from direct colonial rule, these voices were emerging to generate energy as they vibrate across all social strata and formations. Meanwhile, the political potency of music has never been lost on scholars. As Denning wrote, "to argue that decolonization is a musical event, that a musical decolonization preceded and prefigured political decolonization, suggest that empire and colonization was itself a musical event."[4]

In what follows, we examine the above dynamics in light of the immense intellectual productions of a maverick African legend, Fela Anikulapo-Kuti. Although the years of Fela in music precedes the 1970s when he started making waves, here we discuss Fela, not as a jazz, highlife or highlife-jazz artist, but as an African political musician communicating via his Afrobeat sounds. In any case, he had himself described this preceding period as the time he was confused like any other African that have gone through the European taxonomic modernity mechanism through Western education, Christianity and other processes of socialization.

Fela and His Music

As it were with many Africanist scholars like Archie Mafeje, Ali Mazrui, J. F. Ade Ajayi, Kenneth Dike, Wole Soyinka, Ngugi wa Thiong'o, Asante Molefe, Frantz

Fanon, and many others who lived through the early days of Africa's political independence, the total liberation of Africa and the general progress of all black race were the blood upon which the life of the likes of Peter Tosh, Bob Marley, Fela Anikulapo-Kuti, among few other conscious musicians of this period, were drawn. If Achebe, for instance, wrote *Things Fall Apart* to indent the cacophony of the socioeconomic evolution of Nigeria on the literary world,[5] Fela sang about this in *Coffin for the Head of State* and many other records. Likewise, if Cheik Anta Diop, in his *The African Origin of Civilization: Myth or Reality*, lamented about the deliberate ploy of the West to distort African history or send it into oblivion altogether,[6] and theorized the value and efficacy of African civilization to humanity, and Walter Rodney took this to the articulation of the trajectory of the underdevelopment of Africa in his *How Europe Underdeveloped Africa*;[7] Fela not only sang about these in his 1975 *Who No Know Go Know* album and other records, he live though these expressions. And as earlier mentioned, his messages reached wider audience and broader base of accessibility than any of his Afrocentric colleagues in the intellectual community. More than any of these outstanding figures, Fela was able to use the power of language to penetrate the social fabrics of the society. In a society with a widening inequality between those living in affluence and the downtrodden, and palpable divisions along ethnoreligious lines, his music formed a bridge on which all could at least meet, have a common course, and mutual ground of discussion.

The level of penetration that blurs ethnoreligious differences and melt social statuses was made possible by the originality and style of Fela's musical presentations. Since the late 1500s when the coastal states of the area that made up Nigeria today began to have contact with European merchants, and consequently had social and economic exchanges, some English words crept into local languages, and English as a language began to grow gradually as the language of the aristocrats and nobles.[8] By the time this relationship metamorphosed into direct colonization of the whole area known today as Nigeria, English became the official language of the state. Upon independence, it retained both its aristocratic and official state language status. Howbeit, less than 10 percent of the total population at this time were fluent in the language, with vast majority laying claim to the mastery of its adulterated form known as Pidgin English, in their daily social relations. Therefore, while English remained a borrowed language and its speakers perceived as members of the aristocrats, Pidgin English was seen as indigenously made and the language of the common man. It is this language which weaves local words with English through its flexibility, and which by consequence renders communication between two people from different language groups mutually intelligible, that was adopted by Fela in his music. Added to the sensational and emotional power of music, the content of Fela's music sold and endeared him to millions of people within and outside Africa. What the youths, particularly students, and the general public, could not digest from the works of Cheik Anta Diop, Ngugi wa Thiong'o, and other African intellectuals, due to the sophistication of the language employed in their works, accessibility to these works or lack of interest, they learnt through the simplicity and style of Fela's music.

The Whiteman is intrigued by the content and style of his music, the black man is awed by his ability to so vividly anatomize their predicaments under different governments and picture the social ills in the society, all in a simple language. Another conspicuous fact that characterized Fela's success as a musical, cultural and political icon is the sarcasm often employed in his works. Through the adoption of sarcasm as a communication tool and his language usage, Fela eases the mind of his audience to absorb his expression and interpretation of the everyday living experience of the society. This way, while pointing out the ills of postcoloniality in Africa and emphasizing the need to break the jinx of neocolonization, Fela employed the use of words and sounds that are styled to make his culprits even eager to listen to what he had to say.[9]

A good instance of this that could be rightly said to have spanned his audience base was the one titled "Colonial Mentality". This record was released approximately seventeen years after Nigeria's independence and three years after his first "official" ordeal in the hands of the Nigerian government in 1974 and just few months after the invasion of his "Kalakuta Republic" on the 18th of February 1977, in the album he titled *Sorrow, Tears and Blood*. In this particular case, as in many others, the circumstance that surrounded the production of the album plus other factors earlier mentioned, all led to the virality of Fela's messages in this album, particularly the "Colonial Mentality", even among Christians, Muslims, aristocrats, government officials and others whose ways of life and thinking were questioned and derided therein.

More on this will be discussed comprehensively soon. His style of music that uses sarcasm to point out social menace in the society with the view of correcting them—the famous Fela *yabis*—has been identified as the modern reinvigoration of *Efe* music popular among the Egbado of Northwestern Yorubaland.[10] Like Yoruba poets who left tons of materials for generations to remember past events and learn their heritage to build the future,[11] Fela documented the struggle for the decolonization of Africa in songs, in lieu of books. In light of this, and considering that the indigenous language that is garnished into the language of communication in his music (i.e., pidgin) is Yoruba, one can as well adduce the role of an icon of the Yoruba people to Fela. This part might have been distorted or rather, blurred, by scholars and other writers who had worked on Fela because of the preferability of Africanizing the image of the legend, which is understandable given the continental spread of his impact and Afrocentrism of his messages.[12] Aside the use and interpretation of Yoruba words, which could be said to have acquainted many without prior knowledge of the language to some of these words and their usages, Fela's African shrine is partly characterized by the symbolic presence of Yoruba òrìsà like Sango, Ogun, Oya, and others, all of which are worshipped by tourists, visitors and interested others present at the location.

Consider the lines below in his record titled "Water No Get Enemy":

T'o ba fe lo we omi l'o ma lo
If you wan' go wash, na water you go use
[*If you want to take a bath, you need water*]

T'o ba fe se'be omi l'o ma lo
If you want cook soup, na water you go use
[*If you want to cook, you need water*]

T'o ri ba n'gbona o omi l'ero re
If your head dey hot, na water go cool am
[*If you are feeling provoked, water is the antidote*]

The song was released in 1975 as Fela's response to government clampdown on his music and person. It was used 44 years later by Anthony Joshua as his entrance theme to reclaim his lost titles in the heavyweight boxing rematch in Saudi Arabia on December 7, 2019. In analyzing why Anthony Joshua used that specific song, Joe Coleman argues that the song speaks to the "struggles of life and trying to find a way to overcome suffering and perseverance and then expressing your freedom."[13] Choosing this particular song also serves as some kind of homage to Joshua's ancestral home, Africa, and his cultural heritage. Owing to many of the contributions and impacts that Fela's music has on the continued discourse of nation building in Africa, and Nigeria in particular, it cannot be totally out of place to discuss him in the present, rather than as it might be expected—that is, in the past. There is no question that Fela left an indelible print which none has been able to erase since he died.

Many of the elements that testify to this have been written in books by several scholars and writers, and many more are documented on countless media platforms. This is so much so that if the current tempo is sustained into the nearest future, the legend might come to be recognized as the single personality most researched in modern African history. Arguably, this cannot be separated from the fact that he remains the most prolific, phenomenal, opinionated and radical of any known figure of modern African times. It is no news that all of these earned him the title *Abami Eda* (the strange being). Funnily, Obasanjo, who was his arch-enemy, later named himself *Ebora Owu* (the Spirit of Owu). Due to the trajectory of the Nigerian state and the roles played by Obasanjo in this evolution, the two men—Obasanjo and Fela—had it really rough and the appellation ascribed to both sides suggests the intensity of this disagreement. If Fela had not encountered a transformation moment before the appearance of Obasanjo in the scene of Nigerian politics, his relationship with Obasanjo could have been written in a different narrative of history.

Safe the long references and art of an academic, Fela picked on topics that ranged from African culture, politics, the international community, African ethnography, sociology, history and many more, and delivered materials intellectuals have continuously found fascinating and insightful.[14] All of these definitely brought him in contrast to the likes of Obasanjo who were the state being distilled at this time. His uncompromising posture cost him a lot, but also gave him much. For the former, his ordeals in the hands of successive Nigerian governments from 1974 are well documented in books and in the media.[15] Following the trajectory of many of the Nigerian cultural and political nationalists like Sapara Williams, Mojoola Agbebi, Herbert Macaulay, and many more, Fela grew through the colonial structure to come of age at a point to fight the system. So, he came to the conclusion that "experience is what is good and what is bad." Ironically, coming from an elite background, especially one that had members of its family helped propagate Christianity in Yorubaland (present-day western Nigeria) in the main,[16] Fela grew to become a force to be reckoned with in the bid to reinforce African spirituality, culture and civilization, and undo the European taxonomic modernity helped planted by his grandfather. Therefore, in an interview with Collins in 1975, Fela described himself as an African artist: "But you are more than an African artist," Collins queried, "you are a political African artist."

> Oh yes, yes. The political part of it is a necessity. I don't see how an African music today can be about what doesn't affect our lives now. Our music should not be

> about love, it should be about reality and what we are up to now. You see, if you want love in Africa, we have so many women you don't need it (i.e., romance love songs). Even our music before was for purposes like religion, work, and politics. And so Afrobeat is an occasion for politics because that is the occasion we are in now—people suffering.[17]

Traditionally, all African artists are active political agents in their communities. Music, which is a combination of vocals and sounds, could serve a pleasurable purpose, but it is primarily evocative in African ontological connotation. Talking about the essence of sound in itself in this paradigm, Adegbite explained that it is conceived as a metaphysical agent between the human and the spirit world.[18] Fela's position in the above excerpt is given a cultural context when Adegbite further explained that,

> a Yoruba traditional musician will open his performance which is often done spontaneously by studying the psychological situation of the environment in which he is performing. This is because he sees himself dynamically related to a cosmos that is a living dynamic organism and regards musical sound as one of the most effective means of bringing that dynamic relationship into play in practical terms.[19]

The Westernization of African epistemological and ontological interpretation of her environment has greatly eroded this, among other African cultural values. Fela's Afrobeat, both in sound and vocals, could be regarded as an attempt at resuscitating this lost heritage with a modern blend. This is not to say that the performance of other artists like Ebenezer Obey, Orlando Owo, Osita Osadebe, Victor Olaiya, and others at this time were out of tune with the psychological situation of the environment within which they performed; their artistic production did not just speak so much to the social struggle of the black man in general and the Nigerian state in particular. In simple words, their arts were not in realization that something had gone wrong with the social system that produces the political-economic reality of the society. To this extent, they could not perform the political purpose of their essence in the decolonization process of Africa. It should also be noted that while it is true that traditional African music are always divided into genres, each of which serve a special purpose,[20] very few at this time directed their melodic intervention to the decolonization of the newly independent African states. Through his activism, Fela took the anti-establishment inclination of his mother a nudge further, while at the same time bullet-chasing the legacy of his grandfather, J. J. Ransome-Kuti. The grand reality of Fela's life that depicts the power of will and consciousness is that, for many years, he grew witnessing the struggles of his mother and her relationship with the likes of Nkrumah, but only came to know about Nkrumah and the black struggle through a woman he loved, Sandra Smith Iszedore, when he was around thirty-one years of age. It was from this point that Fela began to realize that religion and the educational system introduced by the colonial government are inherently antithetical to the originality of Africa and its development. Hence, if Africa is to be united it has to be thought in schools.[21] School curriculum, he argued, must tell the predicaments of Africa and the need for social emancipation of the people. In this way, he further defined his music as one concerned about happenings in Africa, why Africa is retrogressing, and the reason Africa has not been able to contribute its knowledge to this cosmos even when there are vast untapped knowledge waiting to be put to use in Africa.

Fela lived his musical life at a time Nigeria was experimenting with the supposed independence it got from the British colonial government. He saw the transition of power from the colonial to the Nigerian government. He witnessed how the Nigerian government metamorphosed into a pendulum between civilian rule and military dictatorship. Himself a product of the colonial state, Fela was able to relate well with the daily processes through which the society was striving to become Westernized. The structure of state and economy left by the colonial government to be inherited by the Nigerian government is what Fela and his contemporaries were trying to navigate their life long project through. The experience was vivid: encounter with government bureaucracies and institutions, social relations among the production forces, state-society relations and state relations with the international community. The reality of these constitutes the paradigm through which Fela's music since his 1969 rebirth was made. In this chapter, all are divided into two separate discourse.

Fela and the Political Culture of Africa

> This is about a man who travels the world where the telephones, light supply, transportation systems, and so on. all work in an orderly way. However, when he come back to Africa, he sees plenty of land but no food, plenty of villages but no roads, plenty of open space but no houses. In short, education, agriculture, communications, and the power supply are in confusion.[22]

Post-independence Africa has been an endless promise of a better season.[23] Through the democratization process, which gives the illusion of having a choice to the people on the average of every four years, the people find themselves making and remaking "messiahs" to help salvage the situation. This inclination was transferred to the succeeding military regimes, but similar to their civilian counterparts, the people were often left wide-mouth-opened in about one to two years of the military administrations. The exception, however, was the Buhari/Idiagbon regime that was less tactical and diplomatic, leading to the quick decline of the regime's public image and its legitimacy. From the events of this period, Nigeria would soon become the making of the military.[24] Since the Nigerian political space features military rule, and the only hope of the people has always been to pressure, lobby, and persuade the military regime to hand over power to a civilian government—that is, a democratically elected government—it was only appropriate to be critical of the role of the military in the nature of the democracy it was going to birth. So, following the 1979 democratic transition supervised by the Obasanjo regime, the consequent election that ushered-in the so-called second republic led by the Shagari administration, and the subsequent dealings of the government, Fela couldn't but *Look and Laugh* as he sang *Over take Don Overtake Overtake* to demean and distil the Nigerian government, African puppet-leaders, their foreign friends and other centripetal collaborators.

In a series of records that spanned less than three decades, Fela built his career as an African political musician by writing songs that speak to government corruption, nepotism institutional decay and other elements he considered a sign of societal retrogression. Fela's rebirth as a person and artist, coincided with the post-civil war reconstruction efforts of the Nigerian government following the end of the Biafra crisis and the full materialization of military rule in Nigeria. More than their civilian counterparts, the military rulers wanted total submission, and in addition to the creation of states to achieve this at the regional level by the Gowon regime, dissidents were to be flogged to order.[25] By this, the Nigerian government had already mastered the art of militarizing opposition voices.[26] The situation was similar in other African countries at the time. Since opposition and dissents are considered seditious in many of the post-independence African states, including Nigeria, Fela could not but deal with many running battles with state authorities. This was good for his music and career as he became more sophisticated and acerbic in lyrics and presentation of his art as a career as well as a living experience. Released in 1974 as part of an account of his encounter with the Nigerian government in that year and incarceration at Alagbon prison, the record he titled, *Alagbon Close*, marked a turning point in key areas of his life; and by implication, his spirituality.

In all of his ordeals with the Nigerian government and considering the general look of state-society relations in Africa together with the operationality of the global system, Fela saw the contradictions of life when he discovered that the outside world, which was meant to be the free world where justice and love are administered, is a "craze world," and the "correctional facility" meant to demoralize him was, indeed, the real word. As he captured this in "Beast of No Nation", "The time wey I de for prison, I call am inside world, the time wey I de outside prison, I call am outside world, Na craze world, no be outside world … " In his political struggles, one cannot be wrong to call the government penitentiaries his second home. Fela argued that, although he was put behind bars based on the craziness of the world he lived, prison was a place devoid of the troubles he faced on the outside. In the "craze world," elections were rigged for the preferred candidate of the "soldiers," the economy was nosediving, both the centripetal and centrifugal collaborators of exploitation were milking the state dry and creating a massive level of inequality and poverty-stricken population, justice was exclusive for the influential and those with affluence, dissenting voices were brutally shutdown, government institutions were irresponsible, and so on.[27] The desire and search for a Messiah among the Nigerian population has now grown to a state of irrationality and wind-chasing since the country transitioned to its fourth republic in 1999.

If anything, successive governments often succeed in surpassing their predecessors in whatever reason that made them to lose their legitimacy. So, in "Teacher Don't Teach Me Nonsense," Fela attacked the value of governance in African states. It has now become a trite fact in development studies that culture and traditions cannot be divorced from a nation's developmental strides and societal progress. Fela in the above music record adumbrated the cycle of learning: from childhood when parents and teachers—as one begins to go through the process of attaining Western education—were the instructors of this learning process, to the university when they become lecturers, and government, at the labor market level. For the government which serves as the central productive body of all, Fela not only adduced its training to culture and traditions, he also noted examples of places where these elements have guided their development. Insofar as the instructor of African government and the template of their governance outlook remains that of the white man, Fela argued that Africa's road to development will continue to be famished. An excerpt from the record reads:

Who be our teacher? na Oyinbo	[*Who is our teacher? It's the white man*]
Who be our teacher? na Oyinbo …	
Na all the problems of this world	[*It's all the world problems*]
Na hin we dey carry, for Afrika	[*That Africa shoulders*]

By the time Fela wrote this song in 1986, Nigeria had gone through military rule, sham elections and democracy, economic downturn, foreign debt and obnoxious policies, the last of which was the austerity measures of the Babangida regime having secured a World Bank loan in agreement for the implementation of a Structural Adjustment program template designed by the institution in that same year. By far, this record symbolizes Fela's artistic genius, as he, yet again, was able to relate the reality of the state to his listeners with pleasure. This accurately depicts the characterization of his music. The Babangida Structural Adjustment program, the manipulated elections, the "crazy democracy" in practice, the hope of attaining development through Western taxonomic modernity and all that Fela talked about in this record are subjects that have caught the attention of scholars; none have reached any contrary conclusions different from the ones Fela's voice argued.[28]

For instance, one would wonder while the Western democracy African countries are supposedly trying to operate would recognize a government elected on a known fact of election manipulation or one that took over power forcefully:

Let us think say Oyinbo know pass me
[*Let's assume the White man knows more than I do*]
When Shagari finish elections
[*When Shagari completed the elections*]
Why dem no tell am, say him make mistake-ee
[*Why was he not informed he made mistakes?*]
Say this one no be democracy
[*that what happened was not democratic?*]
Oyinbo dem no tell Army self
[*The Whites failed to tell the Army*]
Na for England-ee, Army no fit take over
[*The army cannot stage a coup in England*]
I come think about this demo-crazy …
[*I then reflect on this "demo-crazy"…*]

If good-u teacher teach-ee something
[*when a good teacher teaches*]
And student make mistake
[*and the students makes some mistakes*]
Teacher must talk-ee so
[*the teacher will enlighten the students*]
But Oyinbo no talk-ee so
[*But the White man refuses to talk*]

This was during the Cold War and Western countries, like their Eastern rivals, were already on the second scramble for Africa.[29] Accordingly, there was no room for strict adherence to any other ideology than propaganda and politics. Western countries supported military rulers and even helped bring down democratically elected governments and other regimes, just so they can make gains in the competition as they did in the earlier scramble. African states became colonized by the scramble for trade by Europeans, and gained their independence on the verge of the Second World War, which signaled the collapse of colonization, only for the same war to lay the foundation for the neocolonialization of these countries by virtue of the new competition it instigated. The real democratization of African states began in the 1990s after the official end of the Cold War in 1992 with the dismantling of the USSR.[30] Even then, the role of the teachers of democracy remained colored with the politics of personal interest. Military regimes might now be unpopular in Africa since the turn of the current millennium, but the democratization process in Africa is clogged with hydra-headed monsters that connect the external machinations to the internal shenanigans. Take the instance of the operational model of the multinational corporations in postcolonial Africa. They represent the same form of their colonial predecessors who were among the leading agents in the colonization project of Western imperial states in Africa and the abusive nature of the colonial governments.[31]

Fela puts the roles played by these multinationals play in Africa succinctly: "Many foreign companies dey Africa, Carry our money go .... Them go dey cause confusion ... Cause corruption ... cause oppression ... Cause inflation ... " Then, he proceeded, in "International Thief Thief (I.T.T.)," to delineate how this is done to undermine the state, the people and the supposed democracy preached by Western countries which are the mother country of many of these companies. In less than two decades afterward, Ken Saro-Wiwa and his nine Ogoni comrades were murdered by the coalition of the Nigerian government and the MNOCs, Shell in particular.[32] The postcolonial condition of African states is so appalling that Fela's understanding of it informed his way of life. Quite unarguably, Nigeria, like other African countries, left colonial rule for what Olaniyan described as the "postcolonial incredible, signally marked by a great variety of morbid symptoms"[33] that put crisis and irrationality in the common daily living experience of the people. Olaniyan's picture of the postcolonial incredible captures the whole essence of Fela's musical flavor and depiction of a craze world. According to Olaniyan:

> The "incredible" inscribes that which cannot be believed; that which is too improbable, astonishing, and extraordinary to be believed. The incredible is not simply a breach but an outlandish infraction of "normality" and its limits. If "belief," as faith, confidence, trust, and conviction, underwrites the certainty and tangibility of institutions and practices of social exchange, the incredible dissolves all such props of stability, normality, and intelligibility (and therefore of authority) and engenders social and symbolic crisis. Evident in Fela's body of work is a gargantuan will to articulate, to name, the incredibility and thereby inscribe its vulnerability. To the extent that Fela's expressed objective is the overthrow or at least the amelioration of the reign of the incredible, he obviously conceives its dominance at the moment as a transition, an "interregnum".[34]

Fela's perception of the reign of the incredible in African politics informed his choice of Kalakuta Republic and the activities promoted there in defiance of the authorities. It is a known fact that during the interregnum, the governing structure of a state is usually in vacuum. To the extent that there was "no Nigerian government" at this time, Kalakuta Republic was to serve as a miniature form of government occupying this void within the space it then covered in Lagos. Before its invasion, devastation and seizure, Kalakuta Republic, organized based on the African communal doctrine promoted by Fela, was noted as a "danger zone" for government officials or institution; implying that this area was designated a sovereign entity within the Nigerian state. Fela's reaction to the developments during the period he lived were, as noted earlier, his expression and interpretation of postcolonial African states, and Nigeria in particular. This interpretations and expressions were all that his Kalakuta Republic, music, and lifestyle represented. Although Fela has transited to the world beyond, Kalakuta Republic (which we refer to as the symbol of the years of interregnum in Nigeria) remains a relic of history, and Fela's general lifestyle that depicts this remains only in memories, Nigeria still functions within this state of interregnum. One cannot think less of this in a country where people are suffering but government officials are smiling, building assets and fortunes on the collective wealth of the people; where the people have no access to clean water, power supply, food, shelter, good roads, cloths, sound health-care facilities, functional education, electing their own representatives and general opportunities.

The incredible during Fela's time, and in this very context, was constituted by the "*ojukoroju* stealing" (glaring acts of fraud and embezzlement), the "follow-follow" tendency, the "paddy-paddy" arrangements, the "government magic" and the brutality of the Nigerian government. These governments, as further described by Fela, following the 1979/1983 elections, are mere recycling of the same cabals among the military and the civilian population. For Fela, "Overtake Don Overtake Overtake" (O.D.O.O.), it is simply "… Soldier Go, Soldier Come, Soldier Go, Soldier Come, Na so Our lives they roll for Africa since dey say we get independence …." Scholars later came to view this in light of the military and civilian regimes being two sides of the same coin. The incredible state, as Fela described it, is controlled by "international rogues" (the so-called public servants, including the political appointees and elected officials, and their foreign collaborators). Two ways in which the legitimization of power is secured by successive governments in Nigeria, like other African states, has been identified by scholars as coercion and manipulation.[35] Fela, in "Coffin for Head of State," showed how the hypocrisy of religion as introduced by the Arabs and Europeans fits into the manipulative instrument of the postcolonial incredible and how militarization of state and steady retrogression characterize postcoloniality in Africa. Since the arrival of Islam in Africa around the seventh century, foreign religions have come to be the basis for social stratification, killings, hate, and other forms of inclinations for separation and inclusion, among Africans.[36]

Christianity came along with colonization and the situation further degenerated. Fela asked if these religions have helped tame the evils in the society. If the answer is affirmative, then Fela's art would not have had any value or relevance in the evolving social milieu. In spite of the fact that the two religions stand for power in modern African states, crime and insecurity have tripled. Fela wondered, in "Look and Laugh," how government manage to spend more money on police uniform than food to feed the people. This is one of the typical colonial law-and-order doctrines post-independent states in Africa have taken hook-line-and-sinker. The United states has the best military and defense system in the world,[37] yet it is threatened by terrorism, homicide, depressed population, crime and other life-threating dynamics which are further complicated by the COVID-19 pandemic in the recent times. Many years after Fela questioned the rationale behind the colonial structure obtainable in post-independence Africa, particularly the justice system, an American rapper, Clifford Joseph Harris, Jr. (T. I.), in his 2014 track "National Anthem," also questioned why the American government keep more money to build and secure American prisons than it spends on preventing the reproduction of the racism and inequalities dynamics that call for this. Further on this, Fela decried, in "Colonial Mentality," how an African would be decked in wigs and sentence his brother to prison. The prison system is not African, and like other inherited structures of the colonial state, it has been further abused by post-independence African governments. It neither reduced crime rate nor better the social foundation of the states.[38] It never worked in the West, even though it could; it cannot work in Africa.

No one could know these affairs better than Fela as he was an active actor in many of the events that constitute news in the state as well as any public analyst whose insights were often pointed and deep. For instance, it should be noted that Obasanjo had just celebrated his one year in office with the invasion of Fela's Kalakuta Republic on the 15th of February 1977, the incident which later killed his mother the following year, that led to Fela's *Coffin for Head of State* in 1981. This was after a long battle for survival upon his release by the Nigerian police following the incidence that cost him almost everything. His refusal to join the FESTAC '77 and his political activism of this period were noted to have been the cause of the invasion that took place a day after the festival.[39] Decades after, Obasanjo's lawyer, Afe Babalola, while defending him at the Human Rights Violation Investigation Commission, popularly known as the Oputa Panel, described the alleged involvement of Obasanjo, who was the then Head of State during the Kalakuta saga, as an unnecessary personalization of the incident against Obasanjo.[40] Either this is true or not, Fela had laid his verdict in several of his songs, from "Zombie," *O.D.O.O.*, "Coffin for Head of State" "Teacher Don't Me Nonsense" and "Sorrow, Tear and Blood" among others, all speaking to the fact that this was a colonial state where repression and coercion of subjects was the hallmark.

His 1977 "Colonial Mentality," which appeared in the powerfully acerbic album, *Sorrow, Tears and Blood*, is even more instrumental in all of these discussion as the frame of the record title succinctly describes the governance structure and functionality in African states, while the album name tags the consequences of this. In less than a decade after the Kalakuta invasion, the Buhari/Idiagbon regime singlehandedly threw Fela to jail on malicious claim of money laundering. The judge in the case later begged Fela for the miscarriage of justice.[41] His cousin, Wole Soyinka, documented this low moment in the history of Nigeria where in the name of fighting corruption and instilling order in the society, the Buhari/Idiagbon regime turned the country upside down, and how he managed to escape the insanity that was let loose.[42] Indeed, there was a precedence to Fela's 1977 ordeals in the Hubert Ogunde's encounter with the colonial government in the 1950s. Ogunde had during this period staged, among others, a play called *Bread and Bullets*. The play illustrated the Enugu coal mine incidence of 1950, apparently in support of the mine workers. He was arrested and charged for sedition by the colonial government.[43]

Fela and the Social Emancipation of Africa

In the face of all this, local production remains as it were in the colonial days. It should be recalled that the collapse of this sector of the economy is a replica of the general relegation of the traditional African heritage.[44] And as Fela himself sang: "De thing wey black no good, Na foreign things them dey like … " (Black things are bad/They prefer only foreign goods). Yet, the colonial state bestowed on Africans, according to Fela in *Coffin for Head of State*, "them dey overdo" (they overdo it). Both the social and the political are known to be inseparable. The social form of a society informs its politics and vice versa. As Olaniyan rightly described Fela's art, his positions on social issues in the society, like on the political scene, were meant to identify the vulnerability of the societal practices that are inimical to Africanity, the mutability of the African civilization, and the development of modern states in Africa; all of this with the view of changing or ameliorating their effects on the society. It was in this sense that Fela viewed music as an instrument for social emancipation because nation building process should be a consensus sojourn in which every element in the society must take active part. The energy of all component units must reverberate the condition of the state in such a way that the society is constantly conscious of its path to the future, to development as well as its place in the global order of things. This became the reality of Fela's philosophy of art after his redemption in Africanity as he began to "think of music as a bearer of African cultural specificity in the global market place of culture."[45]

In light of this, Fela often employed his lyrical stick against his fellow Africans; both the common man and the elites on their social behaviors and implications on the political and economic prosperity of African states. Such was the case with the criticism of foreign religions, especially Islam and Christianity, detailed in his *Coffin for Head of State*, where he questioned the relationship between the prevalence of these religions and insecurity, both economic and social wise, in Africa. Replacing the "Ransome" in his name with "Anikulapo" signaled his realignment with Africa to buttress his Afrocentrism and end the conflicting identity that assailed his attempt to define himself. It was in the same respect that he wrote, in "Gentleman":

> Africa hot, I like am so
> [*Africa is hot but I prefer it*]
> I know what to wear but my friends don't know
> [*I know what to put on but my friend does not*]
> Him put him socks, him put him shoe
> [*he has on his socks and shoes*]
> Him put him pant, him put him singlet
> [*then his pants and singlet*]
> Him put him trouser, him put him shirt
> [*then his trousers and his shirt*]
> Him put him tie, him put him coat
> [*then his tie and his suit*]
> Him come cover all with him hat
> [*he then tops it with his hat*]
> Him be gentleman
> [*this is because he is a gentleman*]
> Him go sweat all over
> [*he begins to sweat all over*]
> Him go faint right down
> [*and he will eventually faint*]
> Him go smell like shit
> [*and he will stink*]
> Him go piss for body, him no go know
> [*He will urinate on himself without knowing*]
> Me I no be gentleman like that
> [*I am not a gentleman like that*]

Fela's depiction of an African man trying to imitate a white man whose climatic condition calls for a different clothing and dressing style, could be taken to imply some metaphorical connotations, aside its literary form. For one, colonization and the attendant modernization it brought about conceived a society where, as Fela mentioned above, everything black is evil and had to be replaced with foreign substitutes. This led to Africans looking up to the outside world, from the west to the east, for their values and interpretation of the self.[46] In the process, African values, knowledge system, heritage and all, became known as the alternative; that is, the substitute to foreign values and ideas, if ever to be considered for any purpose.

With African arts, science and entire civilization intended to be kept in the darkness of history by the colonial powers, aided by their post-independence stooges whom they left in power, Africans were set to commence the journey of identity crisis without even knowing it. Such was the case with Fela's "friends" who defile what their climatic condition demands of them to be comfortable as literarily presented in the "Gentleman" lyrics. And in the metaphoric sense, we see the insanity of implementing colonial policies as well as European taxonomic modernity project in postcolonial Africa. Suit, tie, shirt, socks, and pants are typical European cloths that later came to constitute another symbol of civility, authority, difference, class, and aristocracy in Africa. The reason for this is not far-fetched. These were the picture the Europeans symbolized to Africans, firstly, during the slave trade and later, the colonial experience.

To worsen the situation, the ex-slaves had returned from farm plantations in the Americas to various parts of Africa, with varying degrees of European normality that fascinated the people of Africa. Together with other colonial agents, they became the touchstone of the society as the people were to gradually metamorphose into their state of mind.[47] Since colonization serves as the basis of the transition of the society at this time to civility and modernization, the modernity has to be white in color and Western in orientation. Accordingly, in "Yellow Fever", Fela took on the bleaching practice among Africans as they try to look whiter than the white man in their inferiority complex. An African personality, which every African must portray, according to Fela, is one that is original to African values in social relations. Part of these include the ability to respond assertively to any form of injustice or acts that demean his/her person and Africanity. Owing to the experience of Fela and his personality, employing violence in such a matter is not out of place, because it is a "craze world" the fellow is striving to navigate. Part of the logic of Fela's composition in "Gentleman" is that the postcolonial condition of African states does not require a gentleman approach. Like Malcom X, one of the leading pan-Africanists whose ideas of Africanity and liberation of Africa resonates well with Fela,[48] for the past glory and dignity of Africa to be restored, dialogue and other gentlemanly attributes will do nothing but solidify the position of those who had worked and are still working to undermine the region.

Fela doubted the tenacity of his kinsmen to follow this idea through in songs, particularly as captured in "Shuffering and Shmiling", where he blamed Africans for their abject poverty and sufferings because they will not act appropriately. In the record which has two sides with the same title, Fela returned to the hypocrisy of religion in Africa to show the contradictions between the dominance of Islam and Christianity and the depressing condition of the society. Regardless, Fela observed victims of this human debasement; "the suffer heads" are consoled by the Church and the Mosque with the hope of heaven and eternity as they assured them that the reward for their earthly labor is in these places. This way, while they face neglect by the government, the foreign religions they so much cherish keep them tamed to endure state injustices. Whereas, "Archbishop *na miliki*, Pope na enjoyment, Imam *na gbaladun*. Archbishop dey enjoy, Pope self dey enjoy, Imam self dey enjoy … " (the Archbishop is immersed in revelry; the Pope is filled with enjoyment; the Iman is having fun). In the first side of the record, Fela had, toward the end of the record, implore his listeners to know that in order to change the narrative from being hungry in the midst of plenty, to been satisfied even in the face of little, they "must be ready to fight for am now" (must be ready to fight for it now). This sends a clear message to all, if the personal living experience of Fela says nothing at all about his idea of the mechanism through which African people can be free from oppression, poverty, massive inequality, no light, no water, no food, no house, no road, and no government conditions in Africa. In this album, Fela calls for the real African man characterized in his "Gentleman" record to wake up and charge forward for the redemption of Africa because the power for change resides in the common people. Decades after, the role of religion and social movements in the nation building efforts of postcolonial Africa is still being scrutinized and dissected by scholars from different fields in management and social sciences as well as in the humanities and the arts, with different approaches, with all pointing at similar conclusions.[49] Unlike in the days of Fela, the political consciousness of the people of Africa is hemorrhaging badly that the political culture built through colonial, military, and civilian rules is becoming increasingly dangerous to the people and the notion of Afrocentrism.

Conclusion

Fela's legacy is one too difficult to be fully continued, aside in memory. Quite a number of African artists have attempted to follow the Fela path in one form or the other, but none, including his two sons who have continued the tradition of Afrobeat music, Femi and Seun Kuti, has been able to fully occupy the void he left in the African sociopolitical space of music. In their different styles, Edrees Abdulkareem, Folarin Falana (Falz), Seyi Akinolu (Beautiful Nubia), Damini Ebunoluwa Ogulu Rex (Burna Boy), and others do provide some contexts for the Fela notion of music in their works. However, the now popular Afrobeats, the genre of music which most of these artist play, Pareles warned, should not be mistaken for Fela's Afrobeat. The former which he described as "the computer-driven pop-R&B" not only largely lacks the flavor of Fela's "simmering instrumentals, methodically layering little riffs and long-lined melodies,"[50] it mostly lacks the message and purpose of Fela's music. Put differently, even though these artists do include some of the sociopolitical elements of Fela's music in their arts to raise the consciousness of their listeners, they lack the authenticity of the art as christened by Fela. Budding African artists willing to follow the path of Fela, like the Maberu and the Aluta band of Temitope Fagunwa, are seriously challenged.

For one, unlike in the Fela days, Femi and Seun Kuti who could have hanged on the popularity of Fela to make waves in Africa, and Nigeria in particular, cannot today compete favorably with the likes of Davido, Wizkid, Olamide, and other hip-hop/rap or Afrobeats artists in terms of impact, popularity, and acceptance in the contemporary African music industry.[51] Meanwhile, no African artist could stand the heat of Fela and his music, either in Africa or in the diaspora during his time. Doing things the Fela way means risking it all, which no African artist at the moment seems to be prepared for, for many reasons. Although the fear of persecution by the government could be adduced to the dwindling influence of what Fela described as music in the above—*yabis* as it is popularly known—the most important impediment to its development and continued relevance in the current social milieu is the neglect from the media in the face of intense competition. Due to the changing socioeconomic and political climate of the country, Nigeria, and other African state in general, songs that represent the expression of love, romance, women and pleasure, are the ones making waves today. During the time of Fela, the media through which people could express themselves about the government were very limited. Since government policies, actions, and inactions affect all social strata of the society, and as free beings, the anxiety of expressing this frustration was continually dowsed by the likes of Fela who stood as the mouthpiece of the oppressed and the common man without a voice.[52]

Also, unlike in the recent times, the Nigerian patronage network had not become so sophisticated on a rentier structure that now prevails. Adding to this is the general lethargy of social movements and consciousness in Nigeria and African renaissance in African. A clear testimony to this is the level of activism in African universities today compared to the 1970s and 1990s. Afrobeat, like reggae, does not have audience in Nigeria as it did during this period (i.e., from the 1970s to the 1990s) because of the shift in the social consciousness of the people of Africa. From state to individual level, the idea of pan-Africanism and African revival has turned, more or less, to an abstract assertion.[53] The ills of the society and the irresponsibility of the state are no longer covered by the limited media outlets, but by social media and the internet that provides instant news to the general public and at the same time offer them the platform to react to such a news. As such, the news and criticism of the government have become a daily doze that weakens what one might refer to as Patriotic Immune System of the masses, so much so that the people just want to live through the system. This notwithstanding, a significant voice might still be appreciated, however, the colonial educational structure of the state has caught up with it. Students are seldom concerned about politics and governance but the social form of the society and everything that enhances this, including TV programs and the music they listen to. So, the Nigerian media, as well as their counterparts elsewhere in Africa, would rather dance to this flow so as to remain in business and stay relevant.

The above have greatly torpedoed the popularity of Afrobeat and its *yabis* element in the contemporary African scene. As Fela had accurately predicted, African music is emerging to be the music of the future, but unfortunately not Afrobeat, *yabis* music or in any radical form he had probably imagined. Africans are tired of fighting, pan-Africanism functions as a farce, and Africa is today being prepared for a modern form of colonization—this time not from Europe but China. Fela might not have been perfect and his struggle might not be entirely selfless as noted in some quarters, the fundamental truth, however, remains that, if the path of speaking truth to power was so easy as way of life and making a living, he was the only African who was aware of it. His travails from the above narrative ranged from arrest, prosecution and persecution by different Nigerian governments and the to some extent, the Ghanaian authorities, particularly under the Akufo-Addo regime. Fela's ideas about the reinvention of Africa and the repositioning of its place in the global order of things are somewhat embedded in the creation of a pluriversal world where African knowledge system forms the basis of its societal formation and progress and not the universality of the Western system.[54] African knowledge system is based on history, heritage, and culture,[55] all of which Fela, through his music, advocated to be resuscitated for the birth of a new African personality. Fela music genre might not be popular anymore in this ecological space, but the samples he had produced, like the works of his predecessors who used several versions of poetry to preserve history (both in the political and social scenes), will remain ever relevant in the African development discourse.

Part C

Fela and Felasophy

10

Cultural Imperatives in Fela's Music

Introduction

Music plays an important role in the perpetuation of African culture, through its representation of African heritage, mores, customs, literature, and other aspects of African culture. Idang asserts that music is embedded in the everyday life and activities of African society and people, as stories and religious activities are grounded in the music of that particular culture.[1] Music is attached to several secular and sacred cultural activities in Africa, and an attempt to separate it from these activities may be impossible or possibly the death of one. The importance of music in many African cultures goes beyond the entertainment and self-gratification functions; it exudes a greater purpose of utilitarianism. The concept of utilitarianism encodes that the value of a thing is repose in its function and not only in its aestheticism. Music has played several key roles in the performance and continuance of cultural activities which include initiation rites, rite of passage, agricultural and domestic activities, ritual and religious performances, and national ceremonies. Music is deeply grounded in many other cultures of the world, especially in Africa, and is a rich source of knowledge into the culture that has produced it.

Music is a form of communication between two worlds—the world of the living and the dead. African traditions and ethos are expressed in its art forms, and music takes a front row seat in the promotion of the subject. Oral tradition, which is an essential aspect of African culture due to its insurance of the passage of cultural practices from one generation to the other. Music is connected to poetry in African culture, as one flows into the other in a fluid simulation. Singing is almost like breathing in the African society because the melody and rhythm often accompany their domestic and agricultural activities. This accounts for the several songs in many activities like farming, mining, fishing, hunting, iron works, and so on, which are often in the call-and-response structure. This follows the tradition of a bard or griot in many cultures in West Africa.

The griot is often a praise singer with adequate knowledge of the oral tradition passed down from one generation to another generation through the word of mouth. They often act as chroniclers of culture and history of a particular community who travel from one village to another. Griots are professional historians, storytellers, musicians, and sometimes act as advisers to traditional leaders in the society. Music often combines different aspects of culture as a prop or content to be praised or criticized. When the traditional/religious head in the society errs, the bard is often responsible for the education and perhaps a reminder of the erring person/leader about a previous occurrence with an allusion to the consequences of such action.

Culture is often regarded as the totality of a marked peculiarity shared by a certain group of people, as illustrated by Mbakogu when she traced the connection between culture and development.[2] Culture is the traits and values peculiar to a people, which separate them from other peoples of the world. These values and traits include language, dressing, music, arts, dance, and so on. The list of values goes on to include social norms, taboos, and beliefs. The complex knowledge, arts, belief, laws, customs, and habits possessed by a group of persons in a society mark the purview of culture. Culture encompasses a wide variety of human phenomena, manners, morals, feelings, and emotions which are shared by a particular group of people who possess a common heritage or single ancestry.

Culture is transmitted from one generation to another generation through various means which may include social interaction or participation and impartation from the parents or institution conferred with such functions. There can be no people without a culture, and by implication every group of people in the world has a unique culture and way of expressing their beliefs and values. Africa is a continent of diverse cultures and each is quite unique and different from others; by this, one will navigate culture in its plurality even though there may exist similarities in different regions of the continent. Culture is dynamic in its replication and production due to human contact and interaction with other people of the world. The interaction of different cultures of the world produces new ones, and may either erode the existing ones or promote them. African culture is quite different from other cultures of the world, as it has a distinct belief enshrined in its acquisition and transmission in different art forms. Idang notes that characteristically, culture nurtures values which are simulated in their interactions and connections with different value systems; and their interaction is firmly rooted in the mores of the society.[3] The acceptability of a particular event or action is precedent on the culture of the immediate society which controls those actions through the implementation of rules and regulations that guide social interaction between members of the same community.

The connection between culture and music is sacrosanct; music is intrinsically tied to culture in Africa and its production is a culture on its own. Culture affects music and vice versa, and also influences other cultures that have contact with the music. Culture is an aspect of a society and so the society and its culture influence the production of music. The relationship between these phenomena is symbiotic, through the exploration of musical instruments and performance structures which covers interaction between performers and audience; through this, we can learn so much about the culture of a particular society. Barton discusses how ethnomusicologists explore the impact culture can have on music, and in many cases music on culture, with the inference that music is in essence culture, and its separation from life may not be possible.[4]

The concept of culture as music and music as culture has merit; for some, music is the expression of their culture and who they are, while for some culture is birthed from their music and becomes a culture on its own, having a particular way of dressing, greeting, food, morals and religious beliefs, and so on. Akin Euba provides a powerful ethnomusicological framework by which we can come to terms with the relationship between music and culture, and particularly how music in Africa has evolved. Apart from what he calls the "pre-colonial idioms of music" which grounds "African musical taste," three categories are immediately apparent: neo-traditional art music, Western art music and African-European art music. With Euba, we are better able to place Fela, his musical creativity and performative aesthetics, the relationship between his music and his sociocultural context and how to critical understand Afrobeat. The cultural groundedness of a music, for Euba, goes a long way to determine how the African audience, for instance, relate with it. For instance, a typical African audience, it is to be expected, will favor a piece of music with a large dose of connection with a traditional idiom, musical style and social context than one that possesses a weaker link. Indeed, Euba argues, "in comparing a neo-traditional work with a non-traditional work, an average African listener might make an evaluation based solely on recognition and identity: the neo-traditional work is considered to be 'better' because it is 'African' or because it serves a religious purpose."[5] This same connection to the neo-traditional affects the audience's relationship with the goodness or badness of a piece of music.

> The attitude of modern African audiences to new African art music may also be somewhat related to the erroneous idea that "music is a universal language." Most Africans who did not experience any pains learning their mother tongue, since they grew up with it, are aware, through their study of the English language, that to acquire a speech language with which one did not grow up, one must be prepared to undergo the pain of learning it. The same attitude is seldom applied to music. Because he grew up with the musical language of his home culture, the typical African music lover is often unaware that there are other languages of music or that the acquisition of a non-indigenous musical language could be, if not exactly painful, at least not without effort. Therefore, if a piece of music in a foreign idiom does not appeal to him instantly, he assumes it is because the music is not good. He does not consider the possibility that he might have failed to understand the music, since he assumes music to be a "universal language."

We see there that the kind of African audience which listens to the kind of specially composed, specialist-performed music that is usually presented in a specially appointed concert hall tends either through conditioning or a lack of educational guidance to evaluate music in terms of one or all of the following criteria: (a) its "Africanness," (b) its religiousity, (c) its melodic "sweetness" … (d) the immediacy of its appeal.[6]

It is on this premise that we will discuss the cultural embeddedness of Fela's music, as well as his obligation to his social context and public. Thus, in understanding Fela's music as a balance between African and European art music, Afrobeat retains an essential African disposition: "the relationship of music to its social context, the ethnic delimitation and linguistic basis of musical style, and the role of music in the perpetuation of ethnic beliefs and aspirations."[7] To understand Fela's music therefore, there is a need to know briefly his cultural background and how it is reflected in his lifestyle and music. The relationship between African culture and music is a unique one that is convoluted. Music from time immemorial is constructed and grafted on the culture of the society.

Music is a small fraction of culture, while culture is transposed and transformed through music. Culture refers to the beliefs, customs, and arts of a particular society. In the context of African culture, music is intrinsically woven into the fabric of everyday activities and existence. The different aspects of culture are woven into the music of that culture, and together music opens a door for culture to bloom, while culture offers props and materials for music to thrive. Some peculiar traits of cultures that mark different ones from each other include language, modes of dress, dance, arts and craft, religion, music, food, and so on. These are cultural markers that inform the difference or peculiarity of a culture in the world. In terms of clothing and dressing, the culture of wearing a particular style of fabric keeps evolving to accentuate the age grade and cultural inflections.

Ajayi refers to identity as a set of characteristics that marks an individual or a group of people from another.[8] It is the unique trait that is inherent in the personality of a person. The formation of a personality is hinged on the participation of an individual in the society. Oikelome identifies that identity is the dynamic production of the interface between "self" and the social institution in any society.[9] The discovery of "self" amid several rhetoric of social communication within the society births the personality of a person. The personality of a person or a group of people is situated within the interaction with society. Music has a vital function in the society and involves the identity of the musician, and on this premise the study will take impetus from the identity of Fela Anikulapo-Kuti, which emerged from his musical and cultural ideology.

Identity is an offshoot of one's cultural background and inclination, which starts from the nomenclature one carries. Many Africans have European names as a colonial heritage, which alters the African worldview and identity of the black man who has been divorced from his African roots through a process of renaming carried out by the colonialists. For instance, Fela's middle name, "Ransome," carried the colonial burden of nomenclature with Eurocentric bearings of meaninglessness in the African ethos. From the music which was at the early stage of his musical career, predominantly European in nature due to his education in the colonial state, Fela experienced a double cultural intrusion on his psyche—his African roots and culture—as a constant eruption due to the Western education and culture he was exposed to during the largest part of his formative years. However, Fela was able to shed this colonial heritage and became a staunch cultural nationalist, despising the cultural imperialism in Africa. This is reflected in his music. From their political to the educational, economic, religious and architectural systems, Africans have been culturally displaced by the European cultural hegemony in Africa. Ajayi notes that Fela despised the European manipulation of the African people's psychology, which has affected the growth of the African continent.[10] Fela's ideological proposition is encapsulated in the song "ITT" (International Thief Thief), making reference to the system of human waste disposal, where Fela listed the different names for human wastes and the system of passing the waste.

… Long, long, long time ago	
African man we no dey carry shit	[*In Africa, we do not carry feces*]
We dey shit inside big big hole	[*We use the pit latrine*]
For Yoruba na "salanga"	[*The Yoruba call it "salanga"*]
For Igbo na "onunu-insi"	[*The Igbo call it "onunu insi"*]
For Hausa na salga	[*The Hausa call it "salga"*]
For Gaa land na "tiafi"	[*The Gaa call it "tiafi"*]
…	
Before dem come force us away as slaves	[*Before we were forced into slavery*]
During the time dem come force us away as slaves	
Na European man, na him dey carry shit	[*It is the European who carry feces*]
Na for dem culture to carry shit	[*The European culture permits it*]
…	
During the time dem come colonise us	[*It was when we were colonized*]
Dem come teach us to carry shit…	[*that we were taught to carry feces*]

There is the portrayal of the self and other ideological identities in Fela's music, where he declared the "self" as Africans and Europeans as the "other," and wants the "other" to be banished from his republic. Okeke opines that when the culture of a people is taken away by any means, the people have been totally emasculated, as the society derives essence from the culture.[11] The development of a group depends on their identity and contribution to the political and economic growth of the immediate society.

Fela's Cultural and Musical Background

Fela's artistic development sailed through his traditional and modern musical education, political and activist experiences, and cultural background. African cultures, especially the Yoruba culture from Nigeria in West Africa, have both sacred and secular songs as ritual codes and entertainment texts which draw both the initiate and non-initiate of the culture into the core of the rhythm. These songs can be both lucid and elusive in their semiotic codes depending on the occasion. Olorunyomi attempts to connect Fela with his cultural base:

> In many traditional African cultures, including the Egba Yoruba in which Fela was raised, music and dance are intrinsically tied to everyday experience. This

process could be of a sacred event, thereby incorporating ritual elements, or a secular one, involving music and dance as accompaniments to social gatherings such as sport, general entertainment and, at times, an instrumental jam session.[12]

The Yoruba culture in particular is known for its richness in mythic and ritual lyrical narratives used for the adulation of spiritual deities and human social and political gratification. From the performance of cradle lyrical texts for putting babies to sleep, personal and collective panegyrics and rhythmic narratives of quasi-religious cults, music is a strong medium of communication in the Yoruba culture.

Music is naturally encoded in the Yoruba culture and cosmology, including ritual performances that almost always include songs for invocation and divination. The different traditional Yoruba deities like Sàngó, Ọ̀bàtálá, Ifá, Egúngún, and many others have songs as part of the modus operandi. Olorunyomi narrates that the Ifá system of thought and aesthetics were of interests to Fela.[13] The divining system of Ifá worship and many other African traditional systems of ritual preceded the emergence of Islam and Christianity in the African milieu. Fela, who was raised in the Christian way, renounced this religious heritage and became a believer of the traditional African religion, often making libations and sacrifices to the Yoruba deities before his performances in Afrika Shrine.

The creation and performance of Afrobeat was every bit cultural as it is political. It was a rhythmic means of dispossessing the colonial and neocolonial influence on Fela and his fellow African people. This attempt to shed the colonial baggage on Fela's music resulted in a series of cultural and musical experimentations with different modes and forms of musical instruments.

> The very performance of Afrobeat was political. It was one of Fela's most powerful mediums of social critique and re-imagination. Afrobeat was a new genre blended with essences of Jazz, Funk, Soul and Highlife. Fela's conscious adaptation of African musical traditions like complex polyrhythms and call-and-response patterns carried the sounds of his cultural nationalism.[14]

Through his music, Fela criticized the bourgeoisie culture of the African elite who embraced the colonial culture and had been psychologically colonized to look down on their roots and heritage. This mental colonization makes the African people and government promote neocolonialism in all its manifestations in the continent, counterproductive to the development of the continent. Fela's culture and music was decidedly a counterculture to this European cultural hegemony.

Chief Priest and the Public Bard

The public bard, Fela, was the crusader of the Nigerian masses who were constantly being oppressed by their government and political leaders. Fela's oeuvre maneuvered the rhetoric of the political and socio economic injustice of military juntas in the country. In his songs "Army Arrangement," "Zombie," "Beast of No Nation," and "Alagbon Close" Fela engaged the brutality of the armed forces and security agencies who were supposed to protect the people but were tools to intimidate and suppress the masses from revolutionary activities. Fela raised his musical cudgel against the upper class (politicians and elite), who were promoting the activities of the colonial states in the country by supporting multinational companies in plundering the state's wealth. In "International Thief Thief" (ITT), "Confusion Break Bone," and "Authority Stealing," Fela addressed the African leaders who were embezzling public funds but were never prosecuted. Fela declared that the people are tired and would no longer bear the excesses of these leaders. The public bard earned his place in the hearts of the people as he embraced and recognized the members of the lower class to the detriment of the state.

Fela was making prophesies about the political and economic conditions of the country, and the people were his ardent followers. Olorunyomi described Fela as a poet of hope as well as rage, who regularly encouraged the people to be hopeful in the fight for economic equity.[15] Fela was also an accomplished acerbic humorist, as portrayed in "Jeun K'oku" and "J'ehin J'ehin." He was not shy to point out the fault of the masses in their reluctance to stand for social activism. In "Sorrow, Tears and Blood," Fela criticized the masses' culpability in their own repression, as they are too afraid to seek for justice:

My people self dey fear too much [*My people are too fearful*]
We fear for di thing we no see [*We fear what we cannot see*]
We dey fear for di air around us [*We fear the air around us*]
We fear to fight for freedom
We fear to fight for liberty
We fear to fight for justice
We fear to fight for happiness
We always get reason to fear
We no want die [*We do not want to die*]
We no want wound [*We fear to get wounded*]
We no want quench [*We do not want to die*]

We no want go	[*We are not ready to go yet*]
I get one child	[*I have a child*]
Mama dey for house	[*There is a mother at home*]
Papa dey for house	[*There is also a father*]
I want build house	[*I need to build a house*]
I don build house	[*And then I built the house*]
I no want quench	[*So I do not want to die*]
I want enjoy	[*I need to enjoy a bit more*]
I no wan go	[*It's not time to die yet*]
So, policeman go slap your face	[*So, when a policeman slaps your face*]
you no go talk	[*You keep quiet*]
Army man go whip your yansh	[*A soldier whips your buttock*]
you go dey look like donkey	[*You look like a donkey*]

This culpableness was also narrated in "Shuffering and Shmiling," where the people were still tolerant of the oppressive conditioning by the state. But the bard will not relent in his mission of championing the liberation of his people from hegemonic agencies in the country and continent. Fela created alternative mores which rubbed off on the latter generation of Afrobeat singers in the country. The Afrobeat King transmuted the urban lore and culture to reinvent one that deconstructed the hegemonic mores. This unique culture is represented in his approval and promotion of "igbo" (marijuana) smoking, polyandry, groove, and performance aesthetics.

Fela's obsession with the African culture and ethos were so profound he was bequeathed with the alias "Abami Eda." This name is derivative of the myth of the reincarnation of the Yoruba "Abiku," which Wole Soyinka, J. P. Clark-Bekederemo, Ben Okri, and many other writers have extensively worked on. It elucidates a being who traverses the terrestrial, celestial, and extraterrestrial worlds. The *abiku* is venerated through several ritualistic mediums to appease his restive spirit and voyage in the terrestrial world of the living. Fela as "Abami Eda" becomes a metaphor for his intractable voyage and quest to steer the discourses of socio cultural and economic rhetoric of the state. The *Abami Eda* will continue to plague the mother (African leaders) until his spirit is appeased, and in this case till his people are physically, mentally, and economically liberated.

The system of having a spiritual head that offers libation and leads the ritual and spiritual procession in the African traditional mode of worship can be deduced from the music of Fela's work, which he incorporated into his musical sessions in his commune and club. Okeke elucidates the importance of the oral bard in the primordial African society, who comments and criticizes social and cultural infringements. "Yabis" was a session where Fela acted as both the public bard and chief priest. The yabis session which occurred in 1989 was one of the notable sessions where Fela criticized the dependence on foreign drugs and medical practices. The session was organized after the alleged death of two persons who took paracetamol and died afterward. He draws a parallel between traditional systems of healing and medication with Western medical practices and drugs.

Gardner situates Fela's music and Afrika Shrine within enshrinement lore, which draws from a quasi-religious rhetoric.[16] Afrika Shrine was a signifier of the sacredness of the culture of Fela and his Afrobeat music. Afrobeat becomes the songs of the initiated into the world of socio cultural politics in the Nigerian space. Afrika Shrine is a space for the re-imagination and renegotiation of a culture that communicates with rhythmic codes to the staid discourse of the state cultural imperialism.

The Culture of Fela's Music

One of the focuses of Fela's music was the renouncing of Eurocentric cultural imperialism on Africans and the promotion of Afrocentric views, which calls for the appreciation of African values, culture, traditional life, and medicine. The composition of "ITT" depicted ritual motion, while "Big Blind Country (BBC)" captured the interface of the priest's exploration of myths, African history, and temporal frames. The Chief Priest, Fela, explored, deciphered, and proclaimed in his ritual script (music) as the traditional Babalawo does with his *òpèlè* (divination bead). Cultic codes in Fela's music are explored in his lyrical and visual narratives. Fela's music reverberates the African mystic way of life and values. In "Yellow Fever," "Journey Just Drop," "Big Blind Country," and "Upside Down," Fela explored the theme of cultural alienation of the African people, as Fela's lyrics discussed how Africans have been alienated from their cultural roots. In "Yellow Fever," Fela employed the symbolic medical term "fever" to engage the neocolonial mentality of African women's attempt to be the "self" in the racial discourse and not the "other" whose humanity is weighed by the color of her skin. This self privileges white pigmentation, and acquiring the resemblance of this pigmentation affords the women the status of the self in a male-dominated society.

Fela's music engaged the reconstruction of the black identity that had been displaced by the rhetoric of neocolonial acquired culture and civilization that venerated the continuous dependence of the black people on the benevolence of the white race. Fela's music and his cultural nationalism was a counter discourse to the cultural hegemony of the colonial space and discourses. Fela, in "Gentleman," engaged the mentality of the African man to be like the white "gentleman" who is allegedly the symbol of humanity, completeness and civilization. This effigy is spread through the discourse of portraying the African man as a cannibal, half-human and a nitwit who is incapable of being a "gentleman." The African man has no culture and he is uncivilized, hence, the necessity of his education in how to be a "proper human," which is the preoccupation of colonialism. The West controls the discourse of the "gentleman" and Fela refused this label of being a "gentleman" with white mannerisms and sensibility. He countered the discourse by proclaiming his own identity as an "African man," displacing the Western label of a "gentleman." The gentleman is supposed to act, behave, dress, and even exist in a Euro-Western kind of way. Any attempt to act differently from this norm is perceived as barbaric and uncivilized. Fela criticized the African people's ideology to exist and live as white people in a black body and space.

In "Big Blind Country," the central theme and preoccupation of the Afrobeat singer is the awakening and reorienting of the blind government and people from dogmatic duplication of Western ideologies and epistemologies in the African milieu. Fela was critical of the systems of socialism and capitalism espoused by foreign proponents that were being implemented into the Nigerian space and African setting. He was a proud follower and believer in Kwame Nkrumah's proposal for the emancipation of the black nation and the unification of the black race in the Diaspora. The lyrics of "BBC" satirized the government's uninformed reduplication of ideas and system of governance in Nigeria. The songs were sung in Pidgin, which was notoriously known to be the lingo of the plebeian; the uneducated, uncultured, and uncivilized citizens.

Fela and Pan-Africanism

The notion of an African nation-state was the main thrust of Fela's Pan African ideology expressed in his music, political engagements, and lifestyle. This was mostly influenced by Kwame Nkrumah's works and doctrine, most notably, *Africa Must Unite* (1963), which preached the unification of Africa as one-nation state. Fela advocated for a return to the African utopian (primordial) society, comparing the ruin and decadence of the modernized society ravished by the realities of the aftermath of the first and second world wars. He wanted a return to a society free from all the encumbrances of science and technology, but filled with the basic and simple conceptions of life.

In "Journey Just Drop" (JJD), Fela satirized Africans who travel to these Euro-western countries and return with a different set of values and mannerisms. The "elite" African now has an inferior perception about the African culture, people, and systems. These Africans scorn African communal living and so erect for themselves houses that exclude other members of the society. This is a system of living in the West which privileges the nuclear and solitary type of existence. The system of communal living was notably the suit of the African people; the incorporation of every member of the family into a large communal setting. However, the interaction of the African man with Western culture had made him cynical of the African ethos and mores.

Fela espoused Black Power ideas of cultural pride, black aesthetics, development, and the negritude concepts of the valorization of the black pigmentation and culture in songs like "Gentleman" (1973), "Mr. Grammartology-Lisationalism Is the Boss" (1976), "Mr. Follow Follow" (1976/77), "Johnny Just Drop" (1977), and "Yellow Fever" (1976). Such compositions lampooned the feigned attitudes of many blacks/Africans, and addressed their state of cultural and self-alienation. In "Yellow Fever," Fela criticized the bleaching and toning of the black pigmentation by African women in the bid to look more like white women, while placing value on fair complexions to the detriment of their African configuration. The pigmentation discourse challenges the notion of attaching/defining beauty from Western perspectives. The light/fair skin of the white women as the benchmark for beauty is a narrative that Fela sarcastically satirized. He sang the song to disabuse the black women's mentality and preference for a fairer complexion with the use of several chemical-laced creams to achieve the look. The identities of the blacks are embedded in the "blackness" of their skin, which separates them from every other race in the universe. The black skin pigmentation should be celebrated and nurtured while desire to look fair is a neocolonial baggage and heritage that needed to be stopped.

Fela's song "Lady" has cultural politics as its main subject; directed at the female populace of the African continent. African women's reduplication of Western women's ideas of how to act, and in the portrayal of self-image, is heavily ridiculed. The song is on the same par with "Gentleman," having almost the same trait of portrayal of self-image and identity hinged on the Western discourse of the "acceptable image" of a woman. This particular song had been discussed along the gender discourse of misogyny and patriarchy by many feminists; criticizing Fela's portrayal of the African woman as subservient to the male gender in Africa.

If you call am woman	[*If you call her a woman*]
African woman no go gree	[*The African woman will disagree*]
She go say, "I be lady oh"	[*She will insist she is a "Lady"*]
She go say, "I be lady oh" …	
Call am for dance	[*Call her for a dance*]
She go dance lady dance	[*And she will dance like a lady*]

However, critics who have maneuvered the song along these discourses of feminism, patriarchy, and misogyny failed to consider that Fela was also criticizing the Western notion of how African women's identity and beauty were fashioned along the Western beauty regimen. African women's appreciation and promotion of their heritage and aesthetic configurations were some of the crux of Fela's music; Africans, especially women, should be critical of any image and beauty that alienated them from their biological configuration. The carriage of the African woman should exist on her African terms, and no culture should dictate or influence her identity, especially if it portrayed her existence as the subaltern. The argument that Fela was an unrepentant misogynist is debatable in his song "Shakara Oloje," which criticized both the male and the female African people who were full of pretense and Western affectations. The main point was that Africans should be real and factual with their identity and shun pretentious mannerisms.

Fela and the Utopian African Society

One of the preoccupations of Fela's music is the exaltation of the African culture of communal living, devoid of colonial interference and scientific innovation. Fela's ideology of a one-nation continent—propagated by exponents of pan-Africanism such as Kwame Nkrumah—is explored in the politics and culture of the Afrobeat icon. Fela strove for the unification of Africa as one nation in the establishment of his political party, Movement of the People (MOP). This nation which Fela advocated for in his music is grounded in his establishment of a commune, open and free to all. The Kalakuta Republic is the symbolic one-nation state that Fela sang about. It is the "imagined" utopian African society where there is the absence of the discourses of repression and state economic and cultural subjugation of the masses. Many of his songs addressed the class and economic disparity between the elite and the proletariat. Kalakuta Republic is the symbol of Fela's Marxian philosophy, which must necessarily subvert all forms of state hegemony.

> By appearing in his underwear, though only within his residence, and daring to suggest and remind of the ordinariness of life, in a society where over-clothing—and especially military histrionics—served the semiotics of power, he seemed to have been marked for extinction by the state, and his entire career would be dogged by the sheer wish to defend that alterity.[17]

Through his half-clad nature of dressing in his home and during his musical performances, Fela elevated the primordial system of living and dressing which eschews ostentatious ensemble. The idyllic promulgation of being half-clad is a subtle narrative of the simplicity of life and the criticism of the dependence on European attire and ways of dressing. In the song "Follow Follow," Fela alluded to the acquired ways of dressing that promote Western styles that are often extravagant, while the African styles are pushed to the periphery. Fela discussed that the African man appreciates his African fabric and way of dressing only when he sees it in the Western countries and probably worn by a non-African person. He advocated in "Buy Africa" that the African fabric and clothing should be worn and promoted by the government and the citizens. They should buy these fabrics and wear them to show that these prints are as beautiful as their Western counterparts.

Afrocentric modes of dress were strongly promoted in the music of Fela Anikulapo and was partly the main costume of the icon and his band members, which later included the all-female choreographers and dancers. These women were adorned in African prints sewn in the iro and buba style, with various African hairstyles, beads, and beauty products. The Afrobeat composer himself abandoned his famous one-piece body suit to appear half-naked in long trousers with different African designs and prints woven into them. The musician's trumpet and saxophone were also adorned with different African cultural elements like cowries and shells to depict his cultural heritage.

Traditional rhythms formed the backdrop of Fela's development of Afrobeat. He moved away from his style of music during the Koola Lobitos days to Africa

70, which marked the gradual transition to a syncopated fusion of meters and rhythms. These traditional rhythms reflected his ideology of what an African rhythm should emit, launching the musician and his Egypt 80 band to the center stage of African music. The names of his band changed from time to time to reflect his growth and knowledge of Africa and its epistemologies propagated by the proponents and exponents of the Black Power Movement and pan-Africanism.

Cultural Aesthetics in Fela's Music

The cultural aesthetics of Fela's Afrobeat are immersed in its performance of the narrative of nonconformist and radical rhetoric. Afrobeat is characterized by open engagement with sexual, administrative, and rhythmic politics, which subvert the traditional framings of otherness. Afrobeat, composed by Fela Kuti, transposed traditional musical rhythms and created a musical subculture of "grooving" without state and cultural inhibitions. This musical creation traverses different spheres of cultural and political ideologies which fanned the flame of its volatility in the Nigerian space, and ultimately the world stage. The musical genre engaged Marxian dialectics with their postmodern themes to upturn the socio cultural and economic rhetoric of the elite-dominated society. Afrobeat is steeped in cultural aesthetics, as it maneuvers the different traditional elements of culture as its base and seeks to make projections marked by a liberal space.

> As conceived by Fela Afrobeat is primarily a cultural and political musical practice or—better still—an aesthetics of cultural politics. Its performance is equally characterized by the creation of a liberal cultural space that is admissive of a free discourse of society's fears, doubt, and inhibitions: be it governance, sex, or the yearnings of restive youth in general. Thus, Afrobeat is not simply a musical rhythm but a rhythm of alterity realized largely in song and musical text, but also in cultural and political action.[18]

Afrobeat is steeped in cultural aesthetics, as it maneuvers the different traditional elements of culture as its base and seeks to make projections marked by a liberal space. Afrobeat was more than just a music genre; it was a culture which incorporated different aspects of traditional African culture and infused new ones to create a new subculture. The following have been identified as influences of the African tradition on Afrobeat: the lead and backup singers call-and-response; the fusion of the gong and beaded gourd traditional instruments; the percussive drums; the pitch alternating inflections of Yoruba words and chants speech; and the permutation of different rhythms of music.

Afrobeat and Dance: A Choreography of Culture

Oikelome notes that dance is the unspoken communication of body movement with different gestures, twists, and turns with the accompaniment of music or rhythm.[19] It is an essential ingredient of music and entertainment in Africa. Dance and music are interwoven so closely that to separate one from the other may be a herculean task. In every culture, and especially African culture, music and dance go hand in hand and one often leads to the other. Fela's Afrobeat provoke a kind of dance that is a mixture of traditional steps and choreography which is meant to convey a particular message to the audience.

> The movement is varied with some stamping on the floor with short steps that are ordered and legs moving to the pulse of the music. Each song has its own form of choreography. In "Zombie" we have a complex pattern of basic steps against seemingly independent movements of various parts of the body, which is combined simultaneously with hand and leg gestures. In Each step of the dance is rooted in the African tradition. However, in Water no get enemy, the dance steps are in simple movements with the swaying of the hands in interlocking sequences like that of the cult dance in Egbaland. The swaying of the hands depicts the gentle flowing water from a river.[20]

Oikelome observed that Fela's Afrobeat choreographic performance has sometimes simple and other times complex body movements which are rooted in African cultural steps. The dance, which was popularized by the addition of the Kalakuta Queens, became a meta-language of eroticism and semiotic signs for the elucidation of Fela's thematic preoccupations. The dance, as stated by Olorunyomi (2003), is reminiscent of the cult dance in Egbaland, which employs body politics to enrapture the audience. The body becomes a medium of non-verbal communication between the performers and the audience. The audience's attention is arrested and sustained with the negotiation of anatomical signs of the alluring dancers.

Oikelome notes that Afrobeat is never complete without the dance which is performed by the female dancers. The dance steps are fused to the performance of Afrobeat, which breathes energy into the performance of the music. The dance steps are notably energetic and enthralling, as it pulls the audience into the groove session with the accompaniment of the horns and percussive drums. More often than not, the dance steps reflected the essence and the ideology of the music, and the message is usually clear to the audience through the non-verbal demonstrations of movement. The lyrics of the songs are demonstrated by the mnemonics and paralinguistic elements of the band members and dancers.

> The movements of the dancers are uniform and graceful with expressions more at the hip of the body downwards. At other times, (depending on the intensity of the beat) we see the dancers kneeling down with both hands to the ground in synchronised movement. The movement is varied with some stamping on the floor with short steps that are ordered and legs moving to the pulse of the music. The singers on the other hand gently sway their body to the rhythm coming from the instruments in preparation for the cue from Felá who stands at the middle section of the stage where he directs the whole performance. The intensity of the music also deepens as Felá directs the band with his wave of hands and the swaying of his body and feet.[21]

The dance is encompassing in its communication with the musical texts, the rhythm of the song mixing with the intensity of the body movements. Fela was the master director in the choreographic performance being enacted, as he signaled with his horn for the next step which might have included the audience's participation in the performance. Music and body language are synchronized in a way that grips the attentive listener who catches the meaning of the song and language. Oikelome narrates the significance of the dance to Afrobeat in the songs "Zombie" and "Army Arrangement"; the robotic and chaotic activities of the military and security forces were imitated by the dancers. The performance of these songs provoked attacks on Fela and his commune, which often led to incarceration of the musician and his band members.

Oikelome sees the fusion of the dance steps and music as a performance that has several interpretations which may be studied separately or together as a script; the dance aesthetics enriched the visual aesthetics. The Kalakuta Queens, who were an addition to the band, became the dancers who with their physical appearances became an indispensable feature of the Afrobeat culture. The dancers-cum-backup singers were an integral part of the culture of the Afrobeat music. According to Ayobade (2016), the dancers represented the dialogue that was central to Fela's call-and-response style.[22] Their bodies were both a sensory and visual meta-commentary of the music genre's cultural politics. The Afrobeat genre thrived in the physical and artistic aesthetics of the performers dance. Their dance moves and steps were a culture shock to the Nigerian scenery. Ayobade traced the impacts of Fela's Queens as his dancers and their contribution to the culture of his musical genre. In "Open and Close" and "Jeun k'oku," Fela also gave instruction on how his audience can participate in the dance, which created a subculture of grooving to the throbbing music of the musical icon. The integration of dance and dancers into the performance of his music transformed the Afrobeat genre into a phenomenal culture.

"The Black President" and His Audience

Fela's audience played a crucial role in the performance of his Afrobeat music; as the growth is hinged on audience reception. Fela did not subscribe to other traditional forms of music that catered to and supported the class stratification system. His music was essentially for the marginalized and oppressed people who had no voice. Fela's music and Afrika Shrine became spaces for the re-imagination of a better Nigeria with socio economic emancipation from state-controlled economic dominance. Fela included the audience in the performance of his music; they sometimes interjected and egged him on when he began his yabis session, which was often organized for socio-political commentary. His music was a continuum of social, cultural and political discourses. There is a harmony between Fela and his audience; the audience is familiar with the themes and subject of Fela's music, and were sometimes at the center of his socio cultural criticism and commentary. There is usually a dialogue struck in between these musical performances where Fela asked his listeners questions to gauge their understanding of his discourses, while some of the members of the audience may respond to his musical meditations. His music served as an intoxicating brew for the social critic, unemployed youth and market woman, and an elixir for the oppressed, bruised, and alienated in society.

Afrika Shrine became both a mental and physical space where the masses could escape, even if only briefly, the realities of their society. In the Shrine, they could become anything they wanted—even free from their personal and collective demons. Afrika Shrine was an escapism metaphor where the proletariats (audience) could imagine the perfect egalitarian society.

Afrobeat and Traditional Instruments

The production of any kind of music requires some number of musical instruments; and they may come in different sizes and shapes depending on the type of music to be produced. Fela combined traditional African musical instruments with foreign instruments as a testament to the hybridization of both cultures. The percussive instruments, horns, and strings were imported instruments from the West while the African traditional instruments, including the congas, tap drum, wooden clappers, metal gong (*agogo*), and gourd rattle (*sèkèrè*), were indigenous. The drums highlighted the pulsating rhythm of the music while the metal gong captured the mysticism of the rhythm.

> The African traditional musical instruments sometimes create a scene similar to that of a traditional cult ritual possession found in his native Egba land. This is evident in Fela's use of percussion-dominated rhythms that bears the semblance of religious possession dances. The song starts with the playing of intricate African rhythms on the traditional musical instruments. The frenzy of the event is further heightened at the middle of the performance, with Felá playing the African drums with a higher intensity, followed by ecstatic shouts from the back-up singers.[23]

Afrobeat percussive and indigenous instruments were conspicuously simulating a cultic ambience. Fela kicked off his performances with a high intensity of these indigenous instruments as an introduction to the quasi-spiritual procession style which he cherished, as it denoted his cultural practice. The ingenuity of the Afrobeat musician to carve out a musical ensemble that re-echoed the African identity and ethos was a creative way to push his cultural nationalism ideology. The Western musical instruments used by Fela and his band members had been configured to suit the cultural ideas of the group. The horns were notably adorned with African cowries and shells, while the other instruments had designs, carvings, and inscriptions denoting African aesthetic qualities. As a testimonial of cultural-self representation, African drums were used by the Afrobeat genius to play his diverse folk music within the urban rhetoric of a sophisticated European musical canon.

> The bass drum rhythm has been identified by Steve Rhodes as Egbaesque, with its roots reminiscent of certain rhythms of the Oro cult. What is equally incontrovertible is the choice of most of his simple Egba chants such as "terekute"

> or "jorojarajoro," which are built on harmonics based on the pentatonic scale. It is a format Fela respects and does nor depart from in any fundamental sense.[24]

The drums were very important to Fela and his band to push for the incorporation of African rhythms and sounds, in the making of an eclectic sound that exuded the African ethos in the throbbing and pulsating music. The cultic chants often sung as the chorus in Fela's music were reputably a code of the purely male cult, Oro, which is not of public consumption. However, Fela deconstructed this spiritual and cultural hegemony to make it a site of social, political, and economic discourse. His preference for drums in his Afrobeat genre reflects his culture of creating a polyrhythmic music combining Yoruba chant words that are easily assimilated by both the singers and audience. Furthermore,

> he composed and sung his burgeoning Afrobeat songs, which his mother also encouraged him to do, in Yoruba or Nigerian Pidgin English to celebrate African linguistic creativity, and so they would be easily understood by non-Yoruba speaking Nigerians and Africans.[25]

Performance and Stage: Afrika Shrine and Spirituality

> The name of Fela's night club, Afrospot, where he performed live to his audience, was changed to Afrika Shrine and the interior decorated with the names and statues of Yoruba òrìsà (deities), such as Sàngó, Ògún, and Ifá. Furthermore, the interior of Afrika Shrine was adorned with symbols of African spirituality, rituals, pictures and names of renowned living and dead African personalities and ancestors to give it a sacred ambience and to celebrate African indigenous spirituality and excellence. His Afrika Shrine became a place where radical black nationalist, political, and cultural ideas about the sordid history of slavery, atrocities of colonialism and apartheid, horrors of racism in the U.S., good practices and beliefs in indigenous African knowledge systems, and corruption, social injustices, and mismanagement from the Nigerian government officials and most governments in Africa were discussed by the numerous clients who went there to entertain themselves and philosophize at the same time. Afrocentric books on different subject matters were also sold there.[26]

The use of masks and face paintings from the traditional chalk by Fela and his band members represented the mystic world of the celestial beings that were usually cloaked in mystery. The painting afforded Fela fellowship with the ancestors, playing the medium between the gods and the people. The celebration of fire in his performance is a substrate of Sango, the fire-breathing warlord, while his fixation with masks and chalk painting is reminiscent of the dramaturgy of the Egúngún mask. The sublimity of Fela's spirituality narrates the epoch of his culture, seasoned by the rich African ethological practice.

The Black Power salute was also a tradition of Fela's performance, denoted by the raising of a clenched fist. It is symbolic of a non-oral discourse of power in resident in the black people. Fela's music and performances propagated the Black Power salute as a greeting cipher amongst his followers.

The Hedonist Culture: Grooving and *Igbo*

One of the cultures of the Afrobeat composer was the "grooving" culture, which privileged the hedonistic lifestyle of Fela and his band members. The Indian hemp smoker sang about the legalization of marijuana and openly encouraged the production of this drug which he called "Nigerian Natural Grass" (NNG). This hedonistic lifestyle was one of the reasons the government and Fela had several clashes. The state believed that Fela and his band were enticing youth into a life of pleasure, a lifestyle deleterious to the stability of the nation.

Felagoro, a mixture of Indian hemp and herbs, sold at the Shrine became the "official" alcohol of the musician and his customers. The brew, made from illegal cannabis, was the drink for ushering Fela and his members into drug-induced realms of invincibility and temporary tranquility. The government saw this lifestyle as a threat to the social life of the state and hunted the Kalakuta Republic and Shrine to shut down the spread of this decadent culture rising at a precarious altitude. Even in death, Fela was buried with his signature giant-sized wrap of *igbo* to promote the culture of the Afrobeat icon.

Cultural Imperialism in Africa

"Colo-mentality" was a story of the disenchantment of the realization of Nigerian cultural independence. Fela gave examples of inauthentic cultural values: "Dey" wanted foreign things over African ones; in criminal court, judges donned the "white wig" court dress of their colonizer and "dey" used the British system of justice to judge and jail other Nigerians. Cultural values inevitably shaped the

> form of social institutions. Because colonial cultural values were maintained post-independence by the elite, Fela saw that the relationship between the individual and social institutions had not changed since colonialism's end. (Arogundade 2013, 9)[27]

Fela's preoccupation with the subversion of the colonial cultural hegemony in Africa was very profound in his music. The veneration of the African culture above acquired Western lifestyles is articulated in the song "Colonial mentality." "Colo-mentality" is the attitude of Africans toward Western cultural influences on the system of justice, dressing, products, and services.

> Dem tink say black no good
> Na foreign things them dey like
> No be so? (he be so)

Fela questions the justice system which was a replica of the European type; even from how the judge appears in the custom black robe and white wig with no difference to denote the African system of justice. In the song "Teacher Don't Teach Me Nonsense," Fela espoused that in other countries of the world, culture is the foundation of their political and educational systems:

> Who be government teacher? [*Who teaches the government?*]
> Culture and tradition
> Who be government teacher?
> Cu-ulture and tradition
> Cu-ulture and tradition
>
> Engi-land
> Italy
> Germany
> Na dem culture [*It is their culture*]
> For der Be teacher … [*that is the teacher over there*]

The problem Africa is experiencing, according to the Afrobeat legend, is the replication of Western ideas and epistemologies in Africa. He criticized the adoption of democracy above the primordial African systems of governance.

Linguistic imperialism

Fela recognized that one of the ways to be culturally independent from neocolonial cultural imperialism was to be linguistically African, and this can only be achievable through the promotion and use of African languages which are rich in linguistic aesthetics and reveal a deeper level of code signification and semiotic interpretations. In the song "Big Blind Country," the excessive dependence on English for communication and the government's position on Western products and systems of governance and administration was heavily criticized by Fela. Fela criticized Nigerians and Africans, and the rejection of both the elite and the proletariats of African products in the song "Buy Africa."

Se tiwa nio mio fe
Se tiwa nio mio ra
Se tiwa nio mio se
Tani ma ba wa je
Tani ma ba wa se
Kila se ma lowo l'Africa
Afi ti aba ra ti wa o e
Afi ti aba se ti wa o

Is it made here? I don't want
Is it made here? I won't buy
Is it made here? I won't use
Who will consume our things?
Who will help us do it?
How are we going to make money in Africa
Unless we buy our own things
Unless we do our own things

The purchase and appreciation of European products and goods over African ones espoused the colonial mentality of the inferiority of Africans. Fela noted that when these African products are neglected, the African nation is perpetually enslaved to the European nations whose products are pushing the indigenous ones to the periphery. The lyrics have a double interpretation; the first is thematically realized in the criticism of both the elite and plebeian people's preference for imported Western products which has cultural, political, and socio economic consequences on the continent. Secondly, the linguistic preference for Yoruba and Pidgin diction was a bold stride to subvert the notion of the elite sensibility of speaking the English language as a mark of both economic and educational growth. Fela advocated for the use of African languages in the educational system, governance, administration, and in public spaces.

> In culture, including language, Fela questioned the wisdom of the over adoption and excessive use of colonialist language(s) by governments in Africa. In "Big

> Blind Country" he satirically posited, "In... Nigeria, na Oyibo language we speak, Government style be say, Oyibo ting one better past," which literally translates as, "In Nigeria we prefer to speak the Whiteman's (European/non-African) language(s). The governments believe that European (Western/non-African) things are better." He was convinced that the wider development of African languages for reflecting, articulating, and finding solutions to Black/African problems was key to giving true and effective emancipation to the continent and people from colonialism and neocolonialism. It is because of this conviction that he adopted Yoruba in his songs. Pidgin English created by African creativity became a more convenient lingua franca to transmit his messages to the masses in Nigeria and the anglophone parts of the African diaspora.[28]

In order to fight such injustices, the songs also warned the Black masses to be watchful and grounded in their indigenous and cultural values such as of spirituality, humanism, communalism, and equality.[29] Fela concluded that a "colonized-mentality" influenced the African elite class to think that they were better than their uneducated fellow men, and maintain a superior attitude and social hierarchy. From their sophisticated contemporary houses and European and Arabic names, the elite used foreign things as a precedent for social stratification.[30] In his view, Nigeria would continue to remain in colonial shackles if current social relations perpetuated by colonial social stratification was sustained.

Conclusion

From the purview of ethnomusicologists' appraisal of the connection between music, culture, and the society, music is intrinsically embedded in the culture of a particular group of people. The sustenance of the posterity of any culture depends on the promotion of the art institution, which music belongs to. From this essay, the importance of music has been explicitly stated with lucid annotations from different critics and writers in the fields of anthropology, music, literary theory, and sociology.

This chapter also dwelled on the musical and cultural orientation of Fela Anikulapo-Kuti, drawing from sources that have explored his narratives and song texts. Fela and the culture of his music is precedent on his musical background, political interactions with members of the Black Power Movement and self-cultural realization. Fela was a musical legend whose Afrobeat and lifestyle produced a culture that venerated the liberation of self from the discourse of otherness. His music become a narrative and culture that will continue to attract scholarship due to its postmodern traits, and Afrobeat is a musical culture which will continue to produce diverse rhythms of interpretations.

11

Fela's Thoughts on African Indigenous Knowledge Systems

Introduction

Fela Anikulapo-Kuti ascended musical stardom courtesy of his distinct style of play, which came to life through the introduction of a new musical genre, Afrobeat. His retention of extreme popularity, however, was a product of many factors that combined to project his name into the public domain even long after he was long gone. Fela was a musician with the philosophy of Karl Marx rooted in his aversion to class division, which he believed always constitute threats to the progress of the defenseless masses. As a result of this social principle, he won for himself a cartel of detractors from the highest echelon of power in Nigerian society. His constant criticism of the government meant that he would always attract to himself a body of controversy, which frequently led to immense contradictions between him and the respective government. While governments are readily powerful and have numerous political wherewithal to deploy the state power at their disposal to contain, or more insidiously, silence him, the only weapon Fela had has was his music.

Interestingly, Fela was not a man who bows out when the steam was getting thicker. When the government went very extremely hard on him, Fela became unimaginably harder. The fact that a single individual, whose background was elitist, decided to engage the social class he belonged to for their continued misdemeanor gave him the popularity he had. Fela did not stop at engaging the government in his songs; on the contrary, he became very radical in his activism that was principally directed against them. In fact, the songs he produced were a demonstration of logical protest when intellectually analyzed as there are clear indications that each of them is an evolution from the previous methods and approaches that have refused to force the government into taking the right measures to right their wrongs. Beyond this, Fela's popularity was a product of other significant factors, chief of which was his emancipatory philosophy that is rooted in his interests in de-Europeanization, decolonization, and, therefore, the enthronement of Afrocentric cultures and beliefs. The addition of this to his music, and then lifestyle, increased his popularity across the continent and beyond in a short period. The echoes of freedom whose decibels are arguably incomparable in contemporary time make him continue to get the global attention and accolades that are accorded him in his posthumous existence.

Fela was an admirer of African identity. His radicalism was rooted in an honorable intellectualism. Although he was given all sorts of mnemonic identity that are descriptive of an uncouth individual, the fact that his musical productions are a deviation from the negative images carved for him by the governments, that were always aggressive against the calls for freedom, makes many people who now experience the gross consequences of irresponsible leadership to adore him and make him their most celebrated African musical icon. In the contemporary Nigerian, and by extension the African, music industry, very many musicians dream of being identified with the Afrobeat genre of music, and they gladly celebrate it when they eventually get the opportunity to be seen as one. It is done for a straightforward reason: whoever wins the accolades as an Afrobeat star stands that golden chance of taking on the image of Fela and the immense benefits attached to it. Above all, Fela's interests in African indigenous knowledge systems remain distinct, and these are identified in the rest of this chapter which x-rays his songs by bringing out the inherent element that makes them essentially Afrocentric.

Fela and the Affirmation of African Indigenous Knowledge Systems

Racism perforates every spectrum of African experiences right from the beginning of colonialism and slavery. Strangely, this continued into the postcolonial era because the seed of racial abuse and prejudices that has been planted at the inception of African-European contact had germinated and achieved its full maturity. The magnitude of racial discrimination can be summed up in the sweeping generalization by Europeans that Africans were people without any history of civilization. In what would be discovered eventually, making these wild claims was symbolic to the actualization of Europe's predatory agenda, for it created the moral atmosphere for the justification of the eventual exploitation disguised as a "civilization" project carried out on the blacks. The expansionists needed to declare their prospective preys incapable of independent thought generation and knowledge production to weaken their psychological resolve when dealing with them or to distract the attention of the world from their impending exploitative engagement as this would not only expose their morally weak human and economic philosophy but also showcase them as inherently insidious with zero interest in humanitarian equality or rights. Against this background, the Europeans began the subtle epistemic violence on Africans and their systems.

Even though the concept of knowledge itself is an amorphous one that switches according to the contexts or perception of individuals, Europeans were uncompromising in their intentions to discredit the African knowledge systems by distorting its existential realities. By concluding that the African people were deficient in generating knowledge despite their unimpaired ability to assess themselves and their environment, organize themselves into governing unity, and arrange their environment in ways that are not in contradictions to natural laws and realities, Europeans were especially interested in the subjugation and subduing the African minds so that their colonial systems would thrive, and their economic exploitation agenda would proceed unimpeded. It was for this reason that African knowledge systems, especially African science and technology, were adjudged nonexistent. Subtly and condescendingly, European declared a subtle war against the African ontological reality.

Whereas knowledge production emanates from the reflexive observation about one's environment, the formulation of corresponding hypothesis, and the evaluation of results derived after long-time assessment of natural laws and regulations, the denial of Africans their appropriate knowledge systems reeks of racist prejudices because the generation of knowledge is a relative exercise: what is accepted as knowledge in one group is the accumulation of their social experience and exposure, which naturally cannot be expected to follow the same dynamics that occur in a different context or environment. For a very long time, Africans were forced to deny their knowledge systems and hide their identity in order to celebrate Europe and its cultural achievements.

Growing up in the African colonial environment was, therefore, hard for all Africans, but their level or style of resistance was appropriately different. While some immediately upgraded their lifestyles to accommodate the prevalent subordination of their African identity and knowledge systems, it was a tough pill to swallow for some others who saw that action of acquiescence as an affront to their ontological existent. No sooner had this latter group noted that the meaning embedded in their identity was exposed to unbearable danger than they began to actively engage the colonizers for the reclamation of their African identity. The project of cultural deracination was therefore faced with maximum resistance, and the spark spread across different spectrum where experts in various fields began the process of decolonization with great enthusiasm. Without challenging the apparent misconceptions of the colonial system, African identity was at the risk of extinction, and this would come with very unimaginable consequences for those caught in the web of unfiltered assimilation of Western cultures and systems. Human experiences differ from geography to geography, and it was based on this that several cultural activists became antagonistic of the Europeans who they already discovered were out to uproot their identity entirely.

Among the academics, some anti-European activists deployed their intellectual properties to challenge the colonialists. Eminent scholars, from Kenneth Onwuka Dike, through Cheikh Anta Diop to Valentine Mudimbe, among others, were part of the revolutionary struggle that employed intellectual powers to confront the colonial Europeans. During this period, these African scholars and intellectuals produced many materials that were targeted at the correction of the erroneous assumptions that Africans had no recordable or recorded history. This misconception was challenged and uprooted, and this led to the gradual restoration of the lost African identity. Before long, there was the production of intellectual materials that documented African scientific and technological achievements, which opened the people to the expanse of their African history that was filled with significant greatness. The production of knowledge in this domain would, therefore, provide the needed energy to replicate similar engagement in other spectrums of African existence.

In the music domain, Fela became a force of nature with a strategy that was extensively anticolonial. He used his music very well to reject traces of cultural deracination that the Europeans had successfully planted. Fela became an icon of identity revolution as his music was loaded with emancipatory philosophy as that was principally necessary for Africans and their prospect of achieving real independence. It was evident that the continuation of European philosophy and identity would mean Africans would continue to get second-class treatment unless there were a revolutionary struggle and strategic actions to redirect the continent. Revolutionaries like Fela Anikulapo-Kuti would not be comfortable with the subordination of the African identity by the European colonizers. He, therefore, became an irrepressible voice in the project of decolonization.

The rejuvenation of African identity was pivotal for Africa's psychological independence because the instrument with which people fight for their growth and plan for their eventual greatness lies in their unadulterated mindset about themselves and about the world in which they are culturally programmed. Fela was an intelligent individual who was exposed to a trajectory of African history and Africa's greatness in astronomy and metaphysics, mathematics and logic, philosophy and governance, literature and culture, science, and technology.

On issues that exclusively bordered on African knowledge systems in medical science, healing, for example, Fela produced songs that accentuate the validity of the African ontological system to corroborate the argument that knowledge is relative. The application of it can be geographically specific. Fela says:

English man go say "pile" [*The English call it "piles"*]
Yoruba man go say "jedi-jedi" [*The Yoruba call it "jedi-jedi"*]
Doctors want to do something about it
Doctors must give you "capsule"
Chorus: No solution!
Doctor must give you "tablet" [*Doctor will prescribe tablets*]
Doctor must give you "mixture" [*Doctor will recommend potions*]
Injection must enter your nyash [*Your buttock must be injected*]
Doctor carry you go theater [*Or you go to the operating theater*]
him take de knife slice your nyash [*where your buttock will be sliced*]
I say solution dey for African medicine [*the solution is in African medicine*]
In one week jedi-jedi go start to run away [*Your piles is cured in a week!*]
We must learn to respect our African medicine
Our doctors must go to learn how to make research
but, but, dem go dey perambulate [*But they will be perambulating*]
and dem still dey, same same place [*while still remaining on the same spot*]
Chorus: Same same place!
See jedi [*See piles*]
Malaria
Gonorrhea
And syphilis
Dem no fit do dem [*They can't cure them*]
Me, I dey tell dem [*I keep telling them*]
Our medicine better [*Our medicine is better*]
They get name for am [*There is a name for it:*]
"herbal medicine"[1]

In another critical instance, and to further buttress Fela's recognition of Africa's epistemic difference, He sings:

T'o ba fe lo we omi l'o ma'lo
If you wan' go wash, na water you go use
T'o ba fe se'be omi l'o ma'lo
If you want cook soup, na water you go use
T'o ri ba n'gbona o omi l'ero re
If your head dey hot, na water go cool am
T'omo ba n'dagba omi l'o ma'lo
If your child dey grow, na water he go use
If water kill your child, na water you go use
T'omi ba p'omo e o omi na lo ma'lo
Ko s'ohun to'le se k'o ma lo'mi o
Nothing without water
Ko s'ohun to'le se k'o ma lo'mi o
Omi o l'ota o
Water, e not get enemy!
Omi o l'ota o
Water, e not get enemy!
Water, e not get enemy!

Here, Fela tracked the different symbolic and actual purposes water is used for. For one, it represents African deification of water as matter itself, which is the ultimate grand base for recycling. Based on the premise, some African cultures have deities allocated to water for the celebration of their essence. Within this context, therefore, there are beliefs that water has healing capacity. For Fela, it is not the case that water in itself constitutes the panacea for the myriad of medical challenges confronting Nigeria or the continent. Still, the knowledge of its usage can be very emancipatory. Everyone, regardless of culture or identity, uses water and therefore depends on it for utmost survival. Against this background, Africans usually invest in the phenomenon as one of their reliable sources of sociocultural welfare, which is equally useful for the necessary spiritual and physical healthcare.

From the above analysis, it becomes clear that Fela was greatly concerned about the weakening of African knowledge systems. In medicine, this is even more disturbing where even the contemporary African doctor is opposed to the indigenous knowledge of healing. The colonization of the African intellectual medical experts becomes obvious when one notices that the Western-trained expert recognizes only the European system of healing, even without having sufficient knowledge about the indigenous methods of healing. Like many Africans would bear witness, the method of healing in the Western domain is different from Africa, but what remains constant is that both systems produce results. Treatment of many ailments that require an intense medical process of healing, such as the use of "tablet," "capsules," or the "knife," has been effectively and alternatively in African long before the invasion of the continent by the colonial Europeans. Fela therefore staunchly acknowledged that the fixation on, and promulgation of, Western medicine is a consequence of Europe's hegemonic hold on the ontological and epistemic perception of Africans which denies them their place in human development.

As noted by Olaniyan, Fela concedes that the refusal to reduce African medicine solutions to the concrete proofs found in Western capsules and tablets is an affirmation of the non-standardization of the African method.[2] Although Fela realized that this was not still a convincing basis for subordinating African ontological system, he, however, implored African doctors, with sufficient knowledge and experience, to develop the African systems in ways that will not only make it respectable but also consciously instigate the process of decolonization of the African healing process that had been deliberately distorted or falsely represented in Western racial and medical narratives. Again, this is the demonstration of interest in African epistemic perception and existence. Here, Africans who are borderline European apologists are speedy to sarcastically condemn the African systems because of the projected limitations in its inability to achieve more comprehensive coverage, especially in cases of emergencies. What, however, usually eludes these European apologists is the commonality and collectivism of African knowledge systems.

Unlike the domain of Western medicine, where the knowledge of medical solutions and healing is known only to the select few who are certificated and certified in the field, medical knowledge is shared by virtually all units of African household. Thus, these people are readily accessible at times of emergencies, contrary to the lengthy process or the affordability of the Western medical system. Therefore, the proposition of Afrocentric medical culture is premised on the fact that it holds the potential for context-specific issues where there are solutions to problems facing African people in their environment. The proximity of Africans to nature and their environmental conservation philosophy makes it possible for them to lead a life that factor in that specificity. It is therefore understandable, to a large extent, why Fela became a disciple of Afrocentric cultures. As much as Africa's understanding of science and technology provides solutions for Africans, Fela understood that the quest for external validation of process is another demonstration of a slavish culture where Africans continually conceive themselves as being tied to the apron strings of the European system.

Fela and the Affirmation of African Onomastic Identity

To date, it remains an incontestable fact that Fela represents an embodiment of Africa values and virtues. His successes as an individual and as a music icon were mostly dependent on his ability to interpret hegemonic domination beyond what an average individual was capable of, and the decision to instigate revolutionary actions against instances of repression, oppression, and identity domination. The ideology of imperialism is all-encompassing, and to spot its influence in the different aspects of people's lives, one must be very conscious and clinically observant. From the evaluation of African cultural outlook after colonization and its comparison with what obtains in the precolonial time, one would conclude that the influence of European ideology remains massive and deep. African education, politics, economy, religion, culture, philosophy, and a host of others were severely affected because of the intense infusion of Western ideas into their knowledge systems. The combination of all these formulates what can be conveniently termed identity, and the effort of the predatory Europeans led to the identity struggles that they eventually were immersed in.

On the cultural spectrum, one of the elements of African cultures is the system of name-giving, which is essentially anthropomorphic when contrasted with the Western onomastic systems. Africans give names that reflect the circumstances around the birth of an individual; some names are adjudged naturally and are given to people to locate their identity; some names carry family identity. These realities, therefore, reinforce the usefulness of names in the African family. Fela was born into the Yoruba ethnic extraction. The influence of European philosophy and customs was already apparent in Fela's parents and their dealings. This therefore made it possible for him to be given a European name, and by extension, a European identity. The history of Fela's family shows the deep-rooted immersion in Western identity as his parents and grandparents experienced slavery, which led to their acceptance of Christianity as a religion. The fact that an individual is accidentally born into the Christian family, therefore, mandated them to carry European name, and identity, even against their wishes.

Fela was thus named in Christian tradition with an appendage of Europeanism, which points to his colonial indebtedness. Like many Africans birthed in the postcolonial world, bearing the names of their European erstwhile slave hegemons, this was normalized and considered as a necessary ritual in the process of existence. This normalization, therefore, has affected the people's resolve to protest the loose trace of enslavement, which they, however, have been conditioned to see from a different perspective. Names and naming in Africa are the instant summary of a human's essence. They provide brief, or sometimes expanded, summation about one's family, one's history, and, in some cases, one's spiritual trajectory. For this very reason, names mean entirely different things to Africans. However, this reality eludes so many postcolonial Africans, who now believe that there is nothing inherently special about answering to one's cultural names or means of identification. For this very reason, many Africans are disconnected from their indigenous identity and, in the process, become less significant in the general cultural scheme of thing. The realization that European names, and their imposition, was another consummate plan of getting the African cultural system systematically repressed led nonconformist individuals like Fela to rebuff the idea in preference for the indigenous identity system.

To understand the insistence of Fela on his Yoruba identity, we need to contextualize the context of his birth and the African ontological interpretation of such a phenomenon. Among the Yoruba, there is a general conception about *Abiku* as a spatial-spiritual phenomenon in the culture. The people understand Abiku as a spiritual enigma who choose to create panic in the household where they occasionally surface after transposition. As a spiritually ambiguous creature, Abiku children have attracted to themselves a social rejection because of their apparent predilection to visit tragic experience on their innocent parents. Because their parents, and by extension the society, become tired of their duplicitous existence, Abiku children are given a different form of onomastic identity to taunt them or to blackmail them into staying with their exhausted parents spiritually. Even though they enjoy similar social benefits with the other people in society, their names are signals to their spiritual trajectory in life. Interestingly, Fela Anikulapo-Kuti confessed to being one of these enigmatic children and therefore was bound to be identified as one. Strangely, however, the fact that his parents have been Christianized was going to deny him this cultural identity as his culture-bound identity was suppressed for, or more truthfully, substituted for, the Christian name, Ransome.[3]

The conferment of European naming identity, however, was a demonstration of loyalty to a colonial culture which his father, according to him, was anxious to reciprocate in line with his father before him. This is the way through which Africans retain the Western epistemology. They make frantic efforts to immerse their children in the culture of Europeans, who are, in turn, blackmailed to return the favor to their succeeding generation. Postcolonial Africans find it continuously very difficult to separate culture from religion. Their inability to establish the boundary between their religion and culture has been the predominant reason why the celebration of European cultures continued unchallenged on the continent. Although Fela, as a child, did not have any influence to determine his onomastic identity, he, however, was determined to correct the cultural anomaly in his later life when he understood the permutations of colonialism that informed Africans taking the identity of their erstwhile predators at the expense of their own. The influence of colonialism was so massive that Europeans, disguised as missionaries, took the position of naming their African converts, despite their relatively low understanding of the African ontological reality.

After realizing the effects of carrying European names and identity, Fela protested by giving himself a proper name that confirms his spiritually enigmatic status and subsequently exorcised the colonial name, Ransome, that functions as his middle name. A cultural revolutionary usually appears indifferent to the emotional displeasure of their oppressors when they intend to launch their resistance against them. This, therefore, was characteristic of Fela, who was disproportionately unaffected by the concerns of European apologists as he named himself following the cultural system of his ancestors. He called himself "Anikulapo," retaining the suffix -Kuti in the original family identity. First, the suffix, -Kuti, gives the summary of his status as an Abiku, the spiritually ambiguous child, but the addition—Anikulapo—summarizes Fela's resistance culture and his revolutionary dispositions. The name, Anikulapo, which loosely translates as "one that has control over death," reveals important information about Fela himself. To have declared himself as capable of controlling death suggests something more socially compelling. Fela has asserted himself as a force that cannot be intimidated or forced into silence because he has control over what most humans dread, death. For this very reason, he continued in his fearless engagement of the government and anyone who stood in the way of African emancipation.

It is, therefore, revealing that name means a lot to the African people than can be simplistically summarized in a couple of academic papers. We are provided the opportunity to understand that Fela was unpretentious about his reservations against the European names. He believed that the Europeanization agenda could be quickly promoted through the apportionment of names to the people. In an interview granted to Moore, Fela narrates the following:

> You know what that motherfucker named me? Hildegart! Yes, man. Hildegart! Oooooooh, man! That's how much I wasn't wanted. Me, who was supposed to come and talk about Blackism and Africanism, the plight of my people. Me, who was to try and do something to change that! Oh, man. I felt that name like a wound. My father had rejected me. And my mother too. The one whose very womb had born me. Bear the name of conquerors? Or reject this first arrival in the world? The orishas they heard me. And they spared me. Two weeks after my first birth, my soul left my body for the world of spirits. What can I say? I wasn't Hildegart! Shit, man! It wasn't for white man to give me name. So it's because of a name that I've already known death. Maybe that's why a name is a matter of life or death, more for me than anybody else. What can I say about parents who wanted this motherfucking compromise? You see, my grandfather was just a child when he was captured. He grew up in slavery. He didn't know his ancestors. He didn't even know his real African name. He had to accept Christianity. That's how he acquired Thomas. That's the name the missionaries of Sierra Leone imposed on him.[4]

Fela understood very convincingly that the retention of the European names was a continuation of colonialism, this time not by the Europeans themselves but by Africans. They already accepted European cultural identity at the detriment of their own. Fela established that African names are most especially reflective of the person's social and spiritual growth and can quickly signal to people what is the sociological importance of the individual generally. Thus, when he said that "Me, who was supposed to come and talk about Blackism and Africanism, the plight of my people," it was a way to prove his point about the cultural dissonance between European names and African identity. He demonstrated similar convictions in one of his tracks where he sarcastically explained the effects of colonialism on naming. The track titled "Lady" carefully expresses various contradictions in the contemporary Nigerian sociocultural landscape where the African women reject their Africanness for a European identity. In the song, Fela narrates the cultural dislocation involved in mis-naming:

> If you call am "woman," African woman no go 'gree
> [*If you call her a "woman," an African woman will not agree*]
> She go saaaay, she go say "I be lady o"
> [*She will say "I am a lady"*]
> Chorus: She go say "I be lady o!"
> She go say I no be "woman"
> [*She will say "I am not a woman"*]
> She go say market-woman na "woman"
> [*She will say a market woman is a "woman"*]
> I wan tell you about "LADY"
> [*I want to tell you about "lady"*]
> She go say she equal to man
> [*She says she is the equal of a man*]
> She go say im get power like man
> [*She says she is as powerful as a man*]
> She go say anything man do hinself fit do
> [*She says she can do anything a man can do*]
> …
> She go wan take cigar before anybody
> [*She wants to be the first to pick up the cigar to smoke*]
> She go wan make you open door for am
> [*She wants you to open doors for her*]

This song reveals, among other things, that naming is used as a social tool for the arrangement of the African society. At the risk of being insensitive to the controversy that is already ingrained in the gender scholarship in contemporary time, Fela made remarks about how the postcolonial African woman has become antagonistic to her African social identity, and this, therefore, has provoked the waves of controversy that is commonplace even till date. What Fela was pointing to, with this song, is the place of a name and the allocation of social ideas, duties, and identity to the people who carry the name. "African woman" is a generic name given to women with a particular social disposition and class mentality. And this does not preclude the fact that men are outside of this category. This does not fall within the domain of patriarchy-matriarchy dichotomy as both the men and women have their social responsibility, which can be spotted by the name given to them. Men and women mean different things, and this is reflected in the African ontological reality and existence.

However, the coming of the Europeans fundamentally reconfigured the perception of an "African" woman who now embraces the European identity to adopt all the sociocultural characteristics that come with its adoption. When Fela lamented the level at which African women imbibe the idea of cultural abandonment involved in substituting European names for their African identity, they, therefore, planted the seed of discord that eventually germinated into something more complex and nuanced. This is by no means an attempt to shift any blame on African women. Rather, the analysis is meant to demonstrate how the abandonment of the African name became detrimental to their collective growth. Therefore, the analogy of Fela concerning the adoption of "lady" as a European name was metaphorical, and it was aimed toward the delegitimization of the European identity for Afrocentric cultures and virtues. The affirmation of African onomastic culture is geared toward the emancipation of the people in all aspects of human endeavor.

Fela and the Affirmation of African Education System

Before the intrusion of the West into the African space, indigenous knowledge was the guiding principle for organizing the lives and societies of Africans. The nature of indigenous knowledge makes it possible for people to become part of the process of preservation and transmission as they can access the knowledge generated from their environment without struggling with it. Indigenous knowledge is mostly transmitted orally, and this provides the opportunity for the members of society to get actively involved in the process. Unlike the form of education that can be found in the West, the African indigenous education system portrays a systemic approach where knowledge is transmitted to people directly from their social contact with other members of the society. This, therefore, precludes the attainment of knowledge only in an enclosed structure like the school environment where other different complexities interfere with the medium of transmission. Contrary to the much-touted misinformation that the oral communication of the indigenous knowledge usually inhibits its preservation, the African ontological and epistemological database has existed for a very long period, and its maintenance before the coming of the Europeans into Africa defeat the argument that its survival is not plausible without codification.

Indigenous knowledge enhanced the production of African metallurgy, technology, astronomy, metaphysics, and mathematics. We can therefore say that the Europeanization of the African education system wreaked havoc on the African education system in ways that cannot be superficially observed. Knowledge and its medium of generation and transmission are inseparable. For this reason, the survival of the indigenous knowledge or otherwise in the system of education imposed by the West has been a recent subject of controversy as there are supporters and critics of the system handed down. The indigenous knowledge delineates the technical from the nontechnical, and separates the physical from nonphysical; its attainment is derived from the broad cultural spectrum of the society. Knowledge in the European structure takes a different dimension. African knowledge was, therefore, mostly practical. All spectrum of knowledge in the African ontological arrangement was something every individual could easily relate with and measure their progress because of the practicality. However, the education system of the Europeans has a very different persuasion as it was more theoretical than practical.

The introduction of this type of knowledge led to the displacement of the practical knowledge systems in place in African society. It had a profound impact on the indigenous knowledge systems of Africans as its sustainability in the newly introduced style was not guaranteed. Unlike when Africans could easily access knowledge within the society without particularly getting to any established structure as found in the Western education system, the new system was unsupportive of having such access to knowledge, and this came with profound consequences on the nature of knowledge and the content generally. Many of the custodians of these indigenous knowledge systems were isolated from the system, and this, therefore, began to influence the ways Africans were educated and the content of their education. Knowledge is naturally meant to be local, but the method of schooling imposed does not respect this reality.

From the knowledge of history to ecology, the knowledge of mathematics to astronomy, all these became vulnerable and were immediately at the risk of going into extinction. The installation of the European knowledge systems, therefore, opened another page in the knowledge transmission process in Africa as the early Europeans in the nineteenth century were consciously undertaking the arduous task of maligning the African ontological and epistemological system. African scientific frameworks and dynamics were touted as inferior, the knowledge of ecology was derided, and African knowledge of astronomy, healing, and metallurgy was considered superstitious. All these, therefore, became the background for the erosion of African systems, and it steadily evolved into what became the norm in the contemporary African world, part of what eventually instigated Fela's revolutionary spirit.

Therefore, the deliberate submission of certain Eurocentric scholars like David Hume, Trevor-Roper, Immanuel Kant, and a host of others was an attempt to re-engineer the psychology of the African people so that their knowledge of themselves would erode with time. All these constitute what Fela sums up when he implored the "[Eurocentric] teacher" not to "teach me nonsense" in one of his popular tracks. Although European knowledge systems, which, of course, were etched in their theoretical models, came with expansive branches of knowledge comparatively beyond what was obtained in pre colonial Africa, the results, however, were more disruptive than preventive. While the system can be innocent and inherently advantageous to the promotion of knowledge, generally, the Europeans who introduced it had an insidious mindset. For one, the system that was designed for the education of Africans was naturally ill-conceived. For example, the introduction of the system, despite the awareness of an indigenous one, contradicts the submission that they were genuinely interested in the liberation of the people. This is naturally because the transition of people from one system to the other usually comes with unimaginable consequences. In the case of Africans, for example, the acquisition of education through the newly introduced system did not in itself bring adverse outcomes to the people. However, the sudden change in the content that was transmitted to the people became the very beginning of deliberate miseducation of Africans.

In addition to this, the young Africans who ordinarily were expected to continue with the social responsibility of preserving the African cultures and traditions now found themselves in the European education system within which their indigenous knowledge systems had been delegitimized. Their instant instinctual response was to distance themselves from the African cultural heritage as they are now reconfigured to see nothing appealing and progressive in it. By this distancing, the survival of the African indigenous knowledge systems became very uncertain. The custodians of these systems experienced the harsh effects of the bitter campaigns against them. They were therefore forced to retreat into their closest, waiting for whatever posterity would make of the systems. As the colonizers gained more political power, they ensured that the African epistemology became more frustrated and challenged. More and more, the marginalization of the African education system ironically became an opportunity for the promulgation of the European structures and systems. Before long, many Africans had access only to the form of education offered to them by the available academic institutions, and this made it especially difficult to think of African education systems as viable alternative.

However, the wind of the revolution always blows regardless of the efforts made against it. There are many Africans who became resistant to the superstructure because they had realized that the education system imposed by the West does not reflect the sociocultural dynamics of the people. Apart from the fact that the education content, if locally generated, is usually useful when assimilated, education becomes more impactful if there are immense sociological co-referentiality between education and the society. The observation of these shortcomings inspired these people to undertake revolutionary actions and begin aggressive campaigns against the dominant and hegemonic Western structures. The flame of resistance, therefore, spread like wildfire, and Africa across different fields started to actively resist the system in place. Immediately after the Nigerian colonial experience, individuals like Fela began their anticolonial engagement to complement the efforts put in place in other fields, especially the intellectual. In what would register his contributions to the fight again Europeanization of the African education system, Fela Anikulapo-Kuti made the following remarks in "Perambulator":

As him go to school before
[*If he's ever been to school*]
Dem go teach am plenty things
[*They will teach him a lot of things*]
Dem go teach am plenty English
[*They will teach him plenty of English*]
Dem no go teach am nothing for himself
[*but nothing about himself*]
Dem go give am certificate
[*They will give him a certificate*]
to go carry file for office to be an office clerk
Dem go give am certificate
to make am certified slave
[*to make him a certified slave*]
Dem go give am certificate
to make am "civil servant"
[*to make him a "civil servant"*]
Dem go teach am for dem school
[*They will teach him at school*]
that Mungo Park discovered River Niger

I say when Mungo Park him reach River Niger
[*I say when Mungo Park reached River Niger*]
na African people
[*it was Africans*]
na dem show am de way
[*who showed him the way*]
you see him for dey perambulate
[*or else he would have been perambulating*]
and for still dey, same, same place
[*and still be on the same spot today*].

The above submission follows the understanding that the Europeans are only excessively hegemonic by their deliberate subversion of history in order to perpetuate their harmful agenda.

Fela's interrogation of the Western education system was to reveal its underlying imperialism in a real sense. Fela submits rather implicitly that the essence of European education structures was to frustrate the African knowledge economy and therefore superimpose the Western structures on that of the Africans. The allusion of miseducation that perforates the Western education system serves the contextual importance of delegitimizing it and, by implication, promoting African systems in its stead. While European education would teach Africans of essential things (and by this, Fela meant things essential to the Europeans), such as their language and history, while deliberately refusing to educate Africans about themselves, it is usually not efficient in proffering solutions to the existential challenges of Africans. However, no amount of enlightenment can an education system confer, if it denies the people the opportunity to know themselves, that is, their history. It was, therefore, part of the colonizing mission of Europeans that led to the ascription of greatness and discoveries of the African landscape to European figures like Mungo Park.

Just like what happened in other domains of knowledge generation in Africa, the decolonization project demanded that Africans began to celebrate their past, to contest the deliberate misinformation of the Europeans that led to their aggressive campaigns against the African indigenous systems. To contest the lies spread across different angles about the non-essentialization of the African project, there was an urgent need for the celebration of the African past, at least by their conviction of its greatness. The fact that Fela titled this track "Perambulator" reveals the thematic focus of his songs. His argument that the acquisition of Western education does not stop Africa from hovering around the same point means that the education the African has acquired is ineffective. It is against this background that he insisted that the promotion of the African education systems and structures would bring significant results for the continent. It would, for example, fast-track African development and also enhance the security of the indigenous values. Fela declared that contrary to the false assertions that Europeans gave Africans education or brought them civilization, the opposite was the case. He sings:

Oyinbo no teach us
[*the white did not teach us*]

Oyinbo no teach us nothing
[*the white taught us nothing*]

Chorus: Na we open dem eye!
[*we are the ones who civilized them!*]

Na we open dem eye

Na 500 years slavery cause am
[*Thanks to 500 years of slave labor*]

We teach dem how to do plenty things
[*We taught them plenty things*]

I say we teach dem plenty things]

No be me talk am
[*I am not making empty claims*]

Na books dey talk am
[*These are in authoritative books*]

No be de yeye books you dey read
[*Not the stupid books that you read*]

for de yeye schools for your town
[*in those stupid schools in your town*]

Those colonial schools from that London

I'm telling you now, na we open dem eye
[*I tell you we civilized them*]

The reconstruction of history by the Europeans receives maximum confrontation from the conclusion made by Fela in the above lyrics. Fela insisted that the retrieval of African values lies in the proper representation of African history to avoid further miseducation of Africans. It was therefore desirable that enlightened Africans reverse the case through self-education for the restoration of the values and identity of Africans to be complete. Like many African intellectuals are aware, Fela believed that contact with the European imperialists was the actual point where the history of Africans was rewritten for the good of the Europeans. Africans were established with a track record in different fields of study, and it was their well-developed knowledge systems that helped them build civilizations that contemporary researches now uncover. This Afrocentric nostalgia was to reveal the beauty of the African education system and therefore promote it for recognition in modern times. The style of education that enabled African knowledge to become domestic during the precolonial time was principally encouraged in the songs of Fela so that the people would become all very active in the development of their society using their socially acquired knowledge systems. What remains constant in the crusade of Afrocentric ideologues is the essentialization of the African systems as that would be the weapon against the Europeanization agenda, and would become very resistant to the domination of predatory civilizations.

Fela and the Validation of African Justice System

As one continues to study Fela using different intellectual models for analyzing his life and what he represented, one is exposed to the reality that the entire life of Fela Anikulapo-Kuti is strictly an embodiment of Afrocentric ideas and cultures that reverberate in his music. His unalloyed concentration and commitment to the crusade for the abolition of Eurocentric culture and systems in exchange for the Afrocentric values and beliefs is incomparable. Any fair inquiry into the traditional African values would reveal that the Europeanization agenda was unfair and deserved resistance. To prevent African ideas and identity from entirely getting mesmerized by the Europeans, there must arise specific Afrocentric nonconformists and scholars who would challenge the status quo, not minding the sometimes painful consequences to body and soul. From all indications, the political system introduced by the Europeans was against the social structure available in Africa. By seizing the political system, it became inevitable that other institutions in the society would be affected and reconfigured. One of such affected institutions is the justice system of Africans. Indigenous knowledge systems in African societies recognize a justice system that aligns with the philosophy of the people.

When there is a contravention of societal laws and regulations, there are existing social units that undertake the duty of dispensing justice by giving appropriate judgment. Unlike the Western legal system, which was particularly punitive, the African legal institution was both punitive and corrective. Africans understand that the violation of some established social orders should not automatically warrant severe disciplinary consequences as that would most essentially lay the foundation for extensive hostility instead of facilitating peaceful reconciliation. Subsequent upon this, societal bond and mutual understanding would be affected, and this would further destroy the collective philosophy of communalism upon which African societies stand. For this very reason, therefore, the African legal institution precludes excessive punitive measures, and it rather embraced a more philosophically balanced ideology of remedial and corrective actions. As such, crimes and other instances of violations are settled amicably by the vested authorities. However, there are people who, as a result of their immersion in the Western justice system and ideology, would contend the viability of this system and argue that it is incapable of enhancing representational justice in the contemporary global society.

Whereas there could be some measure of logic in such weak conclusions, a closer evaluation or observation of the inherent logic would reveal its self-destructive nature. Africans, historically, have existed for a very long period before the invasion of the continent by Europeans. Africans have therefore embraced such a justice system which allowed societal harmony. Crimes and violations of the social regulations have not skyrocketed out of proportion because individuals understood and respected the existing social justice system. Therefore, the hypothetical conclusion about the (un)tenability of such a phenomenon or system is modestly shambolic. In fact, to discountenance, the African social justice system reeks of unbridled superordination of the European values. The African justice system was exclusively designed to operate maximally for the people. People are corrected accordingly and implored to desist from acts of rebellion to the existing social norms by appealing to their moral and ideological sense. There are different means of reproach, and it was beneficial for the administration of African body politic and their social existence. Beyond what the European justice system has enabled in terms of bringing sanity to society, the African justice system was sufficiently compelling.

It therefore becomes fascinating when one understands that the irreversible commitment of Fela to the enthronement of indigenous knowledge systems and structures accounted for his defiance of the colonial laws, which undergird the legal systems of the postcolonial African states, and which he believed was too dysfunctional to help build an appropriate civilization for the African people. Even though the arrogant Europeans were convinced that their introduction of Western epistemic principles was for the development of the African countries and people, it comes as no surprise therefore that their subordination of the African ontological reality failed to yield promising results. Instead, their introduced systems were a facilitator of further morally delinquent behaviors. Before colonization, African societies had ways by which the moral fabric of the society was kept intact, and the course of justice served.

Each society assigns deities or other indexes of social principle as a way to prevent people from acting in contravention of the available social regulations. There are indigenous deities allocated to the observation of people who violate these values with a mutual understanding of the probable consequences. Leaders in this period were careful and mindful of their activities, which could jeopardize the collective and common interests of the people. Taboos were created to scare people away from antisocial behavior. This became so established that an individual who contravenes social laws or regulations already understands the consequences without being dragged to courts of law. Therefore, Fela contested, violated, and trampled upon what he saw as colonial laws as a measure of protest. According to him:

> There is the need for the introduction of the use of indigenous languages or mother tongues as the medium of instruction in our society since it is the starting point of the revolution, such that in our courts of law an accused person may have the opportunity of understanding the judicial process. Community courts need to be set up in order to administer petty complaints so as to reduce remanding citizens in detention for long periods without access to justice. An administration of justice that would be corrective rather than punitive should also be devised. If prisons must be built, then they should be such that would be psychologically curative.[5]

This submission demonstrates that Fela was very conscious in his protest against the European justice system. He believed that the African systems, even if guilty of some allegations made by critics, would function effectively in the evolution of a better society than the European ones. Like many Afrocentric scholars or activists, Fela did not contend that the system could be efficient and effective in the European environment. However, it stands no chance of facilitating the organized African society that Africans imagined. Therefore, putting an immediate stop to the promulgation of these European systems was necessary and vital. The Western justice system was so socially incompatible to the advancement of society that the Yoruba developed a saying about it: *A kii ti kootu de ka sore*, which loosely translates to "nobody establishes any friendship after a court trial," means that the Yoruba, for example, are at a loss about the justification for the establishment of a justice system that is exclusively punitive than corrective. They consider it perplexing that instead of creating an atmosphere that would enable people to celebrate each other even after factitious relationships, society is creating an avenue for further division.

Fela understood very correctly that the introduction of such systems would come with aggravating consequences on the molding of the desired African society. Rather than facilitate real growth, Africa and Africans would only be rotating at a spot without any sign of advancement. Using him as a specimen to evaluate the functionality of the European justice system, one realizes that the underlying negative consequences of the Western justice system are overwhelming. The dysfunctionality of the European justice system is evident in contemporary African social reality. The installed justice system does not, in any way, encourage actual justice as it is even complicit in subverting than enhancing it. Modern African society is full of instances of injustices. For an appropriate evaluation of the effectiveness of the European justice system, which people like Fela contested, one should immediately consider the various instances of infringement of the societal laws and regulations that are available today. Across many African countries, cases of inequity, power mismanagement, or blunt disregard for the established rules continue to grow at an exponential rate. Political injustices, moral ineptitude, and social breakdown of the African values are rife. While, quite ironically, all these manifestations seem to indirectly confirm the unsubstantiated hypothesis created by the Europeans that African people are sub humans, they were just the consequences of a legal system unfit for the African realities. There is not a single African country in contemporary time that is free of all these numerous shortcomings.

The social justice system introduced by the Europeans was predominantly meant to suppress the defenseless masses in favor of the aristocrats in the society. For example, the justice system was not as powerful as to challenge the colonialists when they were still in operation in all the African countries. It was this behavior that was inherited by the postcolonial Africans who therefore continued in the subversion of justice. In an interview by Carlos Moore, Fela indignantly lamented:

> You know how people are brought up thinking that jail is just for criminals, man. For people who've "gone against society ...." You know what I mean? That "law and order" shit. But after they put me in that cell with the people they call "criminals", I started thinking: "Who the fuck is Society? Who jails Society when it does horrors to people? Why Society does nothing to help beggars; to provide jobs and keep people from having to steal just to chop? Why don't Society fight against corruption, punish the powerful ...?" I concluded to myself: "Fuck society, man. It's unjust!" I knew I would be in jail for another ten years 'cause the shit they had on me carried ten motherfucking years, man. But still I said, "Fuck society, man .... Fuck! Fuck! Fuck iiiiiiiiit!!"[6]

Just like the inherited capitalism that was apparent in the European philosophy and economic policy, their social justice system is characterized by the principle of stratification and class delineation. The society that claims to pursue justice, under the European justice philosophy, flagrantly refuses to challenge the corrupt politicians, absolves influential people from whatever moral compromises and contradictions they are involved in, becomes indifferent to the poor whose poverty has forced them to take drastic existential measures, and turns a blind eye to the lack of distributive wealth caused by the influential and the affluent.

The understanding of all these, therefore, forced Fela to take an opposing stance against government and crusade for the installation of the African alternative justice system, which he believed stands a better chance of facilitating development beyond what the European system ensures. There is no better understanding of Fela's stance against the colonial legal system and its porosity than when he particularly implored his lawyer, Femi Falana, to prepare himself because he was about to violate colonial laws. Even when his lawyer protested this supposed impunity, Fela retorted that it was Falana's primary job to protect him, his client, even when there are apparent prevarications. According to Falana,

> Fela, for many of us, had a propensity for criminality—for many people. But here was a guy, Fela, who would tell you, Femi, *I wan commit this offense Ah, no nao*. And he would say, "No, I am going to breach the new colonial law, it's your business to defend me." And as far as Fela was concerned, he would do it. And one thing I found very interesting was that he would have done his own work, all you then needed to do as a lawyer was just to look for the law to back up his own defense—a defense that you cannot challenge in any court. And that was how Fela got away with a lot of violations of the legal system.[7]

Conclusion

Generally, Fela Anikulapo-Kuti remained one of the most consistent anti-establishment activists that Nigeria has ever produced in history. He consistently used his musical strength as a combative strategy to challenge oppressive state and irresponsible leadership. Whatever carried the image of state injustice, to the poor, to the less privileged, to any group in whatever form always attracted the attention of the activist, and he dedicated much of his energy to the charitable responsibility of taking charge of the situation of injustice. Considering the courage required to challenge a authoritarian leadership, one can only imagine the extent to which Fela wanted an egalitarian society that would be a better place for all. And, interestingly, the opportunity for this is constant in Nigerian, and by extension the African, situation. The role of the maverick played by Fela recommended his ascension into stardom, especially for those who gladly embraced him. Fela was loved, admired, and cherished even far beyond the confines of his cultural geography. He was a point of attraction to everyone regardless of their creed. The reason for this is simple: Fela spoke the minds of many.

Beyond his activism, however, Fela provided sufficient information and knowledge that beautifully placed him in the category of revolutionaries. This is because his musical productions are appropriate pointers to his cultural activism and identity reclamation agenda. His "Felasophy" is an acute demonstration of a conscious African who did not only understand the complex interplay of globalist politics in the subjugation of the African race and the subordination of their contributions to advancement generally; it is also a reminder of an irrepressible voice of emancipation and an energetic force that is un-subduable. One can only marvel at Fela's lifestyle for the synchronicity of his self-given name—Anikulapo-Kuti (a man in control of death)—his courageous undertakings, his rugged life patterns, and the complexities of his life struggles all appear like a coherently planned game because of their confounding unity. When Fela was not singing a protest song, his actions were interpretable as a protest. When Fela was not engaging the military for one act of brutality or the other, the man's silence was loaded with meaning. Whatever position Fela took up was considered with keen interest by both the African administrators and his dedicated audience.

12

Fela and Pan-Africanism

Introduction

The history of peoples of African descent from the turn of the twentieth century has essentially been one of struggles for self-assertion and recognition. This is singularly an outcome of Euro-American post-feudal (mercantilist) ideologies which saw to the expansion of its interests, beyond its shores, to regions of the global South, enslaving, conquering, subjugating, and forcing its diverse peoples and cultures into "geographical expressions," and creating "empires" for exploitative and commercial expediency. To facilitate and provide an ethical justification/basis for (both public opinion at home and for posterity sake) the dehumanizing conditions required for the success of its empire, this Euro-American colonizing interest resorted to misrepresentations of other people's culture and sociocultural fabrications to keep the colonized in a perpetual state of subservience.

In this colonizing agenda, the humanity of the peoples in the global South was questioned; their cultures were denied, and at best considered inferior and therefore in need of "salvation" and "civilization" or "enlightenment." This saw to the emergence and popularization of unfounded claims of the biological and cultural inferiority of Africans[1] by imperial "scientists" and "anthropologists." These claims crystallized into the colonialist theories of colonial historiography. The bogus claims of colonialist historiography were, however, not designed for the mollification of the morally conflicted Euro-American public alone as it served both in providing steady manpower to man opening colonial posts and as the psychological tool for brainwashing Africans into believing they were inferior. Many Africans at the end of colonial rule had been largely successfully convinced that the very things which made them African were uncivilized and inferior, using a colonialist vocabulary developed for that purpose.

The resultant Euro-American cultural hegemony in the various periods of its continuous expression served to entrench the colonial relationship between the colonizer and the colonized while also influencing the nature of African liberation struggles in colonial and postcolonial times. The liberation struggle was exemplified in the nature of the activities of both early pan-Africanist (pro-black) movements and nationalists who concluded that in "confronting such hubris … performing as modern political subjects involved not only making claims against the state but also claims to recognition as cultural producers."[2]

TsiTsi Ella Jaji, in *Africa in Stereo*, further retraces this cultural approach in black resistance to the turn-of-the-twentieth-century black South African intellectuals who "faced with colonial racism and land expropriation … saw cultural production not only as a means to demonstrate their sophistication as grounds for demanding full human rights but also as a way to raise collective consciousness for concrete political action."[3] In the 1930s, Negritude, as another early pan-African intellectual expression of African and black resistance, identified the consciousness and celebration of cultural and physical aspects of African heritage as a means to offset the bases of white racist discriminations. Leopold Sedar Senghor, one of the chief proponents of the Negritude movement, who was also famous for his artistic (poetry) expression, was known to have been influenced by his significant encounters with African diaspora writers and musicians. Popular black Atlantic music such as blues and Jazz "which Senghor saw in a broader context as an example par excellence of Negritude, his theory of black political aesthetics … was remarkably central to his formulation of the essential characteristics of *l'ame noire*, the black soul."[4]

This tradition of cultural assertion as a pan-African effort toward offsetting the bases of Euro-American cultural hegemony, and halting its consequences on Africa, has over the years taken Afro-cultural artistic forms such as painting, wood and ironwork, poetry, music, dance, and apparel. However, issues around solidarity, appeal, modernism, and the expanding role and reach of media have seen some reassessment in the illustration of the content of this African culture in a way that represents the times without losing its essential futures. This combination of the modern and traditional in music has produced jazz, the blues, reggae, and highlife. It is from these pan-African musical expressions that Fela Anikulapo-Kuti drew inspiration and synthesized his trademark sound, Afrobeat, which naturally represented another arm of the pan-African cultural (artistic) protest. This chapter aims to demonstrate, in some detail, the pan-African inspiration and character of Fela's message delivered in his iconic Afrobeat tunes.

The Ideas and Principles of Pan-Africanism

I learned that pan-Africanism was more than an idea. It was, rather, a movement, founded, some said, at the first African Congress held in the early 1900s. I discovered that the main purpose of the movement was to take back Africa from the clutches of evil men who had plundered and raped her—who had enslaved her people and uprooted them from family, from their homeland, from their cultural traditions, and brought them forcibly to other parts of the world, far away from their ancestral homes, and there to make them into sub-human chattels. In other words, to restore Africa to the Africans at home and abroad, the movement encouraged Africans to unite, to secure equal rights, self-government.[5]

A brief summary is necessary on the origins and motives of pan-Africanism.[6] Although this has been covered in the introduction and the preceding chapters, suffice it to synopsize here that the pan-African movement was a response to the debilitating outcome, for Africa, of the centuries-old relationship between Euro-America and Africa. The attention here is on how this lopsided relationship came to inspire the nature and principles of the pan-African struggle for African liberation. This can be traced to the devices deployed by the Euro-American beneficiaries in implementing and facilitating the unbalanced relationship with Africa.

In "Prospects and Challenges of Pan-Africanism,"[7] the authors highlight four major approaches to the study of pan-Africanism. The achievements of Africans and black people and the expression of black pride are the first articulation of pan-Africanism. The second concerns the back-to-Africa movement. The third involves the study of pan-Africanism as the harbinger of liberation from colonialism, slavery, and racism. The fourth approach involves the study of pan-Africanism as a movement for the political and economic integration and unification of Africa. The four identified approaches can hardly be discussed in isolation, especially considering how each contributed and is intricately linked to the others. However, for the purpose this chapter, such demarcations come in handy in establishing other less conspicuous links between pan-Africanism and some of its expressions. Here, it is the marriage of three of the focus (excluding the second) in these highlighted approaches in their promotion of the African cause through performance art that is demonstrated.

To exploit Africa effectively, Euro-American interests deemed it necessary to attack all that connects the African to Africa. Physically, Africans were removed from the continent and scattered around Europe, and America and the distinctive aspects of their appearance were twisted and explained as evidence of their station as "lesser" human beings. Psychologically, Africans were compelled to accept that their cultures, a way of life, were inferior and therefore had to be shunned and replaced with "superior" European cultures and traditions. It was on this and other bases[8] that Africans were refused basic civil rights and perceived as being unequal.

The cumulative effect this was to have on Africans is first evident in their alienation from one another. This is owed to the growing differences in historical experience and the newly assumed status accorded by place of birth and residence. Second, African people were increasingly being alienated from the contents of their traditions and cultures, such as their indigenous African ontology. This was evident in the growing abandonment of African names, etiquette, languages, among other cultural expressions. The very consciousness of Africans in their Africanness was being eroded and replaced with one that did not do much for their perception of self,[9] which is the ideal springboard from whence other individual and collective socioeconomic advancements can be launched.

What was generally observable was an increasing number of Africans stuck in a sort of cultural limbo, an incomplete state of existence where they were neither African enough nor were they fully accepted as Europeans or Americans. This situation was not limited to diaspora Africans as it was akin to African experiences on the continent. On the continent, the belief in the superiority of white culture had increasingly seen the people substituting aspects of the indigenous culture in alarming degrees. The extent of knowledge, adoption, and command of contents of European culture, such as language, apparel, and other aesthetic aspects, has come to symbolize modernity, class, and status in African societies. Hence, the more non-Western one appeared, the more backward and uncivilized one was considered to be, even in official circles.

Therefore, it comes as no surprise that the ideas and principles of pan-African struggle for African liberation were formulated to ensure black consciousness, African solidarity, equal rights, independence, and self-government. Pan-Africanism had at its core the belief that Africans the world over share not just a common descent but also a common destiny. For blacks to progress, the belief was that they must "unite to uplift."

Over the years, pan-African principles of black consciousness, equal rights, self-government, and independence have recorded successes in three notable phases that also mark its evolution. In the first phase, a number of black intellectual elites met to discuss ideas on how to confront white racism. The second was the period of nationalization of pan-Africanism when the political agitation shifted to a focus on the political independence of individual African territories. The third phase follows the official end of colonialism in Africa and the attempts at unification of Africans.[10]

Music and the Modern Expression of Pan-African Solidarity

Fundamentally, African traditional "belief holds that sound is evocative; that is, it has mystical powers which can be used to evoke psychic forces of tremendous potency ... on the other hand, music as an aspect of sound is regarded in traditional African societies as the immediate expression of Eros; a bridge between ideas and phenomena."[11] As a consequence, music in Africa is woven into every aspect of culture. There are songs for almost every occasion: there are specialized songs for work, those accompanying hunting, marriage, childbirth, and political activities; songs for warding off bad spirits, for praising the good ones, and for eulogizing the dead and the ancestors. These songs or music are mostly linked with a particular dance and are reserved for particular social contexts. They are performed either by individuals directly concerned or by professional musicians for compensation.

The music of Africa is as diverse as the cultures of its regions. And as with culture, they have had some (ancillary) influences on one another both internally and from external sources, depending on the cultures each of the regions were exposed to. Therefore, the regions closest to the Middle-Eastern Islamic world have elements of Muslim traditions—melody, notes, dances, and nasal intonations—in them, while those which remained unaffected by outside factors maintained and transferred their traditional contents for as long as they remained so. This is similar to the experience of African diaspora music, which is a representation of a mixture of traditional African elements with Euro-American influences and experiences that produced reggae, jazz, and the blues.

One of such traditional African music which has maintained its form and purpose is the Yoruba *Oriki*[12] of south-western Nigeria. The *Oriki* combined the creativity of poetry with that of music. In other words, "It is a special praise song, principally for a deity, a king or aristocrat, members of a royal family, descendants of a lineage, or members of a clan."[13] It is an ideal demonstration of functionality in African music. African traditional music is music with reason, music that serves the practical needs of society and not what Tejumola Olaniyan calls the "absolute music" of musicologists which is "instrumental music that is free of any overt connection or association with words."[14] This functionality is further demonstrated in traditional African war chants—a call to action, as in the famed "Ebo landing"[15] that saw captured Igbo slaves marching to their deaths by drowning instead of facing the prospect of life as slaves in the Americas.

In more recent times, music in Africa has been deployed both as a protest medium for demonstrating the existence of a rich African cultural heritage and also to encourage African solidarity by promoting African consciousness. The place of music in pan-Africanism can be traced from the awareness and respect for African art elicited by Afro-Caribbean and African American musicians and performers in the diaspora. From jazz to the blues, samba, calypso, and reggae, they have, in both their artistic feats and cultural messages, promoted the African cause. The successful expression of African artistic capacity represented by the popularity of black music (jazz and blues) influenced pan-African nationalists like Leopold S. Senghor and Kwame Nkrumah, who were a part of the African diaspora community at the time of its rise to prominence. This marked the first diaspora phase.

In the independence era, African musical acts like South African Hugh Masekela and Miriam Makeba, Ghanaian Guy Warren, and highlife originator E. T. Mensah, as well as the Senegalese *Star Band de Dakar* and the Baobab Orchestra, among others, were doing a lot to promote African culture through its music. A bit later on the scene was the West-Indian (Jamaican) reggae icon, Bob Nesta Marley, who also devoted most of his music career to black emancipation, epitomized in such famous titles as "Africa Unite," "Redemption Song," and "Buffalo Soldier" which "maps the routes of a Pan-African imaginary, inscribing both an attachment to the continent and … the originary displacement of the Middle Passage as well as intra-American migrations."[16] This formed part of the second nationalization phase.

The third phase, "end of colonialism and the attempts at unification of Africans," witnessed mass cultural organizations such as the state-sponsored 1966

World Festival of Negro Arts or *le Festival Mondial des Arts Negres* (FESMAN) in Dakar, Senegal, which "provided the first occasion for many black artists across the globe to participate in cultural Pan-Africanism on such grand scale."[17] This was followed by the Second World African Festival of Arts and Culture (FESTAC), which was held in Lagos, Nigeria, in 1977. This provided individual African artists to showcase their talents and in the same vein demonstrate the ingenuity, versatility, and beauty in African culture to the world.

Fela as a Product of Pan-Africanist Thought

The Nigeria of Fela's formative years (the 1940s) was already involved in the broader (global) agitation for the liberation of black people from racism and European domination. By 1923, Herbert Macaulay, grandson of a former freed slave, Reverend and intellectual Samuel Ajayi Crowder, established what became Nigeria's first political party, the Nigerian Democratic Party (NDP), which went on to win three Lagos seats in the Legislative Council. Following the 1930s, political activities in Nigeria became focused on ways to end British rule. The year 1934 saw the emergence of a national party, the Nigeria Youth Movement (NYM), whose members also won elections to the Legislative Council.

After 1940, political activities in Nigeria grew to include many more people. In 1944, a large percentage of the political groups became united under the National Council of Nigeria and the Cameroons (NCNC), led by Herbert Macaulay and Nnamdi Azikiwe. These united groups rallied diverse forces against continuous British rule. These forces included African Second World War veterans, Western-educated people, the media, farmers, market women, and the restless youths. Incidentally, Mrs. Funmilayo Ransome-Kuti, Fela's mother, was also actively involved in this and another aspect of the protest against British colonial rule. Described as the "Lioness of Lisabi," she led the Abeokuta Women's Union to agitate for women's rights and representation in local administration.[18]

Fela's parents were very active nationalists on the local and international scene. His mother, Mrs. Funmilayo Ransome-Kuti, combined her women's activism with an active membership in the NCNC. In her involvement with women activism, she rose to the position of vice president of the Women's International Democratic Federation (WIDF).[19] Her pan-African outlook got her into the circles of the pan-Africanist icon Kwame Nkrumah, whom she later introduced her son Fela to. Fela's father, Reverend Israel Oludotun Ransome-Kuti, was, among other professional preoccupations, an educationist and pioneer chairman of the Nigerian Union of Teachers established in July 1931. He was also an activist and pan-Africanist in his own right.

Therefore, it can be said that young Fela grew up around an atmosphere of revolt against injustice and unfairness. The direct involvement of members of his immediate family ensured that he was not too far away from the influence of such ideals. The extent of the influence of their activities as activists, nationalists, and pan-Africanists on the choice of his musical direction cannot be precisely quantified. There is, however, no question of its role in making him more receptive to such ideas.[20] That and his eventual exposure to the plights of the black person, both at home in Lagos and especially abroad in Europe and America (with the black power movement), where such racial contrast was sharpest, enhanced his propensity to walk the path he chose, the path of pan-Africanism and black liberation.

Fela, even with his activist background, did not immediately embrace the principle of political struggle. It wasn't until his encounter with an African American activist with ties to the Black Panther Party, Sandra Smith, in 1968 that Fela introduced Black Nationalism; its African American Black Power variant,[21] into his music and therefore setting up the ideological base for his Afrobeat. Before this time all Fela was interested in doing music for was to, in his own words, "play, to make bread, to make myself a great artist."[22] But the encounter with Sandra pushed Fela over the cliff. However, it might be overly presumptuous to ascribe Fela's emergence as an Afrobeat-black-rights crusader solely to his encounter with Sandra Smith, notwithstanding the credit Fela gives her for his eureka moment. Fela, as earlier demonstrated, had activist roots, given his parents' (especially his mother's) political predilections. The late Afrobeat icon himself recalls how much pride he derived from their strong sense of obligation to ensuring justice and fairness and in his mother's political victories. To present a better-structured argument, Tejumola Olaniyan presents the three (chronological) stages in the evolution of the ideological discourse in Afrobeat to illustrate other aspects of Fela's multidimensional musical evolution and how these reflect other silent but salient influences that produced the icon. These three distinct stages depict Fela as "the apolitical avant-pop hustler, the afrobeat social reformer, and the afrobeat political activist."[23]

The first phase covers an entire decade beginning from 1958 when Fela went to London for a five-year study period at Trinity College, where he studied music. Here, he is immersed in London's jazz scene, an experience which, combined with an earlier highlife exposure in Lagos, produced his idea of highlife jazz. The second ideological phase commenced with Fela's ten-month sojourn in the United States. His encounter with Black Panther activism in Sandra Smith brought about changes in his musical and ideological trajectories in the direction of black nationalism, pan-Africanism, and Afrocentrism. Upon his return, Fela's musical focus shifted to social activism and cultural nationalism.[24] The third and last phase of Fela's ideological evolutions began in 1974, when he had his first major run-in with state security agents and was jailed alongside other occupants of his Surulere residence for the possession of marijuana. This incident launched a full-fledged anti-establishment rhetoric into Fela's music and earned him the title of "afrobeat political activist."[25]

Olaniyan also raises a critical ecological factor in Fela's emergence. Lagos, unlike Fela's birthplace Abeokuta—a sleepy town about fifty miles north of it—was a postcolonial metropolis which at the time of Fela's arrival was a hot-bed of political activity; the city was at the center of Nigeria's decolonization struggle. This was, however, not the vibe young Fela responded to. "It was that other most significant phenomenon, primarily cultural, which ensnared Fela: the glitzy highlife music scene."[26] If the Lagos before Fela's five-year college period in England introduced him to highlife, it was the rejection of his musical hybrid—the combination of his newly acquired taste in modern jazz and highlife—by Lagos after his return in 1963 which forced Fela to embark on the tour of America in 1969, when he met Sandra Smith Isadora. The view here is that, without the Lagos influence, Fela might still have been a musician, but a completely different type.

Hence, Fela, the highlife and jazz enthusiast, black nationalism and pan-African advocate, afrobeat pioneer, moralist, political and cultural nationalist, is the product of a series of minor and major defining moments in his individual historical development. These range from the nature of his upbringing to the various other experiences and encounters in his adult professional life. And no one incident can lay full claim to Fela's emergence as the afrobeat political activist he became. However, the most notable influence to Fela's musical redirection toward black nationalist pan-African thought remains Sandra Isadora Smith.

Fela and the Pan-African Message

I came back home with the intent to change the whole system. I didn't know I was going to have … such horrors! I didn't know they were going to give me such opposition because of my new Africanism.[27]

In the above quote, Fela recounts the unexpected resistance he encountered on his return from his famous trip to America. In this account, he uses the third-person plural "they" for those who objected and resisted his attempts to spread his newly found ideology of "Africanism." It is partly in determining who "they" in Fela's account are, and why "they" felt the need to muzzle him that we can fully appreciate the (political) message and aspirations of his music. On the other hand is the cultural (unlikely political) significance embedded in his message demonstrated in his "countercultural lifestyle: the nature of the household he ran, the valorization of sexual excess and permissiveness, the culture of marijuana use, and the general flagrant flouting of conventional morality."[28] Therefore, a proper contextualization becomes necessary in developing the right perspective into Fela's message.

The Africa that Fela returned to in 1970 was still grappling with political upheavals: struggling young democracies bedeviled by military interventionism, tyrants consolidating power, and a few countries still undergoing anticolonial agitations. Nigeria itself had just emerged from a brutal three-year civil war (1967–70). The military under Colonel Yakubu Gowon was in charge of a Nigeria undergoing massive revenue influx owing to an oil boom. However, due largely to mismanagement and corruption, the regime failed to capitalize on the opportunity to steer the country toward a path of infrastructural development and economic prosperity. Economic instability was one chief reason put forward by the General Murtala Mohammed-led regime for the bloodless ousting of the incumbent on 30th, July 1975. Another regime change was effected through an assassination carried out a mere six months later (February 13, 1976) by rival factions in a politically divided Nigerian army which saw to the ascension of Lieutenant General Olusegun Obasanjo, the second in command to the slain Head of State. It was General Obasanjo who lifted the twelve-year ban on politics on September 21, 1978, and allowed for a democratic election to be held the following year. Of the fifty new parties formed, only five were approved and registered by the then Federal Electoral Commission (FEDECO). The election produced, albeit with a lot of controversies, Alhaji Shehu Shagari of the National

Party of Nigeria (NPN) as winner and president, ushering in the Second Republic on October 1, 1979.[29]

The elections of 1979 are especially significant in understanding what Fela stood for. This is because, for that election, Fela's party, Movement of the People (MOP), formed the previous year with the intent of contesting the elections, drew up its aims and objectives in a party manifesto that read:

- To fight relentlessly to achieve and maintain the second Independence of the People of Nigeria
- To serve as the positive political vanguard for removing all forms of oppression and for the establishment of a democratic government
- To secure and maintain the complete unity of all the nineteen federal states as one people
- To undertake and encourage cultural research into our traditional heritage, and build up in the people of Nigeria the pride of being African
- To propagate as much as possible in Nigeria the principles of Nkrumahism which are all necessary and relevant to speedy and pragmatic national development
- To support the demand for a West Africa Economic System and an African Central Monetary system and of pan-Africanism by promoting the unity of action among the peoples of Africa and African descent
- To fight continuously to establish the pride of African personality and the pride of all people of African descent[30]

From the seven items listed on the MOP party manifesto, it can be observed that three had national expressions, while the remaining four reflect pan-African objectives. The extent of the importance of this manifesto in itself can be argued to be in its relevance as a document that summarizes the objectives of Fela's musical activism. This forms the basis of an argument that can be effectively delivered based on Fela's reputation as a mere "rabble-rousing radical frequently engaged in charged confrontation with the government"[31] which was already well established by 1978.

In the remaining period of Fela's career and life, from 1979 to 1997, not much changed. Instead, things can be argued to have gotten worse. The Second Republic simply inherited and ran with the same politicians and problems. Comprised mostly of First Republic politicians, it was only a matter of recycling old campaign platforms and renewing old allegiances, and it was back to business as usual. Consequently, the subsequent elections of 1983 became controversial because it was flawed by extensive irregularities. The administration of Alhaji Shehu Shagari was characterized by highly powered corruption, economic regression, and infrastructural decay, and the Second Republic was terminated on December 31, 1983, by a military coup that brought General Muhammadu Buhari into power as Head of State, marking the start of fifteen years of successive military regimes.[32] General Buhari was ousted by another military coup organized by Major General Ibrahim Babangida, who left power for General Sani Abacha in 1993. Together, these regimes accounted for some of the worst years of Nigeria's development. During this period, those in the position of power stole from the polity to enrich themselves and instituted economic programs such as the IMF-induced Structural Adjustment Program (SAP), which forced currency devaluation and other austerity measures imposed on the masses with the guise of pursuing social and economic reforms sliding the country further down the path of economic decline. It was a period in Nigeria's history generally marked by corruption, military brutality, social rot, and political disorder.[33]

It is in response to such backdrop that Fela conceived and delivered his version of Africanism (Afrocentrism and blackism), or what his fans called "Felasophy." Felasophy is captured quite aptly by O. A. Dosumu on his expansion on the "ecology of ideologies," as an "outline of the doctrines of Black Nationalism, Lower Class Partisanship and Libertism."[34] In his rationale, Afrobeat is rooted in "Black Power" as an African American variant of black Nationalism, which, from a global perspective, combines pan-Africanism and Afrocentrism. Hence, as related movements that are somewhat distinct historically, they yet subscribe to the same principles of black unity, pride, and political self-determination that lie at the heart of global Black Nationalist movements. Afrocentrism insists that we draw on the African cultural system as the framework with which to center Africa "in articulating knowledge of(or about) African people."[35] In other words, as Serequeberhan clarifies, Afrocentrism attempts to "uncover and use codes, paradigms, symbols, motifs, myths, and circles of discussion that reinforce the centrality of African ideals and values as a valid frame of reference for acquiring and examining data."[36] In simple terms, therefore, pan-Africanism has at its core an Afrocentric vision that denotes Africa as the center of all pan-Africanist dealings, especially with regard to knowledge and knowledge production. Pan-Africanism unites all Africans and people of African descent around an ideological framework that displaces imperialism and Eurocentric decentering of Africa. It is in this way that Fela unites Afrocentrism and a pan-Africanism through his ideological vocality.

Fela's profound commitment to anti-establishment action, evidenced in Afrobeat's provocative verbal attacks on the insensitive postcolonial state, its beneficiaries, and foreign sponsors, is a reflection of his belief in and struggle toward more equal social and political relations. The political and bourgeoisie classes, both foreign and local—the corrupt politicians, "businessmen," military officers in government positions, and foreign enablers who stand to benefit from and who defend the status quo—make up the unspecified "they" Fela refers to in the statement when recounting the opposition he faced on his return from America in 1970. And collectively, "they" all bore the brunt of Fela's criticisms.[37]

In his capacity as a radical pedagogue, Fela published newspaper articles (under the column "The Chief Priest Says"), delivered university lectures, and also held ideological sessions with core fans. But his main pedagogical tool remained music. With songs like "Teacher Don't Teach Me None-Sense," among others, Fela was able to communicate his Africanism through musical renderings of the Western colonial agenda in Africa and its continued after-effects in the postcolonial era. And his music explained how colonization has brought about the disregard for African value systems and gradual exchanging of these values with subverted adaptations of Western ones. There is also the message that the oppressors never left even with independence but switched places with the new elite and dictators who together in league carry out a reign of oppression.

Conclusion

The movement for the liberation of Africans has had several expressions and titles over time. They are distinctive owing to the difference in historical periods, geographical locations, and the prevailing conditions/thought in their time of expression. These movements—Negritude, pan-Africanism, black Nationalism (black Power), Africanism, and Afrocentrism—have, however, maintained one thing in common: the call for equality and self-determination for Africans. Fela, as a product of more recent expressions of this black liberation movement, was influenced not just through direct contact with elements of its radical wing but also through the achievements and aspirations of others who had taken up the challenge at great personal costs and sacrifice and distinguished themselves.

For several reasons, none of them any less important, Fela was able to transform from the average mainstream musician he was for a time, into a musical political activist, setting himself against a corrupt and vindictive system/establishment, protesting loudly, and calling attention to widespread misdeeds. On the continental and global stages, he strove to enlighten his audience about the existing conspiracy between the West and a class of African elites to perpetuate a system of exploitation with the African masses at the receiving end, in a state of constant wretchedness. For the Nigerian masses he meant also to provide perspective, to rouse their consciousness to the reality of the scheme of things and their place in it. Even in his personal life, he lived his message, embarking on a countercultural display of defiance to adopted European norms and traditions. And in all, he was able to carve a niche for himself as musician's musician, developing his art, creating his unique sound-raising it up to world recognition, and into a legacy that lasts even after his death.

13

Blackism: Fela's Political Philosophy

Politics is found within the dynamics of power relations between the state and its subjects, how the state allocates the benefits and burdens derived from being a legitimate member of the political community. In Harold Lasswell's memorable conception, politics is "who gets what, when and how." Political philosophy investigates these dynamics between the government and the governed, investigating the kinds of power arrangements that enable humans live a good and meaningful life. Ultimately, the political philosopher critically inquires about the nature of good and bad governments, as well as the conditions determining the likelihood of either type.

From Aristotle to Machiavelli, these questions about the foundation for organizing good government are at the fore of any investigation into the nature of human society and the human person, but the differences between Aristotle and Machiavelli are not just in terms of temporal distance. Their political philosophies are marked by a qualitative difference in the understanding of the meaning of politics and the responsibilities of the state, and there is a marked difference in the language of politics that separates Aristotle from Machiavelli. Study of politics in the age of Aristotle was concerned with the understanding and unraveling of politics as the art of good government, what the government does to preserve the fundamental essence of the common good in a way that provides a quality life for the citizens. On the other hand, in Machiavelli's political discourse, there is a radical transformation from this Aristotelian sense of politics into conceiving of politics as raison d'état—reason of state. For him, the ruler seeks to preserve the sanctity of the state's territory while also achieving the domination of the people. In this context, politics empowers the state with the monopoly of the use of coercion.

The colonial state was founded on this latter understanding of politics as the deployment of brute force, the adroit projection of power, and coercion to achieve its interests. The essential tactic of colonialism was to undermine the cultural vitality of the colonized through the use of force to ensure their domination and ability to extract resources. And the colonialists ensured that this happened, to various extents, on the African continent. The African colonial governments fostered a regime of brutality, a specific set of relations of subjection that Mbembe calls the *commandement*.[1] This is a unique idea of state sovereignty that is established through violence, designed to expropriate the colonies and dehumanize the colonized. When colonialism wrapped up its formal presence in Africa, the most significant legacy left behind was an architecture of state violence that was the instrument for colonial law enforcement. In the Nigeria of the 1960s and 1970s, the military establishment stood as the custodian of that retained law-and-order model of the state, accentuated by Nigeria's unraveling development crisis that made it difficult for the military to be at the forefront of any policy initiatives aimed at good governance. While the Nigerian state was situated at the "commanding height" of the oil-driven economy, it was a state that was not conditioned by any ideological objectives that would spell out the relationship between economic means and noneconomic social ends translating into a good life for Nigerians.

Fela's political significance lies in the fact that he represented an acute ideological challenge to the Nigerian state. What Tejumola Olaniyan calls "political Afrobeat"[2] positioned Fela within the critical interstice between the government and the governed as an irritating gadfly that continually stung the Nigerian state into self-conscious awareness about its ideological poverty with regards to the Nigerian masses. By the time Fela had fully taken on his political persona and had appropriately primed his saxophone and the other members of his angry ensemble to ditch out a "dissident tune," the Nigerian postcolonial state was no longer safe to revel in its banality. The rebel had arrived, and this was a rebel with a cause and a mentality armed with grievances! Fela's understanding of freedom had now come full circle, since he had managed to escape from the stern environment of his parents at Abeokuta. The disciplinary regime of the Ransome-Kuti family only succeeded in implanting in the young Fela the means of escape into his own understanding of a space of individual fulfillment. Fela interpreted this space as the satisfaction of his banal desires—drinking, partying, singing, and being about town. This understanding changed when he left for London and had cause to confront the nature of his musical persona. Freedom became a crucial urgency to transform his existential condition into one of meaning. His Lagos and American experiences constituted another phase in this unraveling of the understanding of freedom, when freedom translated into ideological awareness of who he was. This was a critical point in Fela's trajectory of transformation and prepared him for the task of confronting and engaging the Nigerian postcolonial state over the space of freedom for all Nigerians.

Within that contested space, the Nigerian government constrained the yearnings and aspirations of his citizens, limiting their capabilities to become meaningful beings. And this contestation was constructed this way because the juridical freedom that the Nigerian state won at independence, together with the questionable legacy of colonialism, structured the state to deny its citizens room for being and becoming. The Nigerian state had become the heir to the constitutional impunity which defined colonial sovereignty. Within this context, post-independence leadership in Nigeria circumvented the mechanisms that ought to lead to good governance, through the privatization of the commonweal. The gradual prebendalization of public office and resources had reached a height during the Second Republic. The idea of the prebendal state in Nigeria is a unique theory floated by Richard Joseph. In his seminal book, *Democracy and Prebendal Politics in Nigeria*, published in 1987, Joseph provided cogent insights about the nature of the Nigerian state and the political behavior of the Nigerian political elite that could shed further light on the fundamental essence of Nigeria's crippling underdevelopment. Joseph's fundamental question is: "What is the nature of the fundamental processes of Nigerian political life?" According to him, the Nigerian political elites have transformed the Nigerian state and its resources into a clientelist dynamics that enable them to share state resources to their supporters within a system of corrupt entitlement. State offices and positions become *prebends* which public officials and politicians appropriate illegally and deploy not only to further personal benefits but also for other extra-democratic uses.[3]

This comes with the consequence that public office holders consistently work against the democratic will of the citizens in their bid to hold on to political power. Furthermore, it takes little reflection to immediately see the implication this would have on Nigeria's development profile. Essentially, this implies, according to Acemoglu and Robinson, that the politics of the political elites favors extractive structures rather than democratic institutions that could facilitate development and prosperity.[4] Richard Joseph's case study is the Nigeria's Second Republic (1979–83). However, the methodological power of this theory enables us to apply it even beyond this period. Prebendalism allows state actors to undermine democratic imperatives by cutting citizens off from the deployment of resources for infrastructural and developmental purposes. The earlier reference to the opacity of Nigeria's oil industry constitutes a particular case of the Nigerian state acting on behalf of itself. Another example is the ecological degradation of the Niger Delta, which demonstrates how revenues accruing to the state can worsen the condition of its citizens.

Within that contested space, the Nigerian government constrained the yearnings and aspirations of his citizens, limiting their capabilities to become meaningful beings. And this contestation was constructed this way because the juridical freedom that the Nigerian state won at independence, together with the questionable legacy of colonialism, structured the state to deny its citizens room for being and becoming. The Nigerian state had become the heir to the constitutional impunity which defined colonial sovereignty. Within this context, post-independence leadership in Nigeria circumvented the mechanisms that ought to lead to good governance, through the privatization of the commonwealth. The army of the poor, the destitute, the disenfranchised, and the dispossessed were confronted with the choice of either engaging with the state or exiting from it. Most chose the latter option. Resignation was particularly desirable because the state actively cultivated it to take the stress of governance off its back. While some have dropped out in the form of migrating out of the shadow of the Nigerian state, the majority of Nigerians just drop out in place by burrowing out of its reach.[5] Fela's political persona and the nature of Afrobeat ensured that he could not have delinked from the Nigerian state via abject resignation. What Foltz calls "freedom within the African state" opens a space of contestation for the discourse on the meaning and practice of freedom. Thus, "Where not savagely repressed, myriad organizations belonging to the broad category of 'civil society' stepped to the fore, much as civil organizations ranging from syncretist churches to trade unions to ethnic-based 'friendly associations' had helped provide the social infrastructure for nationalist independence movements some 40 years earlier."[6]

Fela was not civil society, even if there is a loose sense of that term that could capture his involvement with the activist-others within this space of contestation. Fela was Fela. His engagement with the Nigerian state was not just at the nodal point of some set of political principles. Rather, he came to the game of political contestation from a deep ideological perspective that combined the philosophical elements of pan-Africanism, spiritualism, and social justice, which he called "Blackism." In Fela's complicated performative practices, blackism is a multilayered array of philosophical dynamics connecting past and present, culture and politics, and modernity and tradition in a complex continuum of relations and interactions that Fela intended to deploy for the understanding of social change and cultural renaissance not only in Nigeria but across the African continent. We can therefore begin to understand the cultural and political significance of his quartet of contemporary black divinities displayed at the Shrine—Malcolm X, Funmilayo Ransome-Kuti, Patrice Lumumba, and Kwame Nkrumah—formidably supported at the supernatural level by Èṣù (trickster god), Ògún (god of creativity and metallurgy), Ṣàngó (god of thunder and progenitor of egúngún performance), and eré ìbéjì (portrait of twins and symbol of fertility). Similarly, we are equally familiar with the pan-African template within which Afrobeat emerged: the constant lyrical references to Africanist and philosophical themes such as social justice, African dignity, African identity/personality, black/African consciousness, the African past, freedom for the continent, and so on that suffuse Fela's songs.

Malcolm X and Kwame Nkrumah constitute two significant ideological pivots in Fela's understanding of blackism. Nkrumah had loomed large in Fela's consciousness ever since his mother introduced to Fela as a young and impressionable boy. His mother's progressive politics connected with Nkrumah's popularity on the continent. Nkrumah's political vision was molded in the years when Africa was in the grip of colonialism, but decolonization was about to commence. He saw Africa as a large, borderless political and ideological whole that had blackness as a common denominator. Pan-Africanism privileges Africa as the symbolic connector of all Africans and African-descended people, seeking to connect the homeland with the diaspora through a broad vision of a shared historical experience, common destiny, and cultural unity. Pan-Africanists like Nkrumah saw colonialism and imperialism as the twin evils that had hobbled Africa's development march for many decades, with decolonization as the condition for a genuine liberation of the continent. This liberation would be sustained by the solidarity of Africans and African descendent people all over the world, with his ultimate political pursuit the realization of a United States of Africa that abandoned national boundaries in favor of economic, cultural, and political unity. Malcolm X's prominence in the American civil right movement did not preclude his association with Africa as the homeland of black people. His black nationalism also gave him the leeway to pursue a vision of trans-Atlantic solidarity of black brotherhood all over the world. This was also the larger vision that motivated Du Bois and Martin Luther King, Jr., as well as the National Association for the Advancement of Colored People (NAACP), the Black

Panther Party, and the Civil Right Movement, and underlaid their struggles for the emancipation of the African American people in the diaspora.

Behind the pan-African ideology is a longing for an ontological image of an undifferentiated African self, whose sociocultural being and historical circumstances serves as a foundation of political and economic solidarity. After his reading of *The Autobiography of Malcolm X*, Fela made the necessary link between Nkrumah's pan-Africanist ideals, Malcolm X's understanding of blackness, the significance of black power, and his own disconnection from Africa and all its cultural and symbolic meanings. In Kwame Nkrumah, for instance, we find two significant but interconnected insights that define his aspirations for the African continent. On the one hand, there is the clarion call for all Africans to unite as the most viable means by which the continent can achieve the gains of the political kingdom. On the other hand, Nkrumah also argued that Africa's postcolonial freedom would amount to a sham if all manifestations of neocolonial manipulations and controls are not completely eliminated. But since the fact of independence for African states interjected the spirit of pan-Africanism, Kwame Nkrumah's advocacy for one Africa had to engage with this fact of the sovereign independence of African states. His strategy was to call for an increasing cooperation and unity among these states as a pan-African strategy of achieving a united front against the neocolonial onslaught. Malcolm X stands today as one of the most significant thinkers of the Black Power movement in the United States. The movement emerged within the context of racial discrimination and the racial ideology which undermined the humanity and racial dignity of the negroes. For Malcolm X, as well as all the other members of the movement—Stokely Carmichael (Kwame Ture), Robert F. Williams, Willie Ricks (Mukasa Dada), and so on—the strategy for reclaiming blackness and the dignity of the negro is a coordinated ideology of self-determination, self-reliance, racial pride and dignity, and self-defense.

It was easy for Malcolm X and even Martin Luther King, Jr, as well as all the participants in the Black Power and Black Nationalist movements to draw a correlation between Africa's decolonization efforts against colonialism and the collective attempts by the negroes to overthrow the racial oppression and the white power structure in the United States. Martin Luther King, Jr., visited Ghana during the latter's independence celebration in 1957. The ideological impression he got from this trans-Atlantic experience had a lot to influence his own brand of radical interrogation of White Power in the United States. It is from this ideological repertoire created by the Black Power movement and the pan-African intellectual and political efforts that Fela drew his ideological strength. Pan-Africanism enabled Fela to achieve an ideological continuum that subsumed Africa and the diaspora. This and many other political influences, from Marcus Garvey, Patrice Lumumba, and Funmilayo Ransome-Kuti, went into the ideological cauldron called blackism. It therefore becomes clear why, for him, there exists an undifferentiated African self that stands as the ontological representation of the black persona wherever it may be found. Indeed, the significance of this ontological understanding of the African self derives from its smoothening over of the polarizing ideological rift that ruptures both the understanding of pan-Africanism on the continent and the Black Power movement in the diaspora. In blackism therefore, we find a unique ontological leap that is strengthened by ideological coherence and is blind to ideological differences.

Blackism, with its philosophic-spiritual elements, possesses a performative framework geared toward constructing, deconstructing, and reconstructing political assumptions and principles and social conventions, norms, and ethos. In Fela's hand, we see a dynamic interplay between the politico-philosophical intent of Afrobeat's dissident tunes and the ritual performances that foregrounded Fela's Yorùbá spiritualism. For the Yoruba, the world is a continuum that defines a metaphysical trajectory linking the dead, the living and the unborn. To connect to this metaphysical plane—what Soyinka calls "the numinous passage which links all: transition"[7]—requires an adaptation of the Yoruba mask tradition into an effective masque performativity that enabled an entry into the world of the ancestors, as well as the capacity to speak to all through the instrumentality of the mask. In the Yoruba spiritual tradition, the mask becomes a spiritual channel for conveying coded messages. It is "a repository of ancient and current knowledge … which makes its language cryptic and its message diverse."[8] For Olorunyomi, Fela donned two masks, both consistent with the Yoruba mask forms. The first mask serves the function of entertainment that the living appropriates for social use, while the other is deployed for ritual purposes.[9] With both elements, Fela was able to reinforce the strident, radical messages of political Afrobeat; he became a medium of the *òrìsà*. As *Abami Eda*, the mysterious, Fela took up the performative license to convey spiritual messages to the world through the strident mouth of the saxophone and through rituals. And he was simultaneously reinforced by the supernatural capacities of the gods to protect against the malicious intents of the postcolonial state.

According to Olorunyomi, Fela's cultural performance rituals were meant to serve the function of cultural validation and the retrieval of cultural identity. Fela's objective was the reconstruction of human social relations in a way that was far from constricting. Fela's ritual dynamics relied on the textual instability and multiplicity of meaning at the core of Ifá to draw his ritual practice into contemporary relevance: "It is this [indeterminacy at the core of interpreting Ifá verses] that Fela seized upon to redirect the energies of the gods, dragging them to do his random battles and battles of other victims of dominant powers that people his diverse narrative texts."[10] In the final analysis, the objective of the deployment of Yoruba spirituality in Fela's masque performativity is to strengthen the ontological affirmation of his idea of blackism—of a radical and creative redefinition of a ritual dynamics that allows the emergence of a core of ancestors that link, across the "numinous passage," the continent and the diaspora in a trajectory of the ontology of blackness.

The creation of Kalakuta Republic and the Afrika Shrine was significant beyond its demonstration of fulminating defiance. Both represented specific inscriptions of Fela's spiritual convictions and philosophical beliefs on society's space. The Shrine is an inscription of alterity, a potent reaction against the denigration of indigenous worship forms.[11] Kalakuta Republic was equally an alternative space of reinvention. Both constituted space for heterodoxy as an alternative imagining of society and its critical constitutive elements. From within both spaces, Fela the Chief Priest spoke stridently, and the "voice of the god(s) that we get to hear at the Afrika Shrine is a class-conscious one, and one that is unapologetic in its partisanship on behalf of marginalized classes, oppressed nationalities and even the aesthetic subculture."[12]

Blackism is a combative philosophy of disruption and of intervention, of dissidence and even dissonance. We must not forget Fela's Marxist inheritance. In Marxist aesthetics, art serves an ideological purpose. Art emanates from within the materialist conception of society and is equally caught in the class struggles. Art, however, play a significant role in the ideological reorientation of the human society, and in the unraveling of false consciousness. Blackism has, at its core, heterodoxy as a principle for constructing and reconstructing alternative social imaginaries. On the continent, blackism would share significant aspects with Afropessimism and Afrofuturism. When Fela peeped through the eyes of the òrìsà to divine the state of the continent, he often saw catastrophe, dislocation, the disarticulation of Africa's being, and her capacity for becoming. But if Fela were alive today and he were to be compelled to abandon his aversion for the cinema to go watch Marvel's *Black Panther*, he would see a lot of correlation between the national strength of Wakanda and the possibility of both national renewal in Nigeria and continental rebirth in Africa.[13]

In the final analysis, the key objective of blackism for Fela was not the need to restore social order; on the contrary, it was to throw it into contestation. In this sense, therefore, we cannot say that Fela's blackism offers any coherent worldview or vision by which we can begin to reinvent the society. Political Afrobeat, and its entire ideological basis, offers only a strident and radical critique. And this is sufficient in and of itself to consider Fela a political philosopher in his own right. After all, one aim of philosophy is the attempt to critically interrogate the intellectual foundations of human life and existence.

14

Freedom and Excesses: Fela and Social Eccentricities

Fela cultivated the character of an iconoclast from the start, a social deviant who intended to shock society into an awareness of its limitations. This required more than Afrobeat's political realization. During his time in the United States, Fela explored the full range of America's counterculture as social deviance. It enabled him to develop a charismatic personality that fed on the excesses of sex and drugs. American countercultural practices of the 1960s were founded on an anti-establishment ethos, and they were equally defined by experimentation with drugs, sexual exuberance, specific forms of music like jazz and funk, an ambivalence about the American Dream, and political activism, especially tied to America's involvement in Vietnam. Fela's creative ingenuity, together with the cultural and traditional repertoire of values, frameworks, and paradigms available, allowed him to create a counterculture on his return to Lagos that was uniquely his own—even when it replicated the basic elements of American countercultural values. That counterculture engaged Lagos society and the Nigerian postcolonial state.

Fela's dynamics of social deviance can be described as a cultivation of excess that tended toward the incredible. The "incredible," to adopt Olaniyan's apt description,

> inscribes that which cannot be believed; that which is too improbable, astonishing, and extraordinary to be believed. The incredible is not simply a breach but an outlandish infraction of "normality" and its limits. If "belief," as faith, confidence, trust, and conviction, underwrites the certainty and tangibility of institutions and practices of social exchange, the incredible dissolves all such props of stability, normality, and intelligibility (and therefore of authority) and engenders social and symbolic crisis.[1]

While it is possible to read Fela's political objective as overthrowing or undermining "the reign of the incredible," his attempt to become a countercultural hero compromised that objective. The paradox is that Fela allowed the "postcolonial incredible," generated by the Nigerian state, to instigate an oppositional framework of social excesses from his antisocial eccentricities.[2] Mbembe conceives this postcolonial incredible in terms of "the banality of power in the postcolony." While the banal speaks to (a) "the way bureaucratic formalities or arbitrary rules, implicit or explicit, have been multiplied," or (b) "what has become rote and hence predictable," it fundamentally signifies "those elements of the obscene and the grotesque that … in fact, are intrinsic to all systems of domination and to the means by which those systems are confirmed or deconstructed."[3] Fela intended to deconstruct this banality of power. His starting point, the starting point for every dimension of his cultural program, was a throwback to the idea of an indigenous cultural system and its traditional elements. For him, this facilitated the process of cultural identity and validation. Fela had a vision, no matter how contrived or inaccurate, about traditional Yorùbá society where conventional boundaries were less constricted than in contemporary society. Drugs, sex, and derision had legitimate places within his vision of tradition and culture.

Literature on Yorùbá cultural performance often references the èfè-gèlèdé performance tradition of Nigeria's Egbado-Yoruba people. In this tradition, the gèlèdé masquerade performance is conjoined with that of an *èfè* (humor) aesthetic in a manner that foregrounds hilarity, bombast, and the grotesque. For any particular outing, the eléfè, or humorist, holds the authority to deride, abuse, and ridicule even the king, while also satirizing social ills.[4] In Fela's hands, the objective of traditional performances was not only inverted but the practices became excessive to the extreme. The aspiration of the gèlèdé performance for social order was reversed in his countercultural dynamics, becoming an incredible subversion of social norms and conventional boundaries. Sex and sexuality were pushed into society's face through Afrobeat lyrics, album sleeves (of "Expensive Shit" and "Shakara," for example), through Fela's outrageous dress sense and semi-nudity, and his *yabis*—lewd banter, ribaldry, and verbal rebuttal. Fela's countercultural movement was a confusing and exciting mixture of defiance, mischief, individuality, creativity, and irreverence. Kalakuta Republic came from Fela's Africanist understanding of communal openness and open-mindedness. It was his attempt to put the pan-African idea of a borderless black or African world into a micro-perspective, welcoming every one of every race. For Fela,

> When I came back home [from the United States], I said to myself: "All African countries should open their doors to Africans from everywhere, especially those in the Americas." That's what I wanted to do if I'd been in power. But I wasn't ….

> So the idea of creating a place open to every African escaping persecution began taking shape in this my mind. Was that my first pan-Africanist idea? Maybe. At any rate, that's how the idea of setting up a communal compound—one like Africans had been living in for thousands of years—came about. A place open to everybody. A real compound, you know. I'd think to myself: "Ah-ah! What is this city shit-o? One man, one wife, one house isolated from everybody else in the neighbourhood? Is an African not even to know his neighbours?"

This countercultural environment was deliberately cultivated at the fringe of society, among the masses that Nigerian society had pushed into abjection. The fringe elements—prostitutes, touts, truants, school dropouts, vagabonds, and all types of free spirits and social rejects—automatically clung to the physical atmosphere of Fela's irreverence. They thumbed their noses at the society that had rejected them in the first place. This counterculture offered relief and social relevance for those who had been consigned to irrelevance due the political economy of the Nigerian state. The freedom that the Nigerian state received from independence did not translate into empowerment for her citizenry; it pauperized them. Drug use, especially the open use of marijuana, became an expression of individual freedom and a significant part of the creative experience for Fela's Afrika 70 band. Songs like "Na Poi," "Going In and Out," "Mattress," and even "Shakara" have lewd sexual undertones that are sometimes coded, as in "Shakara," and usually explicit, as in "Going In and Out." "Na Poi" is a crude but explicit metaphor for sexual intercourse:

> When man see woman, and him hold im hand
> and he carry am go him house
> and he carry am inside room,
> and he lock door
> the thing wey dem dey do
> behind the door wey dem lock
>
> Na Poi!
>
> Fi si
>
> Ibe ko lo fi si yen
>
> Sun mo waju die die
>
> Move am forward small small
>
> O di poi!

Fi ha!

When a man sees a woman, and holds her hand
and takes her to his house
and carries her inside a room
and locks the door
the thing they do
behind the locked door

It's sex!

Put it right in

You're not putting it in the right spot

Move forward a little bit

It's sex!

Do it!

Fela's countercultural persona prompts a revision of our earlier assessment: he transcended his initial desire for a freedom that allowed him to pursue irreverent desires. Imagine Fela as a young boy in primary and secondary school, knowing the punishment for stubbornness and bad behavior, but who still was one of the most likable, boisterous fellows around. Just as his radical and jovial character could have been a deliberate rebellion against his parents' disciplinary regimen, Fela's countercultural dynamics were meant as a shock treatment for Nigerian society's social consciousness. He deliberately undermined society's moral fabric and norms to send a message about society's hypocrisy, especially concerning sex and sexuality.

Kalakuta Republic was rebellion against the state, but it was also a conscious attempt to dilute social conventions along with the norms and ethos that society uses to ensure its own continuity. This does not imply, in any way, that social deviance has no significant role in moving society forward. In understanding social progress, there is a distinct place for social eccentrics who test the boundaries of social conventions, done in a manner that does not lead to the dissolution of society. The issue to examine is the boundary where freedom encounters and intersects excesses, or even the incredible. Fela's idea of the African communal compound was a gross misinterpretation; it was an attempt to fuse communality with an excessive countercultural ethos of Dionysian wantonness. Ultimately, what went on within the walls of Kalakuta Republic, under Fela's firm control, was less extreme than the orgiastic den of unbridled drug use and immorality that society imagined it to be.

Did Fela's countercultural stance compromise his ideological strength, undermining his attempt to champion a logic of contestation that opened up political space for the government to acknowledge that Nigerians had the right to live meaningful lives? This appears to be the case. Fela's decision to abandon the search for social order, pursuing a strategy that reverses and undermines social norms and behavioral convention, stands in the idea of freedom on its head. Social theorists, scholars, and philosophers are motivated to search for means of expanding human freedom because it constitutes the greatest space for the flowering of human ingenuity and possibilities. This requires an understanding of the context within which freedom is sought, and it explores various means by which freedom can be protected, sustained, and enhanced. Postcolonial African society can be defined by a quest for freedom and development. This freedom, following Amartya Sen, can be conceived as the capabilities that individuals possess to pursue individual and collective empowerment and meaningfulness.[5] This implies that the state is responsible for freeing up socioeconomic and political spaces that enhance, rather than restrict, human capabilities.

The countercultural practices that Fela initiated eventually fed into the general disorder that he was protesting in the first place. And there was nothing proposed to replace that which did not enhance freedom in Nigerian society. If there was any vision of an alternative social order in Fela's mind, it cannot be assessed on the basis of "liberal hedonism."[6] Freedom as an individual, social, and national requirement is often considered based on values that make social cooperation possible. Two of those values are decency and civility—but they are precisely the values that Fela's countercultural incredible undermined in his attempt to subvert the postcolonial incredible of the Nigerian state. It was inevitable that Fela's countercultural incredible would bring the wrath of the Nigerian state down on him and his many followers. The circumstances of his death were equally unsurprising. Fela's death was announced on Saturday, August 2, 1997. It was due to complications from HIV/AIDS. He was just fifty-nine years old.[7]

Part D

Fela in the Future

15

Post-Fela: Afrobeats as Memorialization

When Fela Anikulapo-Kuti died in 1997, Nigeria was in the grip of a national crisis, with widespread mass agitation for transition to a democratic dispensation. In 1983, General Muhammadu Buhari came to power, followed by General Badamosi Babangida when he overthrew Buhari's regime as the commander-in-chief of the Nigerian armed forces two years later. Under Babangida, electoral stability was precarious as politicians and political parties were routinely banned and unbanned. This ultimately instigated series of political agitations that eventually led to democratic elections being called on June 12, 1993. The business tycoon and philanthropist Chief M. K. O. Abiola, of the Social Democratic Party (SDP), was presumed to be the winner of the election, but the result was annulled by General Babangida. This set into motion a national crisis, leading to the formation of an interim national government headed by Chief Ernest Shonekan, which only lasted three months before it was toppled by General Sani Abacha. The military ruler died on June 8, 1998, and his junta swiftly collapsed. On May 28, 1999, Chief Olusegun Obasanjo was sworn in as the democratically elected president of the Federal Republic of Nigeria. His election ushered in the Fourth Republic in Nigeria's political history since independence in 1960.

Nigeria's new democratic regime was inaugurated exactly one-and-a-half years after the death of Fela Anikulapo-Kuti, social maverick, Afrobeat maestro, musician, composer, gadfly, and tormentor of the military establishment in Nigeria. It would have made for a momentous event to have Fela witness the inauguration of Chief Obasanjo, a man that was instrumental, as the military president in 1976, to the sacking of Kalakuta Republic in 1977 and Fela's mother being thrown from the first-floor window of Fela's house. What sarcastic or derisive tune would have been released by Fela's Afrobeat saxophone? What would have been Fela's reaction to the many significant political, economic, and cultural events that happened after his death? What would have been his reaction to the various wars that continued occurring on the continent? What about the sit-tight rulers in Cameroon, Zimbabwe, Gambia, and so on?

And what can we say about Fela's relevance today, given that he has been dead for over twenty years and so many things have happened in Nigeria and across Africa between then and now? Similarly, what is the current situation of Afrobeat today, the original musical genre through which Fela lifted his message into the face of dictators and all the enemies of Africa? Fela is a singular figure that history will find difficult to replicate in Nigeria. After his death, there is no other person that has stood up to the government the way he did. None have the same explosive charisma that could sustain another countercultural movement. There has not been another musician so mercurial that has held the imagination of an entire nation for as long as Fela did. It is therefore a mistake to pose the question, as many have, "Who replaces Fela?" The breadth of his contribution to pan-Africanist ideology, to the understanding of black consciousness, to Nigeria's music history, and the trajectory of Nigeria's political dynamics is far too weighty for anyone to fully emulate.

One significant question that grounds the contemporary relevance of Fela is: To what extent has the commencement of democratic governance in Nigeria transformed the space available to Nigerians for self-realization? Put another way, how has democracy enabled the individual capacities of Nigerians to live meaningful lives? Asking the question this way is an attempt to summarize Fela's lifelong objective to stand with the Nigerian poor and dispossessed against the unbridled greed of the Nigerian political class for primitive accumulation. Apart from the ambivalent consequences of his countercultural practices, Fela's political framework remains solid, providing a complete sociopolitical agenda for critiquing postcolonial Nigeria. It is arguable that Fela's voice is still as insistent today as it was three decades ago. It took the government of Lagos State in Nigeria more than seventeen years after Fela's death to confer a posthumous honor on a figure who transformed how we understand the postcolonial, political, and sociocultural character of Lagos.

Nigerians are still not free. The postcolonial state in Africa is still struggling to come to terms with Africa's development crisis. From the Lagos Plan of Action to New Partnership for Africa's Development (NEPAD), the discourse on the urgency of evolving developmental states in Africa ought to be considered side-by-side with the present condition of the ideology of pan-Africanism. It has been argued recently—quite aptly too—that "in the twenty-first century, as Pan-African ideology and consciousness dwindle in both Africa and the

African Diaspora, the appropriation and performance of Pan-Africanism on continental, national, regional, local, and transatlantic levels offer an alternative solution for sustaining Pan-Africanism."[1] This was the direction that Fela wanted pan-Africanism to be taken; this was what Kwame Nkrumah himself intended.

Fela is a notorious figure that the Nigerian political elites love to ignore, and the situation in the country seems worse today because the gap between the government and the governed has not been qualitatively bridged by the inauguration of democracy. All the features of underdevelopment, corruption, public immorality, and social ills of all types which Fela railed against and was tortured for are still present. But Fela's voice, minus his formidable presence, is now heard yearly at the annual FELABRATION musical event, bringing together singers and musicians who wanted to associate with Fela and his ideology. Additionally, Fela's ideological frame of reference—blackism—is still the source of regular colloquiums, conferences, symposiums, and other intellectual gatherings across the world.

Fela's contemporary presence is better maintained through the yeoman efforts of his sons, Seun and Femi Kuti, as well as the emergence of "afrobeats" modeled after Fela's original genre.[2] Femi Kuti has more musical clout in this regard than Seun Kuti, achieving an international stature with his energetic and frenzied style of Afrobeat. As the eldest son of Fela, Femi became a part of his father's band Egypt 80 as an apprentice alto saxophonist in 1977 before starting his own band called The Positive Force. In 1984, Fela was detained on a foreign currency violation charge, which carried a sentence of ten years in jail. Fela went to prison, first at the Kirikiri Maximum prison, then later transferred to the Maiduguri prison in the northern part of the country. This was Femi's opportunity to step up and rescue the situation at the shrine and to affect some critical changes he must have been mulling while undergoing his apprenticeship. Significant among them was dealing with the esoteric ritual practices which defined the Afrika Shrine. Fela was eventually released from prison through a timely coup d'état that brought in General Babangida, whose regime reluctantly reviewed the case (taking another ten whole months to get it done). When Fela returned, he rolled back all of Femi's adjustments to the Shrine, but the crucial point of departure between them was about music and whether it was the appropriate time for Femi to commence his own search for self-realization and self-affirmation. Finally, in 1989 Femi left the Egypt 80, and struck out on his own musical journey, with his own band, *The Positive Force.*

Today, some two-and-a-half decades after he made the decision to leave the Egypt 80 band, Femi Kuti has become the most visible heir of Fela's Afrobeat, the first in the line of all the afrobeats that have since sprung up after Fela's original genre and arguably the most successful of them. Though it took close to ten years for people to take notice of him and his music, Femi finally achieved fame when "Wonder Wonder," a track on his inaugural album, *Femi Kuti* (1995), brought his name and brand of afrobeat home to the Nigerian music scene. In 2003, he got his first nomination for the Grammy award for his album, *Fight to Win*, the first of four nominations he would get without winning (2003, 2010, 2012, and 2013). Femi, like his father, also combines music with activism, but without the strong ideological strength of Fela. "Wonder Wonder" vibrates with the usual Fela thematic concern with African unity and the significance of Nkrumah's pan-African ideals. There is also mention of the ubiquitous issue of religion and its contribution to the impoverishment of the already pauperized masses. In "Africa for Africa" (2010), Femi was also concerned, again like his father, with the tenacity of colonialism and colonial structures on the continent and why Africa needed to put its act together to make progress.

Femi has continued the tradition of nightly performances at what he has renamed the New Afrika Shrine, now located at Ikeja in Lagos after relocation from the old shrine at Gbemisola Street. Although far from the huge countercultural spectacle of Fela, the New Afrika Shrine still constitutes a major showcase that has become a signature part of Lagos' nightlife. It has also succeeded in spawning its own growing informal night economy fed by middle-class patronage, which equally flits dangerously around the shadowy presence of criminality. Enter the Shrine and you are greeted with the usual noisy ambience and the cloudy overhang of marijuana smoke. The performance stage is one huge, electrified space filled by the music ensemble and scantily dressed ladies in garish costumes gyrating to the beats. The contemporary divinities that adorned the old shrine have been multiplied: there is still Malcolm X, Funmilayo Ransome-Kuti, and Kwame Nkrumah, but Patrice Lumumba has been replaced by Martin Luther King, Jr., Marcus Garvey, and Fela himself, as a new divinity. When, on a particular day which the authors witnessed, Femi finally appeared, the hall erupted with several catcalls, hoots, and whistling. When he got ahold of the microphone, he uttered his own signal call: *arararara*, like Fela's "everybody say yea yea!" And the crowd responded: *ororororo*. It was time for him to launch into the yabis before taking up the real and frenzied musical business of the night.

Femi's political activism is not as loud, defiant, politically fierce, and ideologically heavy as Fela's. Still, the New Afrika Shrine, like the old, has also attracted the attention of the government, which has attempted to close it down on a few occasions without success. Contrary to Fela's cultivation of the incredible, Femi's afrobeat lacks the hint of social deviance. In a way that Fela was not, Femi is a "gentleman." Sexuality is rarely ever thrust into society's face. "Beng Beng Beng" (1998) seems about the most notorious of all Femi's songs for its explicit lewdness:

Beng beng beng
Beng beng beng beng beng
Beng beng beng beng beng
The time is 12 midnight my brother
(Beng beng beng)
The girl lay on top my bed now
(Beng beng beng)
The weather outside nah correct weather [*The weather is just the right one*]
(Beng beng beng)
That kind of cold freezing weather [*A very cold and freezing weather*]
(Beng beng beng)
Wey go make your battery dey charge extra [*That gives your "battery" an extra charge*]
(Beng beng beng)
I say everything dey correct order [*Everything was in correct order*]
(Beng beng beng)
She said love me now
She said squeeze me now
Her yansh e just makes me wonder [*Her buttock makes me wonder*]
Her breast be like Dunlop Maria [*Her breast is like Dunlop Maria*]
I say everything dey correct order
Beng beng beng
I just dey go O [*I kept banging*]
(beng beng beng)
Beng beng beng
I just dey go O
(beng beng beng)
Beng beng beng

Apart from this "aberration," Femi's repertoire is filled with lamentations about the condition of Nigeria and postcolonial Africa. His themes range from injustice, betrayal, the daily drudgery of living in Nigeria, and bad government. In "Obasanjo Don Play You Wayo" (2010), Femi called out the political deception of the democratically elected president Olusegun Obasanjo, especially his decision and methods to tackle corruption in Nigeria:

Obasanjo don play you wayo
Obasanjo don play you wayo
He set up EFCC to jail the corrupt leaders
EFCC start to arrest
but dem begin release all these leaders
EFCC find it difficult to jail the corrupt leaders
Because politics in Nigeria
E go hard to jail the …

… friends to the brother to the sister
to the father to the mother to the daughter to the wife of the senator

Obasanjo has deceived you
Obasanjo has deceived you
He sets up the EFCC to jail corrupt leaders
EFCC begins to arrest
but then starts to release them again
EFCC finds it difficult to jail these corrupt leaders
because within the politics of Nigeria
it will be very difficult to jail

… the friends of the brother of the sister
of the father of the mother of the daughter of the wife of the senator

That Fela's Afrobeat has now inspired hosts of artists that inject elements of it into their music is a measure of his continued significance on the global music scene. The challenge is the capacity of any of the new borrowers of Afrobeat to match Fela's energy, experimental genius, and political and ideological profile. Fela casts an exceptionally long shadow. Being "political" seems a profoundly difficult task for any musician or singer today, especially with the common association of musical creativity with crass material acquisition in the music industry. Fela was not only political, he also combined an anti-establishment persona, strong charisma, and a unique ideological bent that attempted to synthesize many currents from Nkrumah to Malcolm X. Breaking out of the popular musical genres in present-day Nigeria such as hip-hop, fuji, and juju in order to deliberately cultivate the sound of Afrobeat seems too much to ask. The risk that took Fela from Lagos to London and then the United States, with all the accompanying existential and ideological anguish, together with the horrors visited on him by the establishment he wanted to rebel against, is just too much to take.

Yet Fela's Afrobeat is the progenitor to many new Afrobeat-inspired musicians. Before Femi Kuti came Tony Allen, Fela's brilliant master-drummer. Tony Allen had a falling out with Fela's Afrika 70 band over issues of royalties and pay. He had been with Fela for twelve years (1968 to 1979). Allen, who gave Fela's Afrobeat its syncopated drum pattern that underscores Afrobeat's originality, had the best chance of success with the first afrobeat clone. He launched his own afrobeat direction with a few initial efforts in collaboration with Fela—*Jealousy* (1975), *Progress* (1977), and *No Accommodation for Lagos* (1979). Allen left the band in 1979, releasing another album, *No Discrimination* (1980), before leaving for Europe. Once there, he made efforts to experiment and expand the stylistic vision of his afrobeat.

After Femi left his father's Egypt 80 band, it was up to Seun Kuti, the youngest son of Fela, to claim the mantle of leadership. Seun has a few albums to his credit—*Think Africa* (2007), *Many Things* (2008), *From Africa with Fury: Rise* (2011), *A Long Way to the Beginning* (2014), *Struggle Sounds* (2014), *Black Times* (2018), and *Night Dreamer* (2019). Unfortunately, he is located in the crowded intersection of his father's legacy, Femi's rising achievements, and the afrobeat produced by contending heirs. There are so many other contenders for the heirship of Afrobeat—Dede Mabiaku (Fela's protégé) and the *Underground African Sounds*, Seyi Solagade and the *Blackface*, Kola Ogunkoya (aka *Gbedu Master*) and *Afrogbedu*, Dele Sosimi and the *Afrobeat Orchestra*, Funso Ogundipe and the *Ayetoro* band, Junwon Ogungbe and the *Life Force Band*, Kunle Adeniran (aka KunNiran) and the *Garetta Beat*, and so on. Some of these afrobeat scions were motivated simply by the powerful Afrobeat influence of Fela himself (Seyi Solagade, Kola Ogunkoya, Juwon Ogungbe, Funso Ogundipe, Kunle Adeniran). But some others took off from direct Afrobeat tutelage in Fela's band. Sosimi began his musical apprenticeship with the Egypt 80 as a rhythm keyboardist and served for seven years (1979 to 1986); he then subsequently became the band leader and music director in Femi Kuti's *Positive Force* from 1986 to 1995 to start out in London as a solo artiste. Dede Mabiaku was with Fela right from 1989, when he was introduced to Kalakuta Republic, and he stayed with him till Fela died in 1997.

Lagbaja (Bisade Ologunde) is one such contender for Fela's legacy. Out of all the heirs to Afrobeat, Lagbaja is the one who seems to have taken the mystical elements of Afrobeat more seriously. "Lagbaja" is a Yorùbá metaphor for the anonymous, denoting anyone, everyone, and no one in particular. Unlike Fela, the masque performativity of Lagbaja is not meant to simulate any spiritualism. In other words, out of the two masks that the Yoruba mask tradition makes possible, Lagbaja adopts the one that is deployed for amusement and entertainment. His masked persona therefore became the aesthetic framework for making political statements. His afrobeat, like Fela's, is therefore meant to represent the facelessness of Nigerian masses made destitute and victimized by the postcolonial Nigerian state. The mystique created by Lagbaja's masked face not only creates a sense of curiosity but also heightens the political profile of the persona. With Lagbaja, we have a significant move away from the explicit political agenda of Fela and Femi to a more flexible musical template with the capacity to fuse seamlessly with the lyrical and aesthetic forms of other contemporary popular music in Nigeria, from hip-hop to juju. This is significant because it also falls to Lagbaja to reconfigure Afrobeat and then reconnect it to the cultural context which Femi and Seun seem to have lost.[3] With popular tracks like "Coolu Temper" (2005), "Konko Below" (2001), "Never Far Away" (2005), "Gra Gra" (2001), "Nothing For You" (2001), and "Toun T'erin" (2000), Lagbaja has cultivated a humorous and relaxed lyrical style that draws cultural sensibility into social commentary.

It would be a disservice to assume that Fela's influence is limited to Femi Kuti, Seun Kuti, and Lagbaja, who each can be regarded as directly incarnating the Afrobeat spirit. Fela's long shadow over the music scene in Nigeria could never be ignored by the younger generation of singers. Evidence of this is the widespread acceptance given to the FELABRATION annual event commemorating Fela's death and his continuing significance in Nigeria's musical and sociopolitical affairs. It has blossomed into a potpourri of contemporary reliving of Fela's memory, not only featuring talks and symposia on relevant matters doing justice to Fela's music, thought, and activism—issues that would have constituted food for his rebellious saxophone if he were still alive—but also bringing together local and international artists demonstrating the vibrancy of his influence over music globally.

The idea for a musical celebration of Fela's Afrobeat and global influence came from his daughter, Yeni Anikulapo-Kuti in 1998. The program became a global celebration in 2015 with several events, especially the symposium, making it a truly engaging musical fiesta. The vision of the celebration—"To have Fela celebrated worldwide"—seems trite since Fela is already a global icon. But the themes of the symposium since 2015, and the caliber of discussants, have continued to relive Fela's political and pan-African legacies. In 2009, the theme was "The Social and Political Influence of Fela on Our Society." And on the panel were Odia Ofeimun, Ben Bruce-Murray, Donald Duke, Femi Falana, and others. In 2010, it was "Music Is a Weapon" (Discussants: Carlos Moore, Dipo Fashina, Yemi Osinbajo, Lesego Rampolokeng). In 2011, it was "Africa and the New World Order" (Discussants: Wole Soyinka, Sanusi Lamido Sanusi, Bola Akinterinwa, Ituah Ighodalo, Rasheed Gbadamosi). For 2012, the theme was "Corruption and the Next Generation" (Discussants: Sola Olorunyomi, Michael Veal, Sefi Atta, Yemisi Shyllon, Olasupo Shasore, and Ndidi Nwuneli). The 2013 theme was "Movement of the People: The Fela and Bob Marley Perspectives" (Discussants: Vivien Goldman, John Collins, Nana Rita Marley, Sola Olorunyomi). The 2017 theme was "Forty Years Post FESTAC 77, AND 20 Years Post Fela: Whither the Pan African Dream?" (Discussants: P. L. O. Lumumba, Kadaria Ahmed, and Jimi Disu).

The Nigerian music scene has flourished beyond what Fela left behind when he died in the 1990s. A flurry of creative and dexterous musical energy has turned hip-hop into a unique style reflecting the Nigerian sociocultural dynamics. From Davido, Burna Boy, and Olamide to Oritshefemi, Patoranking, and Wizzkid—all brand names in Nigeria—music is now defined by a qualitatively different agenda and focus. Through the mediating influence of Femi Kuti, we now have a creative infusion of Afrobeat into the hip-hop genre. Femi Kuti's creative versatility has led to lots of collaborations—between Femi Kuti and Wizzkid, for instance—between his Afrobeat saxophone and the hip-hop frenetic aesthetics. Another Fela feature visible today is a measure of countercultural defiance that has allowed the new generation of Nigerian hip-hop artists to project images and lyricize themes that offend the received morality in Nigeria. While one may recognize that a few of these contemporary performers who have dedicated some of their songs to sociopolitical engagement, it is difficult to see how this music scene replicates Afrobeat's political agenda. One could imagine Fela standing off stage and beckoning to all these artists to remember what he truly stood for, what Afrobeat stands for. He could be signaling that Nigeria is even at a dispensation, notwithstanding its presumed democracy, that is even more precarious than when he confronted its leadership. Only a very few seem to have noticed Fela's insistent gestures in the din of loud music and the existential imperatives of surviving musically in Nigeria. Yet, the FELABRATION provides the platform for all and sundry to continue resignifying Fela's ongoing presence in Nigerian music.

While Nigeria and her political elites and singers were deliberately forgetting Fela and his legacies and creatively sanitizing his memories through the FELABRATION music event, others elsewhere on the globe were keeping alive his deep cultural influence, including the strong political messages that blared from his saxophone and the Afrocentric extent of his message. When, in the year 2000, the theatrical producer, Stephen Hendel, saw a CD collection of Fela's music on Amazon, Afrobeat was about to enter into a rebirth in the United States, far from the native home where an ironic amnesia was proceeding to take hold. When Fela's legacy arrived as an off-Broadway production, after $11 million was raised, the American viewing public would be treated to a staged production of Fela's political Afrobeat, his dedication to social justice, and to the plight of the oppressed. *Fela!*, the musical, would be revealed to the world more than fifty years after he found his Afrobeat tone with Sandra Smith in Los Angeles. It was that initial appeal that brought Shawn Carter (Jay Z), Beyoncé Knowles (his wife), Will and Jada Pinkett-Smith, and other business partners to throw their financial weight behind Hendel for the production of the musical. A "who's who" in the American entertainment world went to Broadway to see *Fela!*—from Alicia Keys and Denzel Washington to Kofi Annan and Michelle Obama, along with hundreds of thousands of fans. *Fela!* has toured dozens of major American cities and has gone internationally to the Netherlands, Canada, the United Kingdom, and even Lagos, Nigeria.

16

Fela as a Legacy

Fela has become a global icon whose significance straddles politics, culture, activism, postcolonial theory, and third-world development. All this despite having been dead for more than two decades and, before dying, the popularity of the dissident tunes of political Afrobeat waning significantly to the point that Fela was nearly transcended by more contemporary musical genres while he was still alive. Toward the end of his life, Fela's creative muse seemed to have abandoned him as his focused narrowed toward the harassment of the Nigerian state. He failed to keep up the prodigious rate of musical production that had reached its height between 1971 and 1975, when he released at least fourteen albums. As this chapter suggests, the essence of Fela's music has all but forgotten now in the frenetic profusion of new popular music forms in Nigeria and on the continent. Increasingly, those who have attempted to stay true to Afrobeat have also been constrained by the same kind of experimental imperatives that Fela himself exhibited insisting that artistry and aesthetics must match and evolve with modern impulses and exigencies.

Yet, Fela's late-life (mis)fortunes or the trajectory of the evolution and dynamics of popular music in Nigeria and internationally do not in any way obviate the legacies that Fela left the world, particularly the way we would relate with the Third World in the grips of postcoloniality. By reason of his aesthetic and political achievements—and shortcomings—Fela himself represented a zeitgeist, embodying a way of coming to terms with what it means to live in a postcolony and what it means to be African. He was a living metaphor for a significant moment in the sociocultural and political history of Nigeria and the continent.

Fela enabled us to think and rethink our lifeworld as a postcolony. His aesthetic and cultural revolutions and engagements remain cogent signposts by which we can achieve a critical understanding of Nigeria and Africa, especially at the critical intersection between neoliberal hegemony and authoritarian state forms on the continent. Afrobeat will forever stand as a model of ideological and cultural intervention and reinvention. Afrobeat got its political force through Fela's projection of a particular aesthetic slant on pan-Africanism to serve as a way of looking at the world and at one another as Africans. Through his pan-Africanist perspective, he offered a critically flawed but interesting ideological variation on black identity, black consciousness, and black power that could be fruitfully compared and contrasted to the efforts of Leopold Sedar Senghor, Aime Césaire, Kwame Nkrumah, Malcolm X, and other black scholars, intellectuals, and philosophers. How, for instance, does Fela's blackism compare with Negritude, the idea of African Personality, and other forms of cultural nationalism? To the aesthetic sensibility of Senghor, Fela's Afrobeat provides a rhythmic and pulsating tapestry of sounds and songs that captivate the mind and instigate the heart toward a rethink of who we are and what we are capable of doing as Africans. While Senghor looked on Africa with a romantic longing, Fela urged us to take a realistic view at ourselves through the postcolonial looking glass.

Senghor is associated with the controversial and notorious "emotion is black" proposition which is taken as a counterpoint to another proposition, "reason is Hellenic." The proposition is often taken to have played into the denigrating racial arrogance underlying Eurocentrism that sees Africans as subhuman in the first place, and hence not given the capacity for ratiocination. To therefore say that "emotion is black" is to be complicit in the ideological oppression of the Africans. Yet, Senghor had a different intention that was supposed to serve the cause of negritude and the African personality. His argument is meant to contest the European appropriation of rationality as the epitome of its power and superiority. In fact, *emotion*, in Senghor's aesthetic philosophy, is meant to constitute a different sense of reason that defines the African's relation to the universe. To the aesthetic sensibility of Senghor, Fela's Afrobeat provides a rhythmic and pulsating aesthetic of sounds and songs that captivate the mind and instigate the heart to rethink who we are as Africans and what we are capable of. It is devoid of all forms of mushy poetic imagination that led Senghor to seek for reason in the depth of some metaphysical essence. Senghor looked on Africa with a romantic longing,[1] but Fela urged us to take a realistic look at ourselves through the postcolonial looking glass. Thus, with Fela, we have a sense of what a militant pan-African sensibility means. It is a sensibility that courageously confronted the hidden assumptions of Western ideology and projects Africanity as a combative ontology that raises an army of pan-African deities, heroes and heroines, activists and revolutionaries to do battle with anything that denigrates the unity of Africa.

Fela's stylistic vision and musical artistry also constitute a significant addition to the understanding of revolutionary music on the continent, in the African diaspora, and more generally in black ideology. Fela belongs in the pantheon of black revolutionary musicians with the likes of Miriam Makeba, Lucky Dube, Bob Marley, Miles Davis, John Coltrane, Sun Ra, James Brown, and Vuyisile Muni. Fela, alongside these other titans, poses a critical challenge to popular music forms in Africa. Afrobeat has become an aesthetic model, setting the standard for perceiving the relationship between art and politics. This genre exists beyond music, also signaling a liberationist sensibility and project. Fela was not just content to play his instruments and sing, and neither did he set out to provide a model for relating musical aesthetics to political (dis)articulations. He may have just wanted to make music and take joy in constant revisions and experimentation with various musical forms, but unfortunately for him, the coalition of cultural, socioeconomic, and political circumstances that defined the historical context he found himself within ensured that he was compelled to relate his music to politics and ideological formations. And his musical experimentation could no longer be just personal or detached from the world. It would rather become a peculiar aesthetic contribution to decolonization and Africa's liberation dynamics.

In liberationist terms, Afrobeat became *subversive* aesthetics with its own unique register that challenges, interrogates, interprets, undermines, and generally deploys cultural and political linguistic forms, folkloric elements, and countercultural rhetoric in the war of liberation. Fela was a modern-day griot, with a leaking "basket mouth" and a formidable musical ensemble—it had more vocal and ideological capacity than the *kora* or the *goje* of the old griots. In "Beast of No Nation" (BONN, 1989), Fela doubled on the griot's function as an aesthetic projection of his time and society to deploy Afrobeat as the "empire sounding back," to use Olorunyomi's graphic description.[2]

These disguising leaders ee-oh, na wah for dem
Dem hold meeting everywhere, dem reach America
(2x)

Dem call the place United Nations
Hear oh another animal talk
Wetin united inside United Nations?
Who & who unite for United Nations?
No be there Thatcher & Argentina dey

No be there Reagan & Libya dey
Israel versus Lebanon
Iran-i-oh versus Iraq-i
East West Block versus West Block East
No be there dem dey oh United Nations
Dis "united" United Nations
One veto vote is equal to 92 … or more, or more
What kind sense be dat, na animal sense (2x)

These disguised leaders are funny
They held meetings everywhere, and even in America

They called the place United Nations
Listen to another animal talk
What's united inside the United Nations?
Who and who are united in United Nations?
Isn't that where Thatcher and Argentina are?
Isn't that where Reagan and Libya are?
Israel versus Lebanon
Iran versus Iraq
East West Block versus West Block East
I hat not where they are, United Nations?
Disunited United Nations
One veto equals 92 votes, or more
What kind of sense is that if not an animal sense?

Thus, Afrobeat's "griotique"[3] sensibility enabled Fela to invert the colonialists' zoo-lexicon to allow the subaltern to speak, not only against the imperialists but also against the internal social and political formations that suppressed capabilities. Bob Marley and his ideological framework of Rastafarianism stand shoulder to shoulder with Afrobeat in this effort. Fela's dissident Afrobeat, in all senses, could be read as a significant attempt to jumpstart the arrested decolonization process that enabled the West to keep foisting its ideological baggage on Africa. In Fela's music, we find a fundamental strain of all the revolutionary sensibility of Africa's most influential thinkers, from Fanon to Nkrumah.

An excursus into Fela's legacy would not be complete without examining his countercultural persona as a rebel and social deviant. This is one of the nodal points in Fela's life that is most debated: To what extent did Fela's charismatic counterculture undermine the achievements of political Afrobeat? The deployment of drug use, explicit sexual references and innuendo, and sexist rhetoric was projected as the image of Fela, the seminude, marijuana-smoking, promiscuous macho-man. A contradiction lies in how someone who held himself as a radical progressive could canvass a position that was founded not only on the rejection of gender equality but ultimately on the very devaluation of the feminine and the abrogation of women dignity. While it may be farfetched to accuse Fela of misogyny, his understanding of gender relations and gender roles was so crude as to reveal a fundamental misinterpretation in how he perceived traditional culture and worldviews and what uncritical uses he put them to. Fela's ideological maturation was founded on the need to elucidate the "fundamentals" of African cultural heritage as a counterpoint to Eurocentric denigration. It must have appeared self-defeating to Fela's cultural sensibility to critique the heritage he meant to project. Fela's entire life could be read as an attempt to champion the cause of humanity, located in Nigeria and Africa, including the rights of women. Except that such an advocacy must not lose sight of cultural fundamentals as Fela perceived them.

The traditional African societies were predominantly patriarchal, and sexism featured prominently, but to conclude that women were just passive receptacles for masculine whims and caprices, as Fela did, is to distort the incredible dynamics of symbiosis, contestation, and negotiation that characterized male-female relations in most traditional African societies. The historical figure of Efunsetan Aniwura, the notorious second Iyalode of Ibadan, demonstrates how a woman in traditional Yorùbá society could, by the force of her achievements and willpower, subvert the traditional African patriarchal dynamics. Efunsetan Aniwura was a power broker par excellence. In fact, Olayinka Oyeleye argues that she demonstrated the "masculinity of domination," to take the issue of women's roles in a traditional context even further, "so much so that she constituted a threat to the reigning Commander in Chief who possibly felt intimidated by her influence and wealth and possibly the fact that she was female."[4] If it is correct to argue, as Veal does, that Fela made the issue of women "a significant arena for articulating issues such as power, cultural identity, spirituality, and aesthetics,"[5] then it remains important for scholars of African and postcolonial studies to keep interrogating how Fela's understanding of gender relationships enables us to further refine and redefine our perspectives on postcolonial gender dynamics at the intersection of tradition and modernity.

Across the globe, Fela's legacies have been dissected, digested, and pushed beyond the boundaries of orthodox interpretations and acceptability. One example suffices: Project S.N.A.P. is a nonprofit organization in the United

States that promotes community values and development through empowering people to collaborate for positive change. S.N.A.P. stands for the core values the organization stand for—Share, Nurture, Act, Preserve. According to its website:

> These values are woven into everything we do at Project S.N.A.P. We are a collaborative team that shares new ideas and perspectives with each other and with our partners. We nurture those ideas and take action to achieve our mission. Every artwork and every message that is submitted to us represents a unique voice, and we work diligently to be sure that we preserve that individual voice in our archives and in our Online Art Museum. (http://projectsnap.org/about-us/)

It is easy to see how this organization can deploy these values against racism and racial discrimination around the world, and it is even easier to see how Fela fits into the S.N.A.P. mission statement. The desire to promote diversity and eliminate racism fittingly led Project S.N.A.P. to develop "The Fela Kuti Mosaic Mural Program" (containing over 2,000 artworks contributed by high-school students) that opens Metro Detroit to Fela's influence in Nigeria and across the world. And that influence reaches to those participants—blacks especially—who have had to resist racism in their own lives across the United States.

In 2003, Trevor Schoonmaker, a curator at the New Museum of Contemporary Art in New York, organized an exhibition titled "Black President: The Art and Legacy of Fela Anikulapo-Kuti," part of a larger "Fela Project" through which Schoonmaker has been able to bring together an international group made up of several photographers, writers, and artists. Schoonmaker's research efforts have produced two books as part of the "Fela Project": *Fela: From West Africa to West Broadway* (2003) and *Black President: The Art and Legacy of Fela Anikulapo-Kuti* (2003). This is only one of so many other global deployments of Fela's music and legacies keeping his memory alive in the continuing fight against injustices, inequalities, racial discrimination, authoritarianism, and all sorts of evils that undermine human flourishing.

Fela Anikulapo-Kuti was an incredible persona that embodied several and severe contradictions—personal, aesthetic, ideological, cultural, and political. It is precisely his complex baggage that stimulated a revolutionary moment in the way we understand postcolonial Nigeria and her relationship with the entire continent. Fela left us with a legacy of artistic, ideological, and cultural frameworks against which we can understand the dynamics of our lifeworld within the context of the global. This justifies his place in the pantheon of the Òrìsà and the discursive space of scholarship.

Notes

Introduction

1. Crawford Young, "Itineraries of the Idea of Freedom in Africa: Precolonial to Postcolonial," in *The Idea of Freedom in Asia and Africa*, ed. Robert H. Taylor (Stanford: Stanford University Press), 10.
2. Ibid., 11.
3. William J. Foltz, "African States and the Search for Freedom," in *The Idea of Freedom in Asia and Africa*, ed. Robert H. Taylor (Stanford: Stanford University Press), 44.
4. Ibid., 47.
5. Ibid., 53.
6. Ibid., 40–1.

Chapter 1

1. Margaret Busby, "Introduction," in *Fela: This Bitch of a Life*, ed. Carlos Moore (Chicago: Lawrence Hill Books, 2009), 9.
2. Moore, *Fela*, 1.
3. Michael E. Veal, *Fela: The Life and Times African Musical Icon* (Philadelphia: Temple University Press, 2000), 6.
4. Ibid.
5. Ibid., 11.
6. Ibid.
7. Tejumola Olaniyan, *Arrest the Music! Fela and His Rebel Art and Politics* (Bloomington: Indiana University Press, 2004), 2.
8. Ibid.
9. Ibid., 1.
10. Sola Olorunyomi, *Afrobeat! Fela and the Imagined Continent* (Ibadan: IFRA, 2005), xxv.
11. John Collins, *Kalakuta Notes* (London: Wesleyan University Press, 2015), 209.
12. Ibid., 2.
13. Ibid.

14 Ibid., 114.
15 Trevor Schoonmaker, *Fela: From West Africa to Broadway* (New York: Palgrave Macmillan, 2003), 8.
16 Tade Makinde, *Fela Anikulapo Kuti: Bruised. Battered. Beloved* (Lagos: LamLam Bookish, 2018).
17 Jawi Oladipo-Ola, *Fela Anikulpao-Kuti: The Primary Man of an African Personality* (Osogbo: Front Page Media, 2011).
18 Temitope Ajayi, "Identity and Ideological Representation in Selected Fela Anikulapo-Kuti's Songs," *Journal of West African Language* 44 (2017): 45.
19 Ibid., 46.
20 Uche Onyebadi, "Political Messages in African Music: Assessing Fela Anikulapo-Kuti, Lucky Dube and Alpha Blondy," *Humanities* 7 (2018): 1.
21 Ibid., 3.
22 Ibid., 7.
23 Ibid., 10.
24 Shina Alimi and Opeyemi Iroju Anthony, "No Agreement Today, No Agreement Tomorrow: Fela Anikulapo-Kuti and Human Right Activism in Nigeria," *The Journal of Pan African Studies* 6, no. 4 (2013): 75.
25 Ibid., 74.
26 Ibid., 80.
27 Ibid., 82–3.
28 Albert O. Oikelome, "Highlife Jazz: A Stylistic Analysis of the Music of Felá Anikulapo Kuti," *The Journal of African Studies* 3, no. 4 (2009): 37.
29 Ibid., 39.
30 Ibid., 41.
31 Ibid., 44.
32 Ibid., 42–3.
33 Olukayode Segun Eesuola, "Behavioural Approach to Political Protest: An Analysis of Fela Anikulapo Kuti 1970–1997," PhD Thesis, Department of Political Science, University of Lagos, 2011, 2–3.
34 Ibid., 4.
35 Ibid., 9.
36 Ibid., 135–73.

Chapter 2

1 Randall F. Grass, "Fela Anikulapo-Kuti: The Art of an Afrobeat Rebel," *The Drama Review* 30, no. 1 (1986): 131–48.

2 Lindsay Barrett, "Fela Kuti: Chronicle of a Life Foretold," *The Wire*, September 2011, Retrieved June 13, 2015.

3 *Bob Marley and Fela Anikulapo-Kuti Research Paper.* 2019. Accessed on the 12th of July, 2019. https://ivypanda.com/essays/bob-marley-and-fela-anikulapo-kuti/

4 *The 10 Best Fela Kuti Songs*. Accessed on the 14th of July, 2019. https://www.okayafrica.com/fela-kuti-songs-10-best/

5 Lindsay Barrett. *Issue 169 in Wire*. 1998. Accessed on the 15th of July, 2019. https://www.thewire.co.uk/in-writing/essays/fela-kuti_chronicle-ofa-life-foretold

6 Ibid.

7 Ibid.

8 Ibid.

9 Ibid.

10 Ibid.

Chapter 3

1 Michael E. Veal, *Fela: The Life and Times of an African Musical Icon* (Philadelphia: Temple University Press, 2000), 26.

2 J. A. Atanda, "The Political Crisis of the Nineteenth Century in Yorùbáland," in *The Collected Works of J. A. Atanda*, ed. Toyin Falola (Austin: Pan-African University Press, 2017), 108.

3 Ibid., 110.

4 Carlos Moore, *Fela: This Bitch of a Life* (Abuja: Cassava Republic Press), 55.

5 Cheryl Johnson-Odim and Nina Emma Mba, *For Women and the Nation: Funmilayo Ransome-Kuti of Nigeria* (Urbana and Chicago: University of Illinois Press, 1997), 42.

6 Veal, *Fela*, 26.

7 Odim and Mba, *For Women and the Nation*, 55.

Chapter 4

1 Sahara Reporters, "The Singing Minister: Unsung Story of Fela's Grandpa," June 13, 2009. http://saharareporters.com/2009/06/13/singing-minister-unsung-story-fela%E2%80%99s-grandpa

2 Wole Soyinka, *Ake: Years of Childhood* (London: Rex Collings Ltd, 1981), 9.

3 Stephanie Shonekan, “Fela’s Foundation: Examining the Revolutionary Songs of Funmilayo Ransome-Kuti and the Abeokuta Market Women’s Movement in 1940s Western Nigeria,” *Black Music Research Journal* 29, no. 1 (2009): 136–8.
4 Carlos Moore, *Fela: This Bitch of a Life* (Abuja: Cassava Republic Press), 58.
5 Justin Labinjoh, “Fela Anikulapo-Kuti: Protest Music and Social Processes in Nigeria,” *Journal of Black Studies* 13, no. 1 (1982): 124.
6 Moore, *Fela*, 83.
7 Michael E. Veal, *Fela: The Life and Times of an African Musical Icon* (Philadelphia: Temple University Press, 2000), 51.
8 Fela himself testified that he was extremely averse to reading. This was not just a normal student’s distaste. He had concluded that novels were too unreal, too glib. His experience with watching Hitchcock’s film, Psycho, reinforced his decision to give up films and novels, and “true books,” to concentrate on history and education. *The Autobiography of Malcolm X*, unlike the stories about Simon Templar, or other literary characters, gripped him from start to finish. This would be mark the literary transformation of his conception of freedom.
9 Veal, *Fela*, 72.
10 Sola Olorunyomi, “On Whose Side Are the Orisa (Gods),” in *Fela: From West Africa to West Broadway*, ed. Trevor Schoonmaker (New York: Palgrave Macmillan), 157.

Chapter 5

1 Kwasi Wiredu, *Cultural Universals and Particulars: An African Perspective* (Bloomington and Indianapolis: Indiana University Press, 1996), 69.
2 Ibid., 70.
3 We are very grateful to the anonymous reviewer for the Ohio University Press for pointing out the significance of these cases to us.
4 See, for example, Robyn C. Spenser, *The Revolution Has Come: Black Power, Gender, and the Black Panther Party in Oakland* (Durham: Duke University Press, 2016).
5 Carlos Moore, *Fela: This Bitch of a Life* (Abuja: Cassava Republic Press), 48.
6 Ibid., 70–1. Emphasis added.
7 Ibid., 81. We can debate whether the “told” was Fela’s interpretation of a counsel offered by his mother, or a subtle command that his subconscious dread of his mother forced him to act upon.
8 Michael E. Veal, *Fela: The Life and Times of an African Musical Icon* (Philadelphia: Temple University Press, 2000), 18.

9 Fela had later ascribed the nature of that marriage to a "colonial mentality": "It was really colonial, inside a court.... Can you imagine me standing in front of a white man to get married?... The marriage was not in my mind, because I cried throughout. I cried throughout because I didn't want to marry in the first place" (cited in Veal, *Fela*, 45).

10 Moore, *Fela*, 187.

11 Sola Olorunyomi, *Afrobeat! Fela and the Imagined Continent* (Ibadan: IFRA, 2005), 163.

12 Ibid., 93.

13 Ibid., 96–7. Emphasis added.

14 Ibid., 107.

15 Ibid., 173–4.

16 Ibid., 252–3.

17 Trine Annfelt, "Jazz as Masculine Space," *Kilden*, July 17, 2003. http://kjonnsforskning.no/en/2003/07/jazz-masculine-space

18 Susan McClary, *Feminine Endings: Music, Gender and Sexuality* (Minneapolis: University of Minnesota Press), 9.

19 Nkiru Nzegwu argues that Fela's understanding of what constitutes proper behavior for an authentic African woman is historically false, since his image of the authentically African was constructed by Christian elites in the nineteenth century. Ironically, his "African woman" is actually constructed from the Western tradition that he so strenuously antagonized. See Nzegwu, "School Days in Lagos: Fela, 'Lady,' and Acada Girls," in *Fela: From West Africa to West Broadway*, ed. Trevor Schoonmaker (New York: Palgrave Macmillan), 135–48.

20 What "unconscious feminists" means is that Fela's Queens, though unlettered in the feminists literature and responding to Fela's masculine dictates, were unconsciously *performing* acts which would later instigate critical studies of their roles in Fela's life and music.

Chapter 6

1 Carlos Moore, *Fela: This Bitch of a Life* (Abuja: Cassava Republic Press), 49–50.

2 Ibid., 85.

3 Kairn A. Klieman, "U.S. Oil Companies, the Nigerian Civil War, and the Origins of Opacity in the Nigerian Oil Industry," *The Journal of American History* 99, no. 1 (2012): 155.

4 Moore, *Fela*, 98.

5 Ibid., 130.

6 Ibid., 146.

7 Mabinuori Kayode Idowu, "African Who Sang and Saw Tomorrow," in *Fela: From West Africa to West Broadway*, ed. Trevor Schoonmaker (New York: Palgrave Macmillan, 2003), 17–18.
8 Moore, *Fela*, 151.
9 Stephanie Shonekan, "Fela's Foundation: Examining the Revolutionary Songs of Funmilayo Ransome-Kuti and the Abeokuta Market Women's Movement in 1940s Western Nigeria," *Black Music Research Journal* 29, no. 1 (2009): 133.

Chapter 7

1 A. Oikelomen, "Performance Practice in Afrobeat Music of Fela Anikulapo Kuti," *Journal of Arts and Humanities* 2, no. 7 (2013): 83. www.theartsjournal.org
2 Sola Olorunyomi, *Afrobeat! Fela and the Imagined Continent* (Ibadan: IFRA, 2005), 25.
3 De-Valera Botchway, "Fela 'The Black President' as Grist to the Mill of the Black Power Movement in Africa," *Black Diaspora Review* 4, no. 1 (2014): 29.
4 Thompson Ewata, "Music & Social Criticism in Nigeria," *International Journal of Humanities and Cultural Studies* 2, no. 3 (2015): 217, http://ijhcschiefeditor.wix.com/ijhcs
5 Oluwakemi Arogundade, "'Anarchy in the Republic': 1974–1977, Fela Kuti and the Spaces for a Nigerian [Re]-Imagination," *The Inquiry: The Journal of the Mellon Mays Undergraduate Fellowship* (St. Louis, The Center for the Humanities and the College of Arts and Sciences, Washington University, 2013), 6.
6 Ibid., 6–7.

Chapter 8

1 Tope Omoniyi, "Hip-Hop through the World Englishes Lens: A Response to Globalization," in *World Englishes and Global Popular Cultures*, eds. Yamuna Kachu and Jamie Shinee Lee (Oxford: Blackwell, 2006), 195–208.
2 Tejumola Olaniyan, "The Cosmopolitan Nativist: Fela Antikulapo-Kuti and the Antinomies of Postcolonial Modernity," *Research in African Literatures* 32, no. 2 (2001): 81.
3 Ibid., 81.
4 Ibid.
5 Pelumi Folajimi, "The New Technologies and the Schism between Popular Music and Elitist/Obscure Drama in Nigeria: Fela Anikulapo-Kuti and Wole Soyinka on YouTube," *Journal of the African Literature Association* 10, no. 2 (2016): 197.

6 Carlos D. Morrison, "Code-Switching: Linguistics," *Britannica Encyclopedia*, n.d., https://www.britannica.com/topic/humanities.
7 E. T. Babalola and R. Taiwo, "The English Language and Code-Switching/Code-Mixing: A Case of Study of the Phenomenon in Contemporary Nigerian Hip Hop Music," *Itupale Online Journal of African Studies* 1 (2009): 1–26.
8 Michael Olatunji, "Yabis: A Phenomenon in Nigerian Contemporary Music," *The Journal of Pan African Studies* 1, no. 9 (2007): 26–46.
9 Adegoke, "Language and Identity Representation in Popular Music," *International Journal of Innovative Interdisciplinary Research*, no. 1 (2011): 155.
10 Stephanie Shonekan, "Fela's Foundation: Examining the Revolutionary Songs of Funmilayo Ransom-Kuti and the Abeokuta Market Women's Movement of the 1940s Western Nigeria," *Black Music Research Journal* 29, no. 1 (2009): 137.
11 Blessing Diala-Ogamba, "Music as Social Poetry: A Critical Evaluation of Fela Anikulapo Kuti's Afro-Beat Lyrics," *The Langston Hughes Review* 21 (2007): 37.
12 Ibid.
13 Michael E. Veal, *Fela: The Life and Times of an African Musical Icon* (Philadelphia: Temple University Press, 2000), 260.
14 Diala-Ogamba, "Music as Social Poetry," 33.
15 Shonekan, "Fela's Foundation," 135.
16 Diala-Ogamba, "Music as Social Poetry," 35.
17 Ibid., 37.
18 Ibid., 36.
19 Ibid., 34.
20 Ibid.
21 Ibid., 36.
22 Ibid., 33–4.
23 Ibid., 34.
24 Temitope Ajayi, "Identity and Ideological Representation in Selected Fela Anikulapo-Kuti's Songs," *Journal of West African Languages* 44, no. 2 (2017): 47–9.
25 Ibid., 47.
26 Ibid.
27 Folajimi, "The New Technologies and the Schism," 197.
28 Ibid., 198.
29 Ibid.

Chapter 9

1 Abimbola Adelakun and Toyin Falola, "Introduction," in *Art, Creativity, and Politics in Africa and the Diaspora*, eds. Abimbola Adelakun and Toyin Falola (New York: Palgrave Macmillan, 2018), 2.

2 Pride Press, "Interview with the Legend Fela Anikulapo-Kuti, About Music, Politics and Freedom," November 7, 2016, https://www.youtube.com/watch?v=LtLJfKDN4x8, Retrieved on August 8, 2020.

3 Adelakun and Falola, "Introduction," 3

4 Michael Denning, *Noise Uprising: The Audiopolitics of a World Musical Revolution* (London: Verso, 2015), 140.

5 Chinua Achebe, *Things Fall Apart* (New York: Knopf Doubleday Publishing Group, 1995).

6 Cheik Anta Diop, *The African Origin of Civilization: Myth or Reality*, edited by M. Cook (New York: Lawrence Hill Books, 1974).

7 Walter Rodney, *How Europe Underdeveloped Africa* (Kingston: Bogle-Louverture, 1972).

8 Abiodun Adetugbo, "The Development of English in Nigeria Up to 1914: A Socio-Historical Appraisal," *Journal of the Historical Society of Nigeria* 9, no.2 (1978): 89.

9 In fact, in a recent article published by Al Jazeera, a writer alludes to the ironic fact that Fela is today being celebrated by those he criticized in his music, while being neglected by the music industry he helped build years ago. See Demola Olarewaju, "How Fela Kuti Came to Be Celebrated by Those He Sang against," *Al Jazeera*, July 15, 2018, https://www.aljazeera.com/indepth/opinion/fela-kuti-celebrated-sang-180713174824360.html, Retrieved on August 3, 2020.

10 Michael Olatunji, "Yabis: A Phenomenon in the Contemporary Nigerian Music," *Journal of Pan African Studies* 1, no. 9 (2007): 26–8.

11 Karin Barber, *I Could Speak until Tomorrow: Oriki, Women and the Past in a Yoruba Town* (London: Edinburgh University Press, 1991); Bolanle Awe, "Praise Poems as Historical Data: The Example of the Yoruba Oriki," Africa 44 (1974): 331–49.

12 Randall F. Grass, "Fela Anikulapo-Kuti: The Art of an Afrobeat Rebel," *The Drama Review: TDR* 30, no. 1 (1986): 131–48.

13 Joe Coleman, "Anthony Joshua's Entrance Music: The Real Meaning behind Fela Kuti's 'Water No Get Enemy' Which Helped Inspire AJ to Win against Andy Ruiz Jr," *Talk Sport*, December 8, 2019, Retrieved on August 3, 2020.

14 Tejumola Olaniyan, "The Cosmopolitan Nativist: Fela Anikulapo-Kuti and the Antinomies of Postcolonial Modernity," *Research in African Literatures* 32, no. 2, (2001): 76–89.

15 Lola Ogunnaike, "Celebrating the Life and Impact of the Nigerian Music Legend Fela," *New York Times*, July 17, 2003, https://www.nytimes.com/2003/07/17/arts/celebrating-the-life-and-impact-of-the-nigerian-music-legend-fela.html, Retrieved on August 8, 2020; Remi Adekoya, Fela Kuti, "Fearlessly Proved the Human Spirit

is Stronger than any Government," *The Guardian*, https://www.theguardian.com/commentisfree/2012/aug/02/fela-kuti-proved-human-spirit-stronger, Retrieved on August 8, 2020.

16 Toyin Falola, *Cultural Modernity in a Colonized World: The Writings of Chief Isaac Oluwole Delano* (Texas: Pan-African University Press, 2020), 5.

17 John Collins, *Fela: Kalakuta Notes* (London: Wesleyan University Press, 2015), 207.

18 Ademola Adegbite, "The Concept of Sound in Traditional African Religious Music," *Journal of Black Studies* 22, no.1, (1991), 52.

19 Ibid., 52–3.

20 Tunji Vidal, "Oriki in Traditional Yoruba Music," *African Arts* 3, no. 1 (1969), 56–9.

21 ReelinInTheYears66, Fela Kuti—Interview 1988, Reelin' in The Years Archive, July 7, 2018, https://www.youtube.com/watch?v=QtiAnjtYdwo, Retrieved on August 1, 2020.

22 Collins, *Fela: Kalakuta Notes*, 38.

23 Kenneth Kalu and Toyin Falola, eds. *Exploitation and Misrule in Colonial and Post-colonial Africa* (New York: Palgrave Macmillan, 2019); Wale Adebanwi, ed., *The Political Economy of Everyday Life in Africa: Beyond the Margins* (London: James Currey, 2017).

24 Ojong Echum Tangban and Chukwuma C.C. Osakwe, eds., *Perspectives in African Historical Studies: Essay in Honour of Prof. Chinedu Nwafor Ubah* (Kaduna: Nigerian Defence Academy Press, 2013).

25 Ibid.

26 In fact, this accounted for the military intervention in the Nigerian politics in the first place. See Adewale Ademoyega, *Why We Struck: The Story of the First Nigerian Coup* (Ibadan: Evans Brothers, 1981).

27 Karl Maier, *This House Has Fallen: Nigeria in Crisis* (Colorado: Westview Press, 2000).

28 See, for example, Bade Onimode, et al., eds., *African Development and Governance Strategies in the 21st Century: Looking Back to Move Forward, Essays in Honour of Adebayo Adedeji* (London and New York: Zed Books, 2004); Toyin Falola and Mike Odey, *Poverty Reduction Strategies in Africa* (New York: Routledge, 2018).

29 Shawn Trenell O'Neal, "The Soundscape of Diaspora and Anti-Colonialism: Historical Significance and Theory," MA Diss, Department of History, University of Colorado, 2016, 9–17.

30 Samuel M. Makinda, "Democracy and Multi-Party Politics in Africa," *Journal of Modern African Studies* 34, no. 4 (1996): 555.

31 Keith Somerville, *Africa's Long Road since Independence: The Many Histories of a Continent* (London: Penguin Random House, 2017).

32 Elias Courson, *Movement for the Emancipation of the Niger Delta (MEND) Political Marginalization, Repression and Petro-Insurgency in the Niger Delta*, Nordiska African Institute, Discussion Paper 47 (Uppsala: Nordiska Afrika Institute, 2009), 10.

33 Tejumola Olaniyan, *Arrest the Music! Fela and His Rebel Art and Politics* (Bloomington: Indiana University Press, 2004), 1

34 Ibid., 2.

35 Archie Mafeje, "The Beast and the Icon: No End to Ali Mazrui's Pax Africana Muddles," *CODESRIA Bulletin* 3 and 4 (2008): 105.

36 Thomas Hodgkin, "Islam and National Movements in West Africa," *The Journal of African History* 3, no. 2 (1962): 323–7.

37 Peter G. Peterson Foundation, "The United States Spends More on Defence than the Next 10 Countries Combined," May 15, 2020, https://www.pgpf.org/blog/2020/05/the-united-states-spends-more-on-defense-than-the-next-10-countries-combined, Retrieved on August 8, 2020.

38 Appiah also gave an empirical narrative of the contradictions between the Western justice system and that of Africans. See Kwame Anthony Appiah, *In My Father's House: Africa in the Philosophy of Culture* (New York: Oxford University Press, 1992), 8.

39 This was also noted by Fela himself. See, for example, Pride Press, "Interview with the Legend Fela Anikulapo-Kuti."

40 Human Rights Violation Investigation Commission, "Former President Olusegun Obasanjo Answers to Fela Kuti's Petition—Oputa Panel," February 15, 2013, https://www.youtube.com/watch?v=6qe44fwMdFE, Retrieved on August 8, 2020.

41 Fela could not but allude to this in the record he released shortly after his ordeal, *Beast of no Nation*, when he refreshed the memory of his listeners on how the judge in his case had confessed to being under pressure and apologized to him to buttress his description of the crazy world he sang about in the record.

42 Wole Soyinka, *You Must Set Forth at Dawn: A Memoir* (New York: Random House, 2007).

43 Collins, *Fela: Kalakuta Notes*, 18.

44 Toyin Falola, "Ritual Archives," in *The Palgrave Handbook of African Philosophy*, eds. Adeshina Afolayan and Toyin Falola (New York: Palgrave Macmillan, 2017), 706.

45 Olaniyan, *Arrest the Music*, 24.

46 Achille Mbembe, *On the Post-Colony* (London: University of California Press, 2001).

47 E. A. Ayandele, *The Educated Elite in the Nigerian Society* (Ibadan: Ibadan University Press, 1974), 5.

48 Grass, "Fela Anikulapo-Kuti," 134.

49 Olufemi Vaughan, *Religion and the Making of Nigeria* (Durham and London: Duke University Press, 2016); Ebenezer Obadare, ed., *The Handbook of Civil Society in Africa* (New York: Springer, 2014); Toyin Falola, *Violence in Nigeria: The Crisis of Religious Politics and Secular Ideologies* (Rochester: University of Rochester Press, 1998).

50 Jon Pareles, "The Legacy of Fela Kuti's Music of Resistance: Hear 15 Essential Songs," *New York Times*, June 10, 2020, https://www.nytimes.com/2020/06/10/arts/music/fela-kuti-afrobeat-playlist.html, Retrieved on August 7, 2020.

51 In fact, on a TV program where Seun Kuti was interviewed, many viewers were surprised to find out that Fela has a son called Seun who is an Afrobeater, let alone having a single album. Seun in turn noted that his music is mainly played and sold outside of Africa. In a way, this signals the real state of Afrobeat in African music and African consciousness. HipTv, "Trending with Seun Anikulapo Kuti (Nigerian Entertainment News)," February 24, 2014, https://www.youtube.com/watch?v=eRjK4aG5imY, Retrieved on August 8, 2020.

52 Owen Jones, "The Story of Fela Kuti 'Gentleman' and 'Zombie,'" *Classical Albums*, https://classicalbumsundays.com/album-of-the-month-fela-kuti-gentleman-zombie/, Retrieved on August 7, 2020.

53 Shireen Ally, "Conversing with 'Pan-Africanism,'" *Africa Review of Books* (2006): 4.

54 See Toyin Falola, *The Toyin Falola Reader on African Culture, Nationalism, Development and Epistemology* (Austin: Pan-African University Press, 2018), 889–910.

55 Ngugi wa Thiong'o, *Decolonising The Mind: The Politics of Language in African Literature* (Harare: Zimbabwe Publishing House, 1981).

Chapter 10

1 Gabriel E. Idang, "African Culture and Values," *Phronimon* 16, no. 2 (2015): 97–111.

2 I. A. Mbakogu, "Is There Really a Relationship between Culture and Development?" *Anthropologist* 6, no. 1 (2004): 37–43.

3 Idang, "African Culture and Values," 97–111.

4 G. Barton, "The Influence of Culture on Instrumental Music Teaching: A Participant-Observation Case Study of Karnatic and Queensland Instrumental Music Teachers in Context." https://core.ac.uk/download/pdf/10884558.pdf&ved=2ahUKEwjWza

5 Akin Euba, "Criteria for the Evaluation of New African Art Music," *Transition*, no. 48 (1975): 48.

6 Ibid.

7 Ibid.

8 Temitope Michael Ajayi, "Identity and Ideological Representation in Selected Fela Anikulapo-Kuti's Songs," *Journal of West African Languages* 44, no. 2 (2017): 43–54.

9 Albert Oikelome, "Performance Practice in Afrobeat Music of Fela Anikulapo Kuti," *Journal of Arts and Humanities* 2, no. 7 (2013): 82–94.

10 Ajayi, "Identity and Ideological Representations… "

11 R. C. Okeke, "Politics, Music and Social Mobilization in Africa: The Nigeria Narrative and Extant Tendencies," *International Letters of Social and Humanistic Sciences* 86 (2019): 28–41.

12 Sola Olorunyomi, *Afrobeat! Fela and the Imagined Continent* (Ibadan: IFRA, 2005), 4.

13 Ibid.

14 Oluwakemi Arogundade, "'Anarchy in the Republic': 1974–1977, Fela Kuti and the Spaces for a Nigerian [Re]-Imagination," *The Inquiry: The Journal of the Mellon Mays Undergraduate Fellowship* (St. Louis, The Center for the Humanities and the College of Arts and Sciences, Washington University, 2013), 6.

15 Olorunyomi, *Afrobeat!*

16 Abigail Gardner, "En' shrine'd: Ushering Fela Kuti into the Western 'Rock' Canon," in *Death and the Rock Star: Ashgate Popular and Folk Music*, eds. Catherine Strong and Barbara Lebrun (Farham: Ashgate, 2015), 135–48.

17 Olorunyomi, *Afrobeat!* 175.

18 Ibid., 173–4.

19 Oikelome, "Performance Practice in Afrobeat Music… "

20 Ibid., 85.

21 Ibid.

22 O. B. Ayobade, *Women that Danced the Fire dance: Fela Kuti's Afrobeat Queens, Performance and the Dialectics of Postcolonial Identity* (Austin: University of Texas, 2016). https://hdl.handle.net/2152/38107

23 Oikelome, "Performance Practice in Afrobeat Music," 92.

24 Olorunyomi, *Afrobeat!* 25.

25 Radio Shrine, "Fela Kuti Speaks," YouTube, accessed January 14, 2011, http://www.youtube.com/watch?v=Lp_xEwQ2Osc

26 De-Valera Botchway, "Fela 'The Black President' as Grist to the Mill of the Black Power Movement in Africa," *Black Diaspora Review* 4, no. 1 (2014): 19–20.

27 Arogundade, "Anarchy in the Republic," 9.

28 Botchway, "Fela 'The Black President,'" 28.

29 Botchway, "Fela 'The Black President,'" 30.

30 Oluwakemi Arogundade, "'Anarchy in the Republic': 1974–1977, Fela Kuti and the Spaces for a Nigerian [Re]-Imagination," in *The Inquiry: The Journal of the Mellon Mays Undergraduate Fellowship* (St. Louis, The Center for the Humanities and the College of Arts and Sciences, Washington University, 2013), 9.

Chapter 11

1 Tejumola Olaniyan, *Arrest the Music! Fela and His Rebel Art and Politics* (Bloomington: Indiana University Press, 2004), 102.
2 Ibid., 103.
3 Carlos Moore, *Fela: This BitcFela's Thoughts on African Indigenous Knowledge Systemsh of a Life* (USA: Lawrence Hill Books, 2009).
4 Ibid.
5 Cited in Sola Olorunyomi, *Afrobeat! Fela and the Imagined Continent* (Ibadan: IFRA, 2005), 36.
6 Ibid.
7 Oladimeji Ramon, "Fela Was My Most Interesting Client—Falana," *Punch Newspaper*, https://punchng.com/fela-was-my-most-interesting-client-falana-2/, Retrieved on August 18, 2020.

Chapter 12

1 The title "African(s)" is deployed in this chapter to represent all Africans; peoples of African descent, dark or light-complexioned, both at home on the continent and outside in African diaspora communities, except where otherwise illustrated.
2 TsiTsi Ella Jaji, *Africa in Stereo: Modernism, Music, and Pan-African Solidarity* (New York: Oxford University Press, 2014), 23.
3 Ibid., 23.
4 Ibid., 66.
5 Simon A. Clark, "Understanding Pan-Africanism," *Caribbean Quarterly* 58, no. 1 (2012): 101.
6 Toyin Falola and Chukwuemeka Agbo, "The Prospects and Challenges of Pan-Africanism," *Oxford Research Encyclopedia of Politics*. July 29, 2019.
7 Falola and Agbo, "The Prospects and Challenges of Pan-Africanism."
8 The difference in both the stages of evolution of African societies and in their technological advancement with their European counterparts was also taken by the latter as evidence of the former's inferiority.
9 A tangible example of this is in the French colonial policy of assimilation which sought to make Frenchmen of its colonial African subjects. This might explain why Negritude as a black-consciousness resistance movement emerged from the French quarter of the European colonial establishment.
10 Falola and Agbo, "The Prospects and Challenges of Pan-Africanism."
11 Ademola Adegbite, "The Concept of Sound in Traditional African Religious Music," *Journal of Black Studies* 22, no. 1, African Aesthetics in Nigeria and the Diaspora (1991): 45.

12 *Oriki* is one of the oldest traditions in Yoruba music.
13 Tunji Vidal, "Oriki in Traditional Yoruba Music," *Journal of African Arts* 3, no. 1 (1969): 56.
14 Tejumola Olaniyan, *Arrest the Music* (Bloomington: Indiana University Press, 2004), 5.
15 Ruth Mayer, "Africa as an Alien Future: The Middle Passage, Afrofuturism and Postcolonial Waterworlds," *Amerikastudien/American Studies* 46, no. 4 (2000): 559.
16 Jaji, *Africa in Stereo*, 1.
17 Ibid., 5.
18 Cheryl Johnson-Odim and Nina Emma Mba, *For Women and the Nation: Funmilayo Ransome-Kuti of Nigeria* (Urbana and Chicago: University of Illinois Press, 1997), 125.
19 Carlos Moore, *This Bitch of A Life* (London: Omnibus Press, 2009), 59.
20 In Moore, *This Bitch of A Life*. Fela is quoted saying his mother took him to some of her political meetings and once much later told him to "Start playing music your people will understand, not Jazz," 56, 57.
21 Oyebade A. Dosunmu, "Afrobeat, Fela and beyond: Scenes, Style and Ideology," PhD. Thesis, University of Pittsburgh, 2010, 143.
22 Moore, *This Bitch of a Life,* 96.
23 Olaniyan, *Arrest the Music!* 3.
24 Dosunmu, "Afrobeat, Fela and beyond," 143.
25 Olaniyan, *Arrest the Music!* 3.
26 Ibid., 88.
27 Moore, *This Bitch of a Life,* 101.
28 Olaniyan, *Arrest the Music*! 166.
29 Dosunmu, "Afrobeat, Fela and beyond," 155.
30 Ibid., 156.
31 Ibid., 157.
32 Ibid., 158.
33 Oyebade Dosunmu, "Afrobeat, Fela and Beyond: Scenes, Style and Ideology," Ph.D. diss, University of Pittsburgh, 2010, 158.
34 Dosumu, "Afrobeat, Fela and Beyond," 20.
35 Molefi Asante, *Afro-centricity: The Theory of Social Change* (Buffalo: Amulefi Publishing Co., 1980), 5.
36 Tsenay Serequeberhan, "Philosophy and Post-colonial Africa," in *African Philosophy: An Anthology*, ed. Emmanuel Chukwudi Eze (Malden: Blackwell, 1998), 33.
37 The "docile" citizenry in Fela's artistic social analogies was not spared in his taunts either. They were subjected to instances of insults and name-callings apparently in a bid to awaken them to the reality of their roles in society.

Chapter 13

1 Achille Mbembe, *On the Postcolony* (Berkeley and Los Angeles: University of California Press, 2001), 25.
2 Tejumola Olaniyan, *Arrest the Music! Fela and His Rebel Art and Politics* (Bloomington and Indianapolis: Indiana University Press).
3 Richard Joseph, *Democracy and Prebendal Politics in Nigeria: The Rise and Fall of the Second Republic* (Cambridge: Cambridge University Press, 1987); Wale Adebanwi and Ebenezer Obadare, eds., *Democracy and Prebendalism in Nigeria: Critical Interpretations* (New York: Palgrave Macmillan, 2013).
4 Daron Acemoglu and James A. Robinson, *Why Nations Fail: The Origins of Power, Prosperity and Poverty* (London: Profile Books, 2013).
5 William J. Foltz, "African States and the Search for Freedom," in *The Idea of Freedom in Asia and Africa*, ed. Robert H. Taylor (Stanford: Stanford University Press), 49.
6 Ibid., 53.
7 Wole Soyinka, *Death and the King's Horseman* (London: Methuen, 1999), 305.
8 Sola Olorunyomi, *Afrobeat! Fela and the Imagined Continent* (Ibadan: IFRA, 2005), 128.
9 Ibid.
10 Ibid., 143.
11 Ibid., 144.
12 Ibid., 146.
13 It will be a debate worth pursuing to see which of T'Challa's or N'Jadaka's (Erik Killmonger) visions of Wakanda best instantiate Fela's radical vision of society.

Chapter 14

1 Tejumola Olaniyan, *Arrest the Music! Fela and His Rebel Art and Politics* (Bloomington and Indianapolis: Indiana University Press), 2.
2 Ibid.
3 Achille Mbembe, *On the Postcolony* (Berkeley and Los Angeles: University of California Press, 2001), 102.
4 Sola Olorunyomi, *Afrobeat! Fela and the Imagined Continent* (Ibadan: IFRA, 2005), 140.
5 Amartya Sen, *Development as Freedom* (Oxford: Oxford University Press, 1999), Amartya Sen, *The Idea of Justice* (Cambridge, MA: The Belknap Press, 2009), and Amartya Sen, *Standard of Living* (Cambridge: Cambridge University Press, 2001).

6 We are grateful to Hannah Trees for this term.

7 It should be noted that Fela's family did nothing to mitigate the news of his death and its cause. The announcement came from Professor Olikoye Ransome-Kuti, Fela's elder brother, a former Minister for Health and a very prominent AIDS activist.

Chapter 15

1 Toyin Falola and Kwame Essien, "Introduction," in *Pan-Africanism, and the Politics of African Citizenship and Identity*, eds. Toyin Falola and Kwame Essien (London and New York: Routledge, 2014), 1.

2 We have deliberately introduced the difference between "Afrobeat" and "afrobeats" as a semantic distinction between the unique and performative political rhythm which Fela consciously created and the spin-off beats which are founded on Fela's tunes but without the intensity of his political activism.

3 Tejumola Olaniyan, *Arrest the Music! Fela and His Rebel Art and Politics* (Bloomington and Indianapolis: Indiana University Press), 186.

Chapter 16

1 Adeshina Afolayan, "L'Émotion est Negre: Senghor and the Poetics of African Identity and Consciousness," *Studies in Social and Political Thought*, no. 13 (2007): 89–107.

2 Sola Olorunyomi, *Afrobeat! Fela and the Imagined Continent* (Ibadan: IFRA, 2005).

3 Ibid., 83.

4 Olayinka Oyeleye, "Feminism(s) and Oppression: Rethinking Gender from a Yoruba Perspective," in *Palgrave Handbook of African Philosophy*, eds., Adeshina Afolayan and Toyin Falola (New York: Palgrave Macmillan, 2017), 361.

5 Michael E. Veal, *Fela: The Life and Times of an African Musical Icon* (Philadelphia: Temple University Press, 2000), 106.

Bibliography

Achebe, Chinua, *Things Fall Apart* (New York: Knopf Doubleday Publishing Group, 1995).

Adebanwi, Wale, ed., *The Political Economy of Everyday Life in Africa: Beyond the Margins* (London: James Currey, 2017).

Adebanwi, Wale and Ebenezer Obadare, eds., *Democracy and Prebendalism in Nigeria: Critical Interpretations* (New York: Palgrave Macmillan, 2013).

Adegbite, Ademola, "The Concept of Sound in Traditional African Religious Music," *Journal of Black Studies* 22, no. 1, African Aesthetics in Nigeria and the Diaspora (September 1991): 45–54.

Adegoke, Adetunji, "Language and Identity Representation in Popular Music," *International Journal of Innovative Interdisciplinary Research* no. 1 (2011): 150–64.

Adekoya, Remi, "Fela Kuti Fearlessly Proved the Human Spirit Is Stronger than Any Government," *The Guardian*, https://www.theguardian.com/commentisfree/2012/aug/02/fela-kuti-proved-human-spirit-stronger, Retrieved on August 8, 2020.

Adelakun, Abimbola and Toyin Falola, "Introduction," in *Art, Creativity, and Politics in Africa and the Diaspora*, eds. Abimbola Adelakun and Toyin Falola (New York: Palgrave Macmillan, 2018), 1–14.

Ademoyega, Adewale, *Why We Struck: The Story of the First Nigerian Coup* (Ibadan: Evans Brothers, 1981).

Adetugbo, Abiodun, "The Development of English in Nigeria up to 1914: A Socio-Historical Appraisal," *Journal of the Historical Society of Nigeria* 9, no. 2 (June 1978): 89–103.

Afolayan, Adeshina, "L'Émotion est Negre: Senghor and the Poetics of African Identity and Consciousness," *Studies in Social and Political Thought*, no. 13 (March 2007): 89–107.

Ajayi, Temitope, "Identity and Ideological Representation in Selected Fela Anikulapo-Kuti's Songs," *Journal of West African Languages* 44, no. 2 (2017): 43–54, Retrieved on August 5, 2020.

Alimi, Shina and Opeyemi Iroju Anthony, "No Agreement Today, No Agreement Tomorrow: Fela Anikulapo-Kuti and Human Right Activism in Nigeria," *The Journal of Pan African Studies* 6, no. 4 (2013): 74–95.

Ally, Shireen, "Conversing with 'Pan-Africanism,'" *Africa Review of Books* (September 2006): 3–4.

Annfelt, Trine, "Jazz as Masculine Space," *Kilden*, July 17, 2003. http://kjonnsforskning.no/en/2003/07/jazz-masculine-space

Appiah, Kwame Anthony, *In My Father's House: Africa in the Philosophy of Culture* (New York: Oxford University Press, 1992).

Arogundade, Oluwakemi. A. "'Anarchy in the Republic': 1974–1977, Fela Kuti and the Spaces for a Nigerian [Re]-Imagination," *The Inquiry* (2013): 1–27.

Asante, Molefi, *Afro-centricity: The Theory of Social Change* (Buffalo: Amulefi Publishing Co., 1980).

Atanda, J. A., "The Political Crisis of the Nineteenth Century in Yorùbáland," in *The Collected Works of J. A. Atanda*, ed. Toyin Falola (Austin, TX: Pan-African University Press, 2017), 108–13.

Awe, Bolanle, *Praise Poems as Historical Data: The Example of the Yoruba Oriki, Africa* 44 (1974): 331–49.

Ayandele, E. A., *The Educated Elite in the Nigerian Society* (Ibadan: Ibadan University Press, 1974).

Ayobade, O. B., "Women That Danced the Fire Dance: Fela Kuti's Afrobeat Queens, Performance and the Dialectics of Postcolonial Identity," Texas ScholarWorks, University of Texas Librares, 2016. https://hdl.handle.net/2152/38107

Babalola, E. T. and R. Taiwo, "The English Language and Code-Switching/Code-Mixing: A Case of Study of the Phenomenon in Contemporary Nigerian Hip Hop Music," *Itupale Online Journal of African Studies* 1 (2009): 1–26.

Barber, Karin, *I Could Speak until Tomorrow: Oriki, Women and the Past in a Yoruba Town* (London: Edinburgh University Press, 1991).

Barrett, Lindsay, "Fela Kuti: Chronicle of a Life Foretold," *The Wire*, September 2011, Retrieved on June 13, 2015.

Barton, Georgina, 2003. "The Influence of Culture on Instrumental Music Teaching: A Participant-Observation Case Study of Karnatic and Queensland Instrumental Music Teachers in Context." PhD Thesis, Queensland University of Technology. https://core.ac.uk/download/pdf/10884558.pdf&ved=2ahUKEwjWza

Bob Marley and Fela Anikulapo-Kuti Research Paper. 2019. Accessed on the 12th of July, 2019. https://ivypanda.com/essays/bob-marley-and-fela-anikulapo-kuti/

Botchway, De-Valera. N. Y. M. 2017. "Fela 'The Black President' as Grist to the Mill of the Black Power Movement in Africa," *Black Diaspora Review* 4, no. 1 (2014): 3–35

Clark, A. Simon, "Understanding Pan-Africanism," *Caribbean Quarterly* 58, no. 1 (March 2012): 99–111.

Coleman, Joe, "Anthony Joshua's Entrance Music: The Real Meaning behind Fela Kuti's 'Water No Get Enemy' Which Helped Inspire AJ to Win against Andy Ruiz Jr," *Talk Sport*, December 8, 2019. https://talksport.com/sport/640264/what-anthony-joshua-entrance-music-meaning-lyrics-fela-kuti-water-no-get-enemy-andy-ruiz-jr-win-saudi-arabia/, Retrieved on August 3, 2020.

Collins, John, *Kalakuta Notes* (London: Wesleyan University Press, 2015).

Courson, Elias, *Movement for the Emancipation of the Niger Delta (MEND) Political Marginalization, Repression and Petro-Insurgency in the Niger Delta*, Nordiska African Institute, Discussion Paper 47 (Uppsala: Nordiska Afrika Institute, 2009).

Denning, Michael, *Noise Uprising: The Audiopolitics of a World Musical Revolution* (London: Verso, 2015).

Diala-Ogamba, Blessing, "Music as Social Poetry: A Critical Evaluation of Fela Anikulapo Kuti's Afro-Beat Lyrics," *The Langston Hughes Review* 21 (2007): 30–9.

Diop, Cheik Anta, *The African Origin of Civilization: Myth or Reality*, ed. M. Cook (New York: Lawrence Hill Books, 1974).

Dosunmu, A. Oyebade, "Afrobeat, Fela and beyond: Scenes, Style and Ideology," PhD Thesis, University of Pittsburgh, Pennsylvania, 2010.

Eesuola, Olukayode Segun, "Behavioural Approach to Political Protest: An Analysis of Fela Anikulapo Kuti 1970–1997," PhD Thesis, Department of Political Science, University of Lagos, 2011.

Euba, Akin, "Criteria for the Evaluation of New African Art Music," *Transition*, no. 48 (1975): 46–50.

Ewata, Thompson, "Music and Social Criticism in Nigeria," *International Journal of Humanities and Cultural Studies* 2, no. 3 (2015): 262–82.

Falola, Toyin, *Violence in Nigeria: The Crisis of Religious Politics and Secular Ideologies* (Rochester: University of Rochester Press, 1998).

Falola, Toyin, "Ritual Archives," in *The Palgrave Handbook of African Philosophy*, eds. Adeshina Afolayan and Toyin Falola (New York: Palgrave Macmillan, 2017), 703–28.

Falola, Toyin, *The Toyin Falola Reader on African Culture, Nationalism, Development and Epistemology* (Austin, TX: Pan-African University Press, 2018), 889–910.

Falola, Toyin, *Cultural Modernity in a Colonized World: The Writings of Chief Isaac Oluwole Delano* (Texas, TX: Pan-African University Press, 2020).

Falola, Toyin and Chukwuemeka Agbo, "The Prospects and Challenges of Pan-Africanism," *Oxford Research Encyclopedia of Politics*. July 29, 2019. https://doi.org/10.1093/acrefore/9780190228637.013.718

Falola, Toyin and Kwame Essien, "Introduction," in *Pan-Africanism, and the Politics of African Citizenship and Identity*, eds., Toyin Falola and Kwame Essien (London and New York: Routledge, 2014), 1–10.

Folajimi, Pelumi. "The New Technologies and the Schism between Popular Music and Elitist/Obscure Drama in Nigeria: Fela Anikulapo-Kuti and Wole Soyinka on YouTube," *Journal of the African Literature Association* 10, no. 2 (2016): 189–208.

Foltz, William J., "African States and the Search for Freedom," in *The Idea of Freedom in Asia and Africa*, ed. Robert H. Taylor (Stanford, CA: Stanford University Press), 40–61.

Gardner, Abigail, "En' Shrine'd: Ushering Fela Kuti into the Western 'rock' Canon," in *Death and the Rock Star: Ashgate Popular and Folk Music*, eds. Catherine Strong and Barbara Lebrun (Farham: Ashgate, 2015), 135–48.

Grass, Randall F., "Fela Anikulapo-Kuti: The Art of an Afrobeat Rebel," *The Drama Review: TDR* 30, no. 1 (Spring 1986): 131–48.

HipTv, "Trending with Seun Anikulapo Kuti," February 24, 2014, https://www.youtube.com/watch?v=eRjK4aG5imY, Retrieved on August 8, 2020.

Hodgkin, Thomas, "Islam and National Movements in West Africa," *The Journal of African History* 3, no. 2 (1962): 323–7.

Human Rights Violation Investigation Commission, "Former President Olusegun Obasanjo Answers to Fela Kuti's Petition—Oputa Panel," February 15, 2013, https://www.youtube.com/watch?v=6qe44fwMdFE, Retrieved on August 8, 2020.

Idang, Gabriel E., "African Culture and Values," *Phronimon* 16, no. 2 (2015): 97–111.

Idowu, Mabinuori Kayode, "African Who Sang and Saw Tomorrow," in *Fela: From West Africa to West Broadway,* ed. Trevor Schoonmaker (New York: Palgrave Macmillan, 2003), 16–24.

Jaji, TsiTsi Ella, *Africa in Stereo: Modernism, Music, and Pan-African Solidarity* (New York: Oxford University Press, 2014).

Johnson-Odim, Cheryl and Nina Emma Mba, *For Women and the Nation: Funmilayo Ransome-Kuti of Nigeria* (Urbana and Chicago: University of Illinois Press, 1997).

Jones, Owen, "The Story of Fela Kuti 'Gentleman' and 'Zombie,'" *Classical Albums*, https://classicalbumsundays.com/album-of-the-month-fela-kuti-gentleman-zombie/, Retrieved on August 7, 2020.

Joseph, Richard, *Democracy and Prebendal Politics in Nigeria: The Rise and Fall of the Second Republic* (Cambridge: Cambridge University Press, 1987).

Kalu, Kenneth and Toyin Falola, *Exploitation and Misrule in Colonial and Post-colonial Africa* (New York: Palgrave Macmillan, 2019).

Klieman, Kairn A., "U.S. Oil Companies, the Nigerian Civil War, and the Origins of Opacity in the Nigerian Oil Industry," *The Journal of American History* 99, no. 1 (June 2012): 155.

Labinjoh, Justin, "Fela Anikulapo-Kuti: Protest Music and Social Processes in Nigeria," *Journal of Black Studies* 13, no. 1 (September 1982): 119–34.

Mafeje, Archie, "The Beast and the Icon: No End to Ali Mazrui's Pax Africana Muddles," *CODESRIA Bulletin 3 and 4* (2008): 104–5.

Maier, Karl, *This House Has Fallen: Nigeria in Crisis* (Colorado: Westview Press, 2000).

Makinda, Samuel M., "Democracy and Multi-Party Politics in Africa," *Journal of Modern African Studies* 34, no. 4 (December 1996): 555–73.

Makinde, Tade, *Fela Anikulapo Kuti: Bruised. Battered. Beloved* (Lagos: LamLam Bookish, 2018).

Mayer, Ruth, "Africa as an Alien Future: The Middle Passage, Afrofuturism and Postcolonial Waterworlds," *Amerikastudien/American Studies* 46, no. 4 (2000): 555–66.

Mbakogu, I. A., "Is There Really a Relationship between Culture and Development?" *Anthropologist* 6, no. 1 (2004): 37–43.

Mbembe, Achille, *On the Postcolony* (Berkeley and Los Angeles: University of California Press, 2001).

McClary, Susan, *Feminine Endings: Music, Gender and Sexuality* (Minneapolis: University of Minnesota Press, 1991).

Moore, Carlos, *Fela: This Bitch of a Life* (Abuja: Cassava Republic Press, 2010).

Morrison, Carlos D. "Code-Switching: Linguistics," *Britannica Encylcopaedia*, n.d., https://www.britannica.com/topic/humanities

Nzegwu, Nkiru "School Days in Lagos: Fela, 'Lady,' and Acada Girls," in *Fela: From West Africa to West Broadway*, ed. Trevor Schoonmaker (New York: Palgrave Macmillan), 135–48.

Obadare, Ebenezer, ed., *The Handbook of Civil Society in Africa* (New York: Springer, 2014).

Ogunnaike, Lola, "Celebrating the Life and Impact of the Nigerian Music Legend Fela," *New York Times*, July 17, 2003. https://www.nytimes.com/2003/07/17/arts/celebrating-the-life-and-impact-of-the-nigerian-music-legend-fela.html, Retrieved on August 8, 2020.

Oikelome, Albert O., "Highlife Jazz: A Stylistic Analysis of the Music of Felá Anikulapo Kuti," *The Journal of African Studies* 3, no. 4 (2009): 37–54.

Oikelomen, Albert O., "Performance Practice in Afrobeat Music of Fela Anikulapo Kuti," *Journal of Arts and Humanities* 2, no. 7 (2013): 82–94. www.theartsjournal.org

Okeke, R. C., "Politics, Music and Social Mobilization in Africa: The Nigeria Narrative and Extant Tendencies," *International Letters of Social and Humanistic Sciences* 86 (2019): 28–41.

Oladipo-Ola, Jawi, *Fela Anikulapo-Kuti: The Primary Man of an African Personality. The Narrative and Screenplay* (Osogbo: Front Page Media, 2011).

Olaniyan, Tejumola, "The Cosmopolitan Nativist: Fela Antikulapo-Kuti and the Antinomies of Postcolonial Modernity," *Research in African Literatures* 32, no. 2 (2001): 76–89.

Olaniyan, Tejumola, *Arrest the Music! Fela and His Rebel Art and Politics* (Bloomington and Indianapolis: Indiana University Press, 2004).

Olarewaju, Demola, "How Fela Kuti Came to Be Celebrated by Those He Sang against, *Al Jazeera*, July 15, 2018. https://www.aljazeera.com/indepth/opinion/fela-kuti-celebrated-sang-180713174824360.html, Retrieved on August 3, 2020.

Olatunji, Michael, "Yabis: A Phenomenon in Nigerian Contemporary Music," *The Journal of Pan African Studies* 1, no. 9 (2007): 26–46.

Olorunyomi, Sola, "On Whose Side Are the Orisa (Gods)," in *Fela: From West Africa to West Broadway*, ed. Trevor Schoonmaker (New York: Palgrave Macmillan, 2003), 157–71.

Olorunyomi, Sola, *Afrobeat! Fela and the Imagined Continent* (Ibadan: IFRA, 2005).

Omoniyi, Tope, "Hip-Hop through the World Englishes Lens: A Response to Globalization," in *World Englishes and Global Popular Cultures*, eds. Yamuna Kachu and Jamie Shinee Lee (Oxford: Blackwell, 2006), 195–208.

O'Neal, Shawn Trenell, "The Soundscape of Diaspora and Anti-Colonialism: Historical Significance and Theory," MA Diss, Department of History, University of Colorado, 2016.

Onyebadi, Uche, "Political Messages in African Music: Assessing Fela Anikulapo-Kuti, Lucky Dube and Alpha Blondy," *Humanities* 7 (2018): 129–48. https://www.mpdi.com/journal/humanities, Retrieved on August 5, 2020.

Oyeleye, Olayinka, "Feminism(s) and Oppression: Rrehinking Gender from a Yoruba Perspective," in *Palgrave Handbook of African Philosophy*, eds. Adeshina Afolayan and Toyin Falola (New York: Palgrave Macmillan, 2017), 349–70.

Pareles, Jon, "The Legacy of Fela Kuti's Music of Resistance: Hear 15 Essential Songs," *New York Times*, June 10, 2020, https://www.nytimes.com/2020/06/10/arts/music/fela-kuti-afrobeat-playlist.html, Retrieved on August 7, 2020.

Peter G. Peterson Foundation, "The United States Spends More on Defence than the Next 10 Countries Combined," May 15, 2020, https://www.pgpf.org/blog/2020/05/the-united-states-spends-more-on-defense-than-the-next-10-countries-combined, Retrieved on August 8, 2020.

Pride Press, "Interview with the Legend Fela Anikulapo-Kuti, about Music, Politics and Freedom," November 7, 2016, https://www.youtube.com/watch?v=LtLJfKDN4x8, Retrieved on August 8, 2020.

Ramon, Oladimeji, "Fela Was My Most Interesting Client—Falana," *Punch Newspaper*, October 17, 2017. https://punchng.com/fela-was-my-most-interesting-client-falana-2/, Retrieved on August 18, 2020.

ReelinInTheYears66, Fela Kuti—Interview 1988, Reelin' in The Years Archive, July 7, 2018, https://www.youtube.com/watch?v=QtiAnjtYdwo, Retrieved on August 1, 2020.

Rodney, Walter, *How Europe Underdeveloped Africa* (Kingston: Bogle-Louverture, 1972).

SaharaReporters, "The Singing Minister: Unsung Story of Fela's Grandpa," June 13, 2009. http://saharareporters.com/2009/06/13/singing-minister-unsung-story-fela%E2%80%99s-grandpa

Schoonmaker, Trevor, *Fela: From West Africa to Broadway* (New York: Palgrave Macmillan, 2003).

Sen, Amartya, *Development as Freedom* (Oxford: Oxford University Press, 1999).

Sen, Amartya, *Standard of Living* (Cambridge: Cambridge University Press, 2001).

Sen, Amartya, *The Idea of Justice* (Cambridge, MA: The Belknap Press, 2009).

Serequeberhan, Tsenay, "Philosophy and Post-colonial Africa," in *African Philosophy: An Anthology*, ed. Emmanuel Chukwudi Eze (Malden, MA: Blackwell, 1998), 9–22.

Shonekan, Stephanie, "Fela's Foundation: Examining the Revolutionary Songs of Funmilayo Ransome-Kuti and the Abeokuta Market Women's Movement in 1940s Western Nigeria," *Black Music Research Journal* 29, no. 1 (Spring 2009): 127–44.

Somerville, Keith, *Africa's Long Road since Independence: The Many Histories of a Continent* (London: Penguin Random House, 2017).

Soyinka, Wole, *Ake: Years of Childhood* (London: Rex Collings Ltd, 1981).

Soyinka, Wole, *You Must Set Forth at Dawn: A Memoir* (New York: Random House, 2007).

Tangban, Ojong Echum and Chukwuma C.C. Osakwe, eds., *Perspectives in African Historical Studies: Essay in Honour of Prof. Chinedu Nwafor Ubah* (Kaduna: Nigerian Defence Academy Press, 2013).

The 10 Best Fela Kuti Songs. Accessed on the 14th of July, 2019. https://www.okayafrica.com/fela-kuti-songs-10-best/

Thiong'o, Ngugi wa, *Decolonising The Mind: The Politics of Language in African Literature* (Harare: Zimbabwe Publishing House, 1981).

Vaughan, Olufemi, *Religion and the Making of Nigeria* (Durham and London: Duke University Press, 2016).

Veal, Michael E., *Fela: The Life and Times of an African Musical Icon* (Philadelphia: Temple University Press, 2000).

Vidal, Tunji, "Oriki in Traditional Yoruba Music," *African Arts* 3, no. 1 (Autumn 1969): 56–9.

Young, Crawford, "Itineraries of the Idea of Freedom in Africa: Precolonial to Postcolonial," in *The Idea of Freedom in Asia and Africa,* ed. Robert H. Taylor (Stanford, CA: Stanford University Press), 9–39.

Index

www.ingramcontent.com/pod-product-compliance
Lightning Source LLC
Chambersburg PA
CBHW052213300426
44115CB00011B/1670